Secret Fleets

Fremantle's World War II Submarine Base

Lynne Cairns

EasyRead Large

SECRET FLEETS

FREMANTLE'S WORLD WAR II SUBMARINE BASE

Published 2011 by the
Western Australian Museum
49 Kew Street, Welshpool
Western Australia 6106
www.museum.wa.gov.au

Digital edition released 2013.

First edition published 1995 as *Fremantle's Secret Fleets*.
Copyright © Western Australian Museum, 1995, 2011.

Designed by Tim Cumming.
Printed by Southwind Productions, Singapore.

National Library of Australia
Cataloguing-in-Publication entry
Cairns, Lynne.
Secret fleets: Fremantle's World War II
submarine base / Lynne Cairns.

2nd ed.
ISBN 9781920843526 (pbk.)
ISBN 9781920843571 (epdf)
Includes bibliographical references and index.
Subjects: Navy-yards and naval stations—
Western Australia—Fremantle—History. World War,
1939-1945—Naval operations—Submarine.
World War, 1939-1945—Western Australia—
Fremantle. Fremantle (W.A.)—History.

Western Australian Museum.
Dewey No. 940.5451099411

TABLE OF CONTENTS

ACKNOWLEDGEMENTS	iv
INTRODUCTION	ix
CHAPTER ONE: The Development of the Submarine	1
CHAPTER TWO: Australia's Early Submarines	18
CHAPTER THREE: World War II Begins	35
IMPORTANT DATES	48
CHAPTER FOUR: Japan Enters the War	60
CHAPTER FIVE: Australia Prepares for Invasion	73
THE PORT OF FREMANTLE	91
CHAPTER SIX: The US Submarines come to Fremantle	98
THE SUBMARINES AT ALBANY	115
CHAPTER SEVEN: 1942: Submarines on the Offensive	120
PREMISES USED BY THE UNITED STATES NAVY	134
CHAPTER EIGHT: 1943: The Fremantle Submarines at War	140
THE SUBMARINE REPAIR UNIT AT NORTH WHARF	158
CHAPTER NINE: Meanwhile, on the Home Front	163
CHAPTER TEN: A Submariner's Life	184
WAR TIME MARRIAGES	206
CHAPTER ELEVEN: Early 1944: The Allies Fight Back	217
UNITED STATES NAVY ACCOMMODATION	232
CHAPTER TWELVE: Late 1944: British Submarines Arrive	235
TRENCHANT SINKS ASHIGARA	252
CHAPTER THIRTEEN: Clandestine Operations	258
THE BRITISH MINIATURE SUBMARINES	284
CHAPTER FOURTEEN: The War Comes to an End	292

CHAPTER FIFTEEN: Remembering the Submarine Base	319
CHAPTER SIXTEEN: Submarines Return to Western Australia	334
CONCLUSION	349
APPENDIX	362
ENDNOTES	393
SOURCES AND SUGGESTED READING	430
Index	455

During the war, Fremantle played host to over 170 Allied submarines, with submarines of the United States, British and Dutch navies making a total of 416 war patrols out of the port between March 1942 and August 1945.

The Fremantle Port was closed, and barbed wire and sentries appeared at various strategic points, transforming it, almost overnight, from a relatively quiet place to the largest submarine base in the Southern Hemisphere. The secrecy surrounding the operation of the Fremantle submarine base meant that its existence was little known at the time and, until now, has been largely forgotten by history.

The Royal Navy submarines Totem and Tapir. (Royal Australian Navy Public Affairs, HMAS Stirling.)

The British submarine tender HMS Adamant at North Wharf. (West Australian Newspapers – War 897.)

ACKNOWLEDGEMENTS

The first edition of this book was published as *Fremantle's Secret Fleets* in 1995, only fifteen years ago. With the rapid development of computer technology and the internet, however, records that were virtually impossible for a researcher based in Western Australia to access can now be located. In this new edition I have been able to include a much more detailed account of the activities of the Fremantle-based submarines, but even authoritative sources differ at times, so it has not always been possible to find out exactly what really happened. Readers who are interested in looking more fully into any aspects of the topic may find the bibliography helpful.

I thank again all those people who helped me produce the original edition, with a special mention of Ben Green who scanned all the photos but wasn't included in my original list. This time around, I wish to thank Sally May and Michael Gregg of the Western Australian Museum's Maritime History Department for their support. Sally May was responsible for the original concept and title, and read the manuscript this time, while Michael Gregg not only tracked down a number of new submarines, but made corrections to my final list and conducted a check of the final proofs. Michael has researched the Fremantle Harbour and Slipway records, compiling a database of shipping arrivals and departures that will surely become a marvellous research tools for anyone doing Western Australian maritime history. I would also like to thank Tim Cumming for his attractive design and Ray Coffey for his editing and support.

United States submarines at North Wharf at the end of World War II. A submarine tender (possibly USS Anthedon) is at the wharf. (West Australian Newspapers – War 906.)

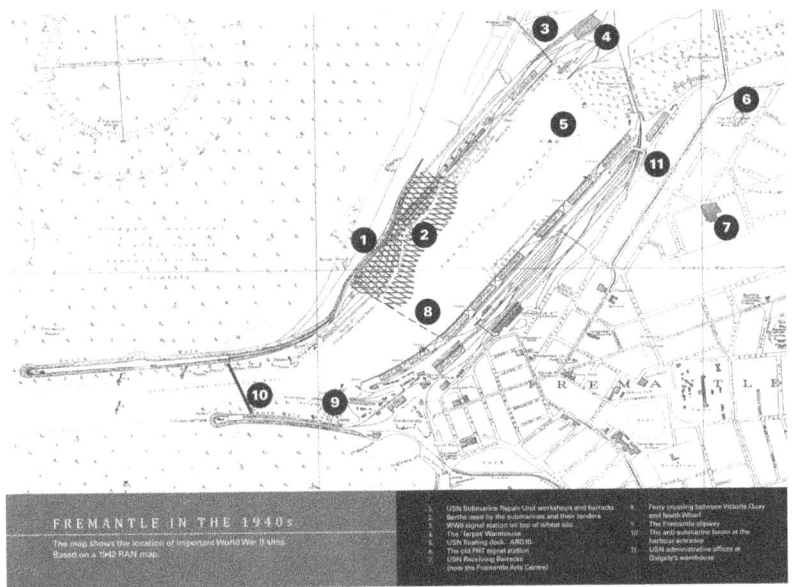

Aerial photograph of Fremantle Harbour in February 1945, showing boom defence nets in the foreground. Looking west to Gage Roads. (Western Australian Museum, courtesy A.J. Seymour – MHD 320/014.)

INTRODUCTION

In 1995, fifty years after the end of World War II, in the first edition of this book, published as *Fremantle's Secret Fleets,* I wrote: 'The idea of the battlefield as an arena for adventure and the proving of "manhood" has surely been relegated to the realm of fiction and fairy-tale, by the real or vicarious experience of modern warfare ... the shifting economic alliances and horrific civil conflicts of recent decades must have killed forever the naive view that wars are fought between the forces of good and evil.'

The dreadful events of the first decade of this new millennium, and the rhetoric accompanying the 'war on terror' have, sadly, proven that this is a forlorn hope.

The experience of war has profoundly influenced the development of Australia's dominant traditions. Fascination with war and glorification of war were part of the European inheritance of the early white settlers. To Britain and her neighbours, success in war was the measure of a nation's right to independence, and skill and courage in war the measure of a man. Thus, the Great War role of Australian soldiers at Gallipoli and in France was seen as crucial to Australian nationhood. Indeed, Anzac Day has often been referred to as a celebration of the true birth of the nation.

In the decades after the Great War, heroic statues of the bronzed, slouch-hatted Anzacs who had gone away to fight and often die in a distant war were erected in towns all over Australia. It was an image that dominated the childhood memories of the generation of Australian men who joined the Second Australian Imperial Forces (2nd AIF) and sailed off to fight for 'Mother England' during the first years of World War II. Unlike the earlier conflict, however, war was not to remain safely on the other side of the globe. In 1942, the women and men who stayed at home were to face the threat of invasion, and the alarming prospect of a war fought on Australian soil.

In the post-World War II period there was a tendency to ridicule Australia's fear of invasion, but in the decade and a half since the first edition of this book appeared, Australia has rediscovered its World War II history. The debate about the 'Battle for Australia' continues, but it is generally accepted that in the early months of 1942 Australians at home faced a perceived, if not real, threat of invasion.

When Japanese records became available they showed that, after consideration, the Japanese High Command had decided in 1942 against mounting a full-scale invasion.[1] The Allies, of course, did not know this at the time, so the near certainty of Japanese incursions into Australian territory was accepted, not only by the Australian population but also by the Allied commanders. For the general public the future looked very grim, as the rapidity of the Japanese advance and the fall of well-fortified Allied bases exposed the vulnerability of Australia's unprotected coastline.

Of course, until the Japanese conquest of South-East Asia most of that region was controlled by European powers. It is sometimes forgotten, now that they have become sovereign nations, that when World War II broke out Britain held Malaya (now Malaysia), Burma (Myanmar) and Singapore; Timor was a Portuguese possession; and France ruled a large part of South-East Asia, including Vietnam and Cambodia. The Netherlands controlled all the islands that were to become Indonesia (known as the Dutch East Indies), and the United States of America had military bases in the Philippines, Hawaii and a number of small islands in the Pacific.

The United States submarine Puffer operated out of Fremantle during 1944 and 1945. (Western Australian Museum, courtesy William Pouleris – MHA 4561/18.)

Indeed, it was less than 40 years before World War II, that Australia itself had ceased to be just a collection of Britain's colonial possessions, and many Australians, including the country's leaders, still looked to Great Britain's military and naval strength to ensure the nation's security.

Then, in February 1942, Britain's 'impregnable' fortress at Singapore fell and with it went all hope of protection from Britain, which was fighting for its own survival against the might of Germany and struggling to hang on to Burma in the East. The rest of Indochina was already under Japanese domination, and the Dutch, embattled in the Indies, had already lost their homeland to the Germans. The ships of the United States Navy had been driven out of the Philippines and were retreating towards the Australian mainland. Allied resistance was faltering, and there was every possibility that Japan might continue its southward push and occupy part of the Australian mainland.

People in Australia, and particularly Western Australia, only needed to glance at a map to be aware of their vulnerability should the Japanese maintain the momentum of their early successes. With the newspapers belatedly reporting Japanese atrocities in China and Korea, Australians had few illusions about what they could expect under Japanese rule.[2] Meanwhile, northern Australian ports were being bombed. As a result of the post-war tendency to play down the seriousness of Australia's position in the early 1940s, the number of enemy attacks, and the extent of damage inflicted on Darwin, Broome, Wyndham and other targets in northern Australia, comes as a surprise to most Australians.

The general perception at the time was that Australia, or part of it, may have fallen to the enemy but for the assistance of the Americans, and in the light of the information available in 1942 this seems to have been a reasonable assessment. If the US had decided to draw back from the South Pacific and concentrate on defending Hawaii and the US mainland, Australia would have been open to harassment, if not invasion.

When the US forces came to Australia in 1942, however, it was not just an altruistic rescue operation. It was a matter of mutual need. All the other Allied bases in the south-west Pacific region had fallen to the enemy and Japanese submarines were already attacking America's west coast. If the war was to be kept a safe distance from the homeland, the US needed a secure base (and a local source of provisions) in the South Pacific from which to carry the war into enemy-held territory. Australia was really the only choice. That the two countries shared a common language and ethnic background was an added bonus.

United States forces played a dominant role in the war with Japan, particularly in the western Pacific region. Australian military leaders were generally subordinate to the United States Command under General Douglas MacArthur, and thousands of US troops streamed into Australia. Though the American submarines were only a small part of this force, they played a vital role in defeating the enemy.

The first United States submarines arrived at Fremantle, Western Australia, with the submarine tender USS *Holland* on 3 March 1942, and the base was still in operation when the war ended. During those years the port played host to 168 Allied submarines, together with their support vessels and land-based facilities. Personnel from the Australian

Defence Forces, government departments and private industry were involved in setting up, maintaining and supporting the submarine base, which was to become the largest in the Southern Hemisphere. Some of these submarines only came to Fremantle for maintenance, or en route to other bases, but 154 submarines of the United States,[3] British[4] and Dutch[5] navies made 341 war patrols from the port between March 1942 and August 1945. Some Fremantle-based submarines also made patrols from Darwin or Exmouth Gulf.

(top) The Dutch submarine KX1 was taken out of service after arriving from Sri Lanka in March 1945. After being stripped, the submarine sank in Fremantle harbour. The photograph shows it being raised. (Western Australian Museum, courtesy M. Sweetman – MHA 903B/35A.)
(Bottom) Walter Murray snapped the Royal Navy submarine Totem lying at the Fremantle wharf

on 25 August 1946. (Western Australian Museum, Murray Collection – MHA 4504/79A.)

During the latter half of 1942 and early 1943, a second important base was set up in Queensland's capital, Brisbane, which, for a brief period during the most intense preparations for the Allied resurgence in the Pacific, was to outstrip its western counterpart. As in Western Australia, setting up the Brisbane base involved the cooperation of local government and industry. Brisbane was also General MacArthur's headquarters at the time, so the role of the submarines was overshadowed by the large numbers of servicemen and equipment building up there for the Allied push to drive the Japanese out of the territory they had conquered in the Pacific.[6]

If the war against Japan is seen simply as a Pacific Ocean conflict, Brisbane, on Australia's Pacific coast, seems an obvious choice for a submarine base. The strategic importance of the Fremantle base is, however, one of the best-kept secrets of World War II.

There are two elements that explain why Fremantle was chosen for a major submarine base. The first is to do with geography. It can be seen by the map of Australia and its near neighbours directly to the north that the territory captured by the Japanese in early 1942—in particular Indonesia and Timor—is directly north of Western Australia, and very close. It is easy to forget this fact, a fact which also explains why so many Western Australians holiday in Bali.

Then we must look at the historical setting. In 1942 that tourist industry did not exist. The Dutch, British, French and Portuguese colonies were exotic, faraway places visited by few English-speaking people. Apart from the normal maritime activities of the local people, travel among the islands was mostly the province of pearlers and other exploitative adventurers, using small steamers or sailing vessels. There were no regular passenger flights into the region. It was, after all, only twelve years since Charles Kingsford Smith had made the first long-distance flight across the Pacific. At that time, even in Europe and the United States, only the wealthy could afford to travel by air.

Australia's north was equally undeveloped. The important ports that now lie on the north-west coast were not to be developed until vast iron-ore deposits were discovered in the region decades later. In 1942, Darwin was the only important port between Brisbane and Fremantle, and it was already under attack and possessed little infrastructure. Fremantle was closer than any of the alternative sites to the important oil fields and other resources of Japan's new conquests.

With the dominant role of Hollywood in popular culture, the American experience of the war with Japan has overshadowed other accounts, and many people simply know of it as 'the Pacific War', with little or no acknowledgement that there was a 'western front' to this conflict. The Japanese-held territories formed a barrier between the Pacific and the strategically important Indian Ocean. The Suez Canal was under threat from Axis forces in North Africa and the Middle East, and Japan already held most of South-East Asia. Part of

Burma was in Japanese hands and Britain was involved in a desperate struggle to prevent the Japanese from taking the remainder of that country. If Burma fell, it would cut lines of communications with China, still fighting its long war against the Japanese invaders, and India would also be vulnerable. Indeed, in 1944 there was an attempted invasion of Indian territory.

India had been on the path to a negotiated independence when World War II began, but this was postponed when the British viceroy declared war without consulting Indian leaders. Britain relied heavily on Indian troops, especially in Burma, but the people really had little incentive to continue fighting for the British Empire, and some advocated throwing off the colonial yoke and negotiating a peace with Japan. A pro-Axis group was already in existence. If Burma fell and India was neutralised, the eastern Indian Ocean would be open to the enemy, so a base on Australia's west coast made sense.

After the war, Australian historians showed little interest in the role of Allied submarines in World War II. As the Royal Australian Navy had no submarines of its own, except for an old Dutch submarine used for antisubmarine training, the existence of the base at Fremantle was not relevant to Australian naval history.

The location of the base in Western Australia also explains this lack of interest. The state was still seen by the rest of Australia, including the federal authorities, as a backwater. As records dealing with the eastern states are more numerous and accessible, later writers have tended to perpetuate this view. For instance, to American writer John Hammond Moore, Western Australia seems to have been almost invisible. In *Over-sexed, Over-paid and Over Here*, his history of the Americans in Australia from 1941 to 1945, 'Freemantle' [sic] and 'United States Navy submarines' each receive two page-number references in the index. Under 'Sydney', there are twenty-three references.

Then there is the position of Fremantle itself. It lies at the mouth of the Swan River, some nineteen kilometres from the state capital, Perth. So, unlike Brisbane, where the submarines were seen travelling down the Brisbane River from their base at New Farm, or docked at the historic graving dock where the Queensland Maritime Museum now stands, at Fremantle the submarines had immediate access to the Indian Ocean. Only those living or working near the port would have seen much of their activity. With censorship and security provisions keeping precise information out of the contemporary press, the existence of the base would rarely have been brought to the attention of the people of Perth.

But the very nature of submarine warfare, together with the strategies and internal politics of the United States Command, also tended to hide the submarines' vital role in the defence of Australia. Submarines go about their deadly business silently and invisibly. While it would have been difficult to hide the presence and movements of a large fleet of surface warships in Fremantle harbour, with submarines it was easier to keep the exact number secret, and to mask their arrivals and departures. Even the submariners had little knowledge of the movements of the rest of the fleet. Each submarine crew was virtually isolated during patrols, and while on shore would only meet men from the other boats then in harbour.

Nevertheless, the people of Fremantle must have noticed the changes to the city as the United States Navy (USN) moved in and took over sixteen warehouses and a number of other buildings. Civilian contractors were involved in the construction of new buildings on North Wharf and various other venues, including the former asylum and old women's home in Finnerty Street, which now houses the Fremantle Arts Centre. By 1944, over two hundred civilian workers were employed directly in USN facilities.

The harbour soon became a place of barbed wire, searchlights and sentries, off limits to most civilians. The Royal Australian Navy was responsible for harbour control and defence, including the anti-submarine boom defence net system at the entrance to Fremantle Harbour. An elaborate boom defence system was also installed in Cockburn Sound in the latter years of the war, with the aim of making the sound into a safe haven for Allied shipping.

It was also in Cockburn Sound that commandos from the Services Reconnaissance Department's Z Special Unit (Z-Force) were trained in preparation for daring cloak-and-dagger operations behind enemy lines.

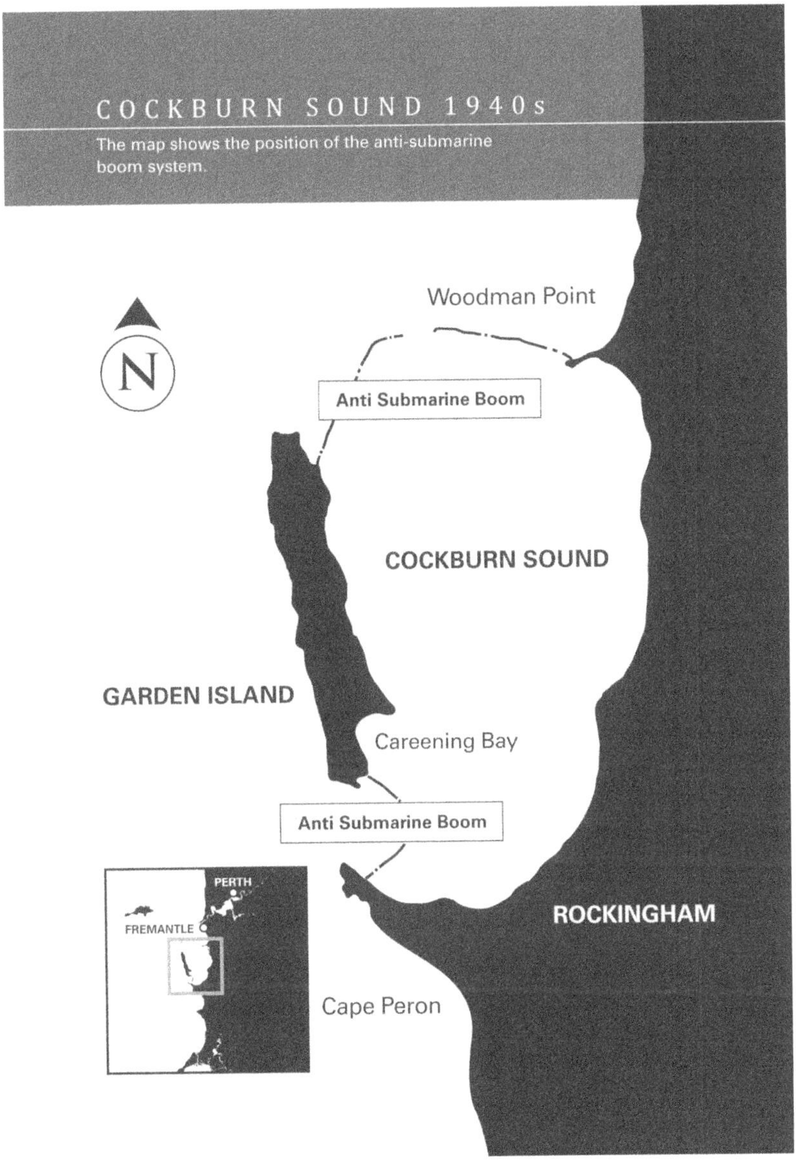

COCKBURN SOUND 1940s

The map shows the position of the anti-submarine boom system.

Woodman Point

Anti Submarine Boom

COCKBURN SOUND

GARDEN ISLAND

Careening Bay

Anti Submarine Boom

PERTH
FREMANTLE

ROCKINGHAM

Cape Peron

Victoria Quay after the war, with British T and V class submarines berthed alongside the coastal steamer Kybra and Fort Providence. (Western Australian Museum – MHD 355/030.)

Three different types of midget submarines were used for training at Careening Bay: the submersible boats (SBs or 'Sleeping Beauties'), and the larger Welman and Welfreighter types. The most famous clandestine operation out of Fremantle was the tragic Operation Rimau, a Z-Force mission that departed from Garden Island aboard the British submarine *Porpoise* on 11 September 1944.

The Western Australian experience of World War II is an important part of Australian maritime history, because the perceived threat was of a seaborne invasion of the unprotected northern and north-western coasts. So vital were the control and ownership of ships and boats that many private craft were confiscated, requisitioned or even destroyed, and Australian companies with no previous boat-building experience were called on to build vessels of up to three hundred tons for use by Australian forces.

In 1995, because the Fremantle submarine base had played such a vital role in the nation's defence, it was considered important that its history be recorded while the memories of participants could still be tapped. Sadly, many of those who provided personal information about their experiences in World War II have passed away. At that time, pressure of time and financial restraints limited what research could be achieved, but new material has become available since then and the original account has been expanded to include relevant information.

At the beginning of this new edition, you will find two new chapters that tell the fascinating stories of the evolution of submarines, and of Australia's submarines before World War II.

The final two chapters are also new. Where the submarine base had almost faded from popular memory in 1995, the presence of the Australian Oberon-class submarine *Ovens* on the historic WWII slipway at Fremantle is now a constant reminder that submarines played a part in the port's history, and in the maritime history of the nation. The story of how it came to be there is told in 'Remembering the Submarine Base'. The final chapter looks at Australia's experience with submarines since the war, and how submarines—our own Australian fleet—are once again based in Western Australia.

The role of the World War II submarine base at Fremantle is closely linked to a number of connected themes in Australian history, such as auxiliary, women's and intelligence services, and the impact of the war on civilian life and industry in Australia. For readers who would like to investigate some of these topics, or to find out more about submarines and World War II history, additions have been made to the original bibliography. As a great deal of information can now be found on the internet, I have included a list of the websites that I have found to be most useful.

General arrangement drawing of the Royal Navy's first submarines, the Holland class. (Western Australian Museum – MHD 376/06.)

CHAPTER ONE

The Development of the Submarine

We tend to think of the submarine as a modern phenomenon, like aircraft and motor vehicles, but the story of its development goes back to the 16th century. Even earlier than that, Leonardo da Vinci, for one, had toyed with plans for a submarine.

Englishman William Bourne designed a submersible boat in 1578. The bilges were fitted with leather ballast tanks and the operator had access to air through a hollow mast. It had no means of propulsion and seems never to have been built, but in 1605 a German doctor and mathematician named Magnus Pegelius built some kind of submersible. Little is known about this craft, which apparently sank. Some fifteen years later, in England, Cornelius van Drebbel took the idea a step further by designing an oar-propelled submersible, possibly based on Bourne's design, which he tested on the Thames.

The next advance seems to have been in 1653, when a Frenchman named De Son built a submersible at Rotterdam. This 72-foot vessel, the first mechanically powered submarine, was propelled by an internal paddlewheel driven by clockwork, which was not powerful enough to make it work.[1] Then, between 1690 and 1692, the French physicist Denis Papin designed and built two submersible craft. These box-like vessels appear to have had no means of propulsion, but Papin's use of a centrifugal pump to equalise pressure was innovative.

Over a century later, in 1776, American David Bushnell's one-man, pedal-operated *Turtle* was used during the American War of Independence in an attempt to sink a British warship, HMS *Eagle.* Despite the failure of the mission, the potential use of submarines in warfare had been demonstrated. The *Turtle,* shaped like two turtle shells joined together, was apparently about three metres long, made of steel-reinforced wood, with a covering of tar.

In 1800 another American, Robert Fulton, who was living in Republican France, built the *Nautilus.* This craft still had no mechanised means of propulsion, being driven by a hand-cranked screw propeller. It was shaped like a teardrop, with two horizontal fins on the rudder to control the angle of dive, which have evolved to become a modern submarine's diving planes. On the surface, the vessel was wind-propelled using a collapsible sail. When France rejected the project Fulton tried to interest the British in the submarine, but it was eventually abandoned.

In 1837 a South American submarine, the *Hipopotamo,* was tested in Ecuador, and in 1850 Bavarian Wilhelm Bauer produced the *Brandtaucher* (also called *Le Plongeur Marin),* which was designed for use against a possible blockade of the German coast. The German navy was interested in the submersible but it sank during trials and was lost, though the crew survived. Bauer offered his services to Austria, England and finally Russia, where he built *Le Diable Marin* in 1856.

During the 1860s submarine design advanced quite rapidly. In 1863 in France, Charles Burn and Simon Bourgeois produced the 140-foot *Plongeur,* which was propelled by a compressed-air-powered reciprocating engine. The submarine, which could travel at 5 nautical miles (9km) per hour and dive to a depth of ten metres, was armed with a ram and an electrically fired spar torpedo. Unfortunately it proved difficult to handle.

Then, during the American Civil War, a series of submersibles was developed by Confederate interests in an attempt to break the Union blockade. In 1862 the *Pioneer,* built by Hunley, McClintock and Watson, was launched in the Mississippi River, but it had to be scuttled when the Union forces advanced on New Orleans. Another Confederate submarine, *Bayou St. John,* was built about that time but little is known about it. The *Pioneer's* inventors then joined with others to produce the *American Diver.* Once again, although they had experimented with electromagnetic and steam propulsion, it was hand cranked. After one unsuccessful attempt to attack the Union blockade, the submarine sank, but the next Confederate submarine, launched in 1863, was more successful. Named *H.L. Hunley* after its designer, it was a hand-propelled craft, twelve metres long with a top speed of 4 knots (7.4km) per hour. The vessel was taken over by the Confederate military and operated as a Confederate army vessel. Several disastrous trials were conducted, in one of which the designer, H.L. Hunley, lost his life. Then, in February 1864, the *Hunley* was successful in sinking the Union vessel USS *Housatonic,* though it was lost in the process. The wreck of the *Hunley* lay on the bottom for 131 years, until it was found in 1995. The remains of the *H.L. Hunley* were recovered in 2000.

The Confederate forces also had a semi-submersible steam-driven torpedo boat, the *David,* which was built in 1863 by T. Stoney. A cigar-shaped vessel that operated very low in the water and burned anthracite coal, which gives off little smoke, the *David* seriously damaged the Union ironclad steamer USS *New Ironsides* in Charleston harbour. In 1864 it was used to attack USS *Memphis* and the USS *Wabash.* There is no record of what happened to the vessel, which may have been captured by Union forces when Charleston was taken. The Union forces were also interested in submarines. In 1862 there was the *Alligator,* which sank before it underwent its final tests, and ten years later the navy showed an interest in another unsuccessful model, the *Intelligent Whale.*

In 1864 Spain produced the first combustion-powered submarine, *Ictineo II,* designed by Narcis Monturiol. Driven by a steam engine on the surface, underwater it was propelled by an air-independent power system utilising peroxide as a fuel. The chemical process also provided oxygen for the crew and the auxiliary steam engine. During tests the *Ictineo II* could submerge to 27.5 metres and stay underwater for up to seven and a half hours. Monturiol also pioneered double-hulled construction. A replica of *Ictineo* is on display at Barcelona.

Two years later German engineer Karl Flach built the *Flach* for the Chilean government. It was launched in May 1866, but after several successful tests it sank in Valparaiso Bay, taking Flach, his son and nine others to their deaths. The Chilean government hopes to find and raise the submarine.

During the 1870s two important inventions contributed to the advancement of submarine technology. They were the self-propelled torpedo and the petrol-combustion engine. Robert Whitehead produced the first successful, self-propelled torpedo for the Austrian imperial navy in 1866. The British bought Whitehead's torpedoes and began producing their own in 1872.

The internal-combustion engine had been around for quite a long time, but the use of petrol only came into use from the mid-19th century. In 1863 Jean Joseph Étienne Lenoir produced a three-wheeled carriage powered by a petrol engine with a primitive carburettor. Four years later, German engineer Nikolaus August Otto developed and patented the four-stroke engine. In 1870 Siegfried Marcus used a petrol engine to power a small vehicle, beginning the development of the automobile.

With these new developments there was a proliferation of submarine projects across Europe and the Americas, and by 1880 forty-two such projects were underway, fifteen of them producing finished submarines.[2] Other designs were soon being developed, and by the turn of the century the concept of the submarine was well established.

In America, the most successful submarine designer was Irish-born John Philip Holland. In 1875 he unsuccessfully submitted his first submarine designs to the United States Navy. The Irish republican revolutionary group, the Fenians, became interested. They provided funds for development of the design, resulting in the *Fenian Ram,* launched in 1881.

It took some time, however, for the new technologies to come into use. In 1881 fifty human-powered craft were built in Poland for the Russian government, but the same inventor produced an electric submarine three years later. The Peruvian government's *Toro Submarino* was built in 1879, and that year the steam-driven *Resurgam,* designed by George Garrett, was launched in Britain.

With backing from Swedish industrialist Thorsten Nordenfelt, Garrett then developed the Nordenfelt No 1, which was steam powered and armed with a Whitehead torpedo and a machine gun. It was sold to Greece for £9,000 in 1886. The firm went on to produce two submarines for the Ottoman Empire. In 1890 two Nordenfelt-type submarines were built in Germany.

In 1890, the Spanish navy's electric-powered submarine, designed by Isaac Peral, became the first to launch a torpedo while submerged. Another electric submarine, the French *Gymnote,* launched in 1888 and fitted with a periscope, served with the French navy until 1907. France was the first nation to add submarines to its naval forces, followed by the United States.

The success of American John Philip Holland has tended to overshadow some of these valuable contributions to the evolution of the military submarine. After the *Fenian Ram* Holland had fallen out with the Irish revolutionaries, but he continued his work, going on to produce, in 1897, the first petrol-powered submarine. In 1900 it was bought by the United States Navy and became USS *Holland,* America's first navy submarine. Six more of the submarines were ordered.

HM submarine Holland I, 1902. (Western Australian Museum – MHD 376/07.)

Simon Lake was Holland's only rival in America. He built his *Argonaut Junior* in 1894 and *Protector* in 1901. Though neither vessel was accepted by the

USN, Lake continued to make valuable contributions to the development of the submarine. Certain innovations, such as a flat keel, diving planes on the conning tower and a lockout chamber for divers to exit, first appear in his *Protector.* The submarine was sold to Russia in 1904, and he went on to design submarines for the Austro-Hungarian and Russian navies. In 1914 a Simon Lake submarine pushed the maximum diving depth down to 78.03 metres.[3]

In June 1900 France commissioned the *Narval,* a double-hulled, steam and electric submarine with a range of over 160.09 kilometres on the surface and over 16 kilometres underwater. The *Narval* was followed, in 1904, by the *Aigette,* which used a diesel engine when traveling on the surface. Seventy-six of these submarines were built by 1914. The danger of fire aboard a submarine lessened as diesel engines began to replace petrol engines.

Producing functional military submarines, and getting them accepted by the world's navies, were two different things, however, and in 1901, the year the Commonwealth of Australia was proclaimed, the ethics of using submarines in naval warfare was still being debated.

The Dutch submarine Luctor et Emergo during trials in 1906. The vessel was commissioned into the Royal Netherlands Navy as Onderzeese Boot 1, or O1. (Western Australian Museum, courtesy Willem Broertjes – MHA 4592/23.)

The world's great naval traditions had evolved over centuries dominated by the sailing ship, and were comparable to the rules of land warfare, soon to be overturned forever in the World War I trenches. Ideally, a ship was expected to identify itself by flying its nation's flag before engaging the enemy. Approaching an adversary by stealth was 'not quite cricket'. Civilian vessels were not to be attacked unless they were known to be supporting the enemy by carrying armaments or other war materials. To prove this, the vessel had to be boarded and searched, and the safety of passengers ensured, either by providing lifeboats or taking them on board. These provisions, probably never universally adhered to, were impractical in the case of submarines and defeated the whole rationale for deploying them, which was to destroy enemy shipping by stealth.

These concerns, as well as political conservatism, had caused some resistance to the introduction of submarines into the Royal Navy. But other countries, especially France, were including them in their fleets and Britain could not afford to be left behind. In 1901, although Admiral Arthur Wilson is reputed to have referred to the use of submarines in war as 'underhand, unfair and damned un-English', Britain began building five of the American Holland submarines under licence from the Electric Boat Company. These led to the development of an improved series of classes, starting with the

A-class and progressing to the E-class, which was to be the most successful.[4]

The Russian, Japanese, Netherlands and German navies also acquired submarines in the early 1900s. The Imperial Russian Navy launched its first submarine in 1902, and an improved model the following year. They also acquired the German-built *Forelle* and two American-built submarines, which took part in the Russo-Japanese war of 1904-1905. More improved classes were developed and, by 1908, Russia's Baltic fleet included 17 submarines.

By 1904, when John Philip Holland set up a new company and began building submarines in Japan, that country had already acquired some seven submarines. Japan's interest had been evident as early as 1897, when Japanese naval officers went to the US to examine the recently launched *Holland VI*. In 1903 Japan bought the *Protector,* built by Simon Lake, and the *Fulton* from the Electric Boat Company the following year. Five more submarines were ordered from the two suppliers.

The Dutch and German navies had to wait until 1906 to add submarines to their fleets. The first Dutch navy submarine was a Holland boat, built under licence in the Netherlands and launched in 1905. After trials, it was bought by the Royal Netherlands Navy and commissioned in 1906 as the *Onderzeese boot 1,* later renamed *O 1.* In the years leading up to WWI, the Netherlands commissioned three more submarines, *O 2, O 3* and *K 1.*[5]

The first boat for the German navy was completed in 1905 and launched in 1906. It was the double-hulled Karp-class submarine, *U-1,* which was driven by a kerosene engine. It was armed with a single torpedo tube, and could travel at 10.8 knots (20km/h) on the surface and 8.7 (16.1km/h) when submerged. By 1912 Germany had begun to make up for lost time in building up her submarine fleet, and by the beginning of World War I had 29 submarines ready to go into action and another nineteen being built.

Rapid improvements in submarine design continued to be made during the years leading up to World War I, by which time all the major combatant navies had established submarine fleets. In addition to Germany's 29, Britain's submarines numbered 77, with another 15 being built. France had 62 and Russia 58. Of the Ottoman Empire's seven, only two were in service.[6]

The last known image of RAN Submarine AE1 tied alongside the portside of HMAS Encounter in New Guinea waters. (Western Australian Museum, courtesy Australian War Memorial – MHK D14/002.)

CHAPTER TWO

Australia's Early Submarines

In 1913 the Royal Australian Navy (RAN) ordered two of the British E-class submarines. The two submarines, *AE1* and *AE2,* were commissioned in February 1914 and arrived in Sydney on 24 May.[1] These submarines were 55.17 metres long, with a beam of just under seven metres. Like all the recently designed submarines of the time, they were powered by diesel engines for surface travel and by electric motors when submerged. They could reach speeds of 15 knots on the surface and ten knots underwater, and were armed with four 18-inch torpedo tubes.[2] The submarines' officers were all from the British Royal Navy (RN), with the crew made up of both RAN and RN sailors.

In Australia, the outbreak of war brought an immediate need to forestall Germany's use of its south-west Pacific possessions as bases from which to harass Allied shipping. At that time, Germany controlled the eastern half of New Guinea and most of the islands to the east, including the Bismarck Archipelago, Nauru, Samoa and some of the Solomon, Caroline and Mariana Islands. First colonised as a commercial venture by a German company in 1884, East New Guinea was formally taken over by the Imperial German government in 1899. The German navy's East Asia Squadron was in the region when war was declared.

The two RAN submarines were part of the Australian fleet sent to take control of these German colonies, and both were involved in the campaign to occupy German New Guinea. While patrolling St George's Channel near the Duke of York Islands on 14 September 1914, however, *AE1,* commanded by Lieutenant Commander T.F. Besant, RN, disappeared without trace off the Bismarck Peninsula. It was the first Allied submarine to be lost during the war.[3] The wreck of the *AE1* has never been found.[4]

AE2, commanded by Lieutenant Commander Henry Stoker, RN, returned safely to Sydney, and in December 1914 it went to Albany to join the second Allied convoy that was assembling there before taking Australian troops overseas. From there the submarine was towed across the Indian Ocean to join the British squadron that was about to take part in the Gallipoli campaign.[5]

Turkey, then part of the Ottoman Empire and allied to Germany, held the approaches to the Black Sea from the Mediterranean, blocking the route to Russia. Britain decided to force a way through the Dardanelles, the narrow strait connecting the Aegean Sea and the Sea of Marmara, and attack the Turkish capital, Istanbul. In March 1915 a large Allied fleet attempted the task, but it had not progressed far into the strait before three battleships were destroyed by Turkish mines and another three badly damaged. The plan was then abandoned in favour of the alternative: a disastrous land offensive that was to indelibly imprint the name Gallipoli, and the date 25 April 1915, on the Australian psyche.

Just days before the Gallipoli landing, *AE2* was ordered to slip through the Dardanelles and disrupt Turkish shipping in the Sea of Marmara during the Allied assault. Besides creating a diversion, it was hoped that if the mission were successful other submarines could follow to harass Turkish shipping and prevent enemy reinforcements being sent to the front. Previous attempts by British and French submarines had failed.

AE2 off Aden en route to Gallipoli in 1915. In the background is HMT Berrima which had towed AE2 from Albany to Aden. (Western Australian Museum – MHD 0092/01.)

On 24 April 1915, the submarine slipped into the Dardanelles under cover of darkness and managed to progress some 6 nautical miles (11.11km) into the strait before a damaged hydroplane forced it to return to Mudros for repairs. At two-thirty am on the following day, 25 April, Stoker made his second attempt. The submarine began to creep through the strait on the surface, but at about 4am it was forced to dive to avoid enemy fire. A couple of hours later *AE2* reached Chanak, where the strait is at its narrowest. At this point, the submarine encountered and torpedoed the Turkish gunboat *Peyki Sevket.* Then, while manoeuvering to avoid an enemy destroyer, *AE2* ran aground right under the guns of a Turkish fort.[6]

> Fire was opened on us from all sides, the captain said the sea was one mass of foam caused by the shells fired at us but luckily we were not hit, but we could hear inside the boat the shrapnel dropping on us like a lot of stones ... the captain said the boat had to come off wether [sic] the propellors [sic] got damaged or not. With this he sped up the motors to their speed limit which brought us safely off and down to 90ft [27.43 m] again.[7]

Despite a second grounding, *AE2* reached the Sea of Marmara to become the first Allied vessel to pass through the Dardanelles. At dusk on 26 April, Stoker sent a wireless telegraph message to inform his superiors that *AE2* had successfully completed its mission.[8]

Meanwhile, the initial landing at Gallipoli had exposed the Allied troops to devastating enemy fire. Recent studies have suggested that poor planning and ignorance of the topography led to the landing at Anzac Cove being made in the wrong place. The Anzacs, facing an entrenched enemy, had been unable to advance very far up into the ridges and ravines by the day's end. The divisional commanders on the ground could see the situation was very bad and sent a message to General Birdwood, the British commander of the Anzac forces, suggesting that a strategic withdrawal would be advisable.

Birdwood reported to General Hamilton, the British commander, who was in the process of discussing the suggestion with his senior officers when the news of *AE2's* success was reported to him. It was difficult for the general to accept the possibility of withdrawing before the campaign was really underway, and the prospects of getting the troops out safely and efficiently were not promising. Though there is some argument about how much Stoker's message really influenced Hamilton's decision, it did give the general something positive to offer the embattled army. His '...dig, dig, dig...' message to Birdwood has often been quoted. The important part of the message explained that it would take at least two days to re-embark the forces, but the news that *AE2* had got through would have cheered the troops.[9]

Over the next four days, Turkish ships were busy trying to find and destroy *AE2,* and although the submarine eluded them it was unable to sink any more enemy vessels. Finally, in an encounter with the Turkish torpedo boat *Sultanhisar, AE2* was so badly damaged that it was necessary to abandon ship and scuttle it by venting the tanks. Stoker and his crew were taken prisoner and endured three and a half years in captivity, during which time three men died.[10]

Unlike the British submarines that followed, *AE2* was unable to return in triumph, and the fact that it was an Australian submarine that first forced a passage through the Dardanelles seems to have been forgotten. Stoker missed out on the Victoria Cross awarded to the commanders of those later submarines, but went on to enjoy a long career as an actor, director and writer in the theatre and film world, as well as serving again in senior roles during World War II.

AE2 drifted down onto the muddy floor of the Marmara Sea, where it was to lie undisturbed for eighty years. In 1995 the wreck was located by Selçuk Kolay, director of the Rahmi Koç Museum in Istanbul, lying in 86 metres of water.[11] An Australian dive team was involved in confirming the identification of the wreck, and a replica of the conning tower, complete with marine encrustations, has pride of place in the Western Australian Maritime Museum's Naval Defence Gallery.

The activities of submarines during the war again raised the question of ethics. The Allies were outraged when

German submarines sank the liner *Lusitania* and other passenger vessels. Though the threat of US intervention forced Kaiser Wilhelm to clamp down on the controversial tactics for a time, he was to authorise unrestricted submarine warfare later in the war.

In the years after the end of World War I, the ethics of submarine warfare were still being debated during international conferences, and the leading nations tried to formulate rules to cover use of this new and deadly weapon. Great Britain, for one, suggested banning submarines completely and was prepared to dispense with her fleet if the other nations agreed, but no binding agreement could be reached. The effectiveness of submarines in war had been fully demonstrated and no nation could really afford to be without them.[12]

The RAN was convinced of the need to replace its two lost submarines, so as early as 1915 the British Admiralty was approached for advice about what type of craft would be most suitable. The Australian Government was still influenced by the ambitious Henderson Report of 1911, which envisaged an expanded navy with six submarines and naval bases near the main capitals, including one in Cockburn Sound, south of Fremantle.[13] A more realistic plan suggested that only two submarines should be obtained, at an estimated cost of £200,000. Nothing was done at that stage, and when, in 1919, Britain offered a gift of six J-class submarines, they were quickly accepted.

The J-class submarines, first commissioned into the RN in 1916, had served in waters around Britain during the war, and one boat, the *J6*, was lost in the North Sea. It was replaced by the *J7*, which was slightly different, so Australia's new submarines were *J1*, *J2*, *J3*, *J4*, *J5* and *J7*. There had been some advances in design since *AE1* and *AE2* were built, and these submarines had improved armaments, a longer range, and a surface speed of 19 knots (35km/h).

Other than the crew of *AE2*, who had just returned to Britain after their release from captivity, Australia had few trained submariners at that time, so the submarines' crews were made up with volunteers from the RN. Once again the senior officers were all British, but one Royal Australian Naval Volunteer Reserve (RANVR) first lieutenant and nine sublieutenants were Australian. Accompanied by the new depot ship HMAS *Platypus,* the six submarines left Britain in April 1919. Unfortunately the vessels had not undergone thorough refits before being turned over to the RAN, so they all required extensive refits on arrival in Australia.

The RAN seems to have had little understanding of the maintenance requirements of a submarine fleet, and had underestimated the support facilities needed to keep six submarines in working order. Despite these problems, and delays in obtaining new batteries from the United Kingdom, four of the submarines took part in exercises during 1920. The post-war economy was deteriorating rapidly, however, and drastic cuts in funding soon reduced the navy's ability to maintain the fleet. Consequently, as the submarines became due for refits each one was laid up. By 1925 all had been laid up, and they were all stripped and their hulls scuttled between 1926 and 1929. *J3* and *J7* ended their days as breakwaters in Port Phillip Bay, Victoria and the others were scuttled at sea outside Port Phillip Heads..

Despite the financial constraints, the Australian Government still believed the navy needed a submarine arm, so in 1925 an order was placed for two new submarines to be built in the UK by Vickers. A new ocean-going design was chosen, which was more suitable for Australian conditions than the smaller submarines intended for coastal defence.

Australian submarines HMAS Otway and HMAS Oxley in England. The O-class submarines were technically advanced but unreliable and costly to maintain. They were returned to the Royal Navy. (Western Australian Museum, courtesy the Royal Australian Navy – MHA 4600/16.)

The new submarines, (1) and *Otway* (1), were launched in mid 1927, and after being fitted out and undergoing sea trials, they set out for Australia on 8 February 1928. These O-class submarines were 83.82 metres long and 8.5 metres in beam, with a range of 13,679.4 kilometres. Unfortunately the diesel engines were of a new and unproven design, and they were found to be defective. Only eight days out on their voyage, serious fractures were discovered in the engines of both of the submarines. The two vessels continued to Malta, where they were held up for about nine months while major repairs were done. It was a full twelve months before they reached Sydney on 14 February 1929, and this long delay in delivery, plus news of the faulty engines, attracted a great deal of criticism towards the government.

Economics had sealed the fate of the J-class submarines, but the new submarines sailed into an even worse economic environment, with the world moving rapidly into the major financial crisis remembered as the Great Depression.

Once again, planning for the submarines' care and deployment was inadequate, and though they took part in exercises with the fleet, in May 1930 *Oxley* and *Otway* were placed in reserve. The following year the Australian Government transferred the submarines to the Royal Navy because it was not possible to maintain them in light of the severe economic situation. Both submarines served with the RN in World War II, *Oxley* being lost off Norway in 1939.[14]

There was no likelihood that Australia would attempt to expand its navy while the Great Depression ran its course, and meanwhile the rising power and aggressive stance of Nazi Germany was bringing the world to the brink of war. When World War II finally came, the RAN had no submarine fleet. It was left to the submarines of the United States, Britain and the Netherlands to defend Australia from under the sea.

'EMPIRE AT WAR' screamed the West Australian newspaper on 4 September 1939. (Western Australian Museum, courtesy West Australian Newspapers – MHS 226/07.)

CHAPTER THREE

World War II Begins

On 3 September 1939, Australia followed Great Britain into World War II. There was no question of an independent stance. The 'mother country' was at war and, as in 1914 when the prime minister Andrew Fisher pledged 'our last man and our last shilling', the Menzies government, with the support of the Opposition, did not hesitate to follow suit.

Within hours of the declaration of war a British liner, the *Athenia,* had been sunk by the German submarine *U-30,* and by the end of the week, what was to become known as the Battle of the Atlantic had begun. Lasting throughout most of the war, it was not so much a battle as an ongoing struggle to protect Allied merchant ships against Germany's attempts to prevent indispensable supplies reaching British shores. The solution was for the merchant ships to travel in convoys under the protection of naval vessels, but there was still a terrible loss of ships and the merchant seamen who sailed them. The German U-boats were a formidable weapon in this war of attrition.

In Australia, the armed forces were quickly put on alert and, within a few days, thousands of men rushed to enlist. The government quickly introduced national security regulations, concentrating a great deal of power in the Federal Executive. Censorship and price controls were introduced, and the police, briefed by military intelligence, began rounding up 'enemy aliens' for internment. As the war progressed, the Commonwealth government acquired additional powers, giving it control of all the nation's resources. Under the legislation that was introduced, individual Australians could be required to provide goods or services, or to work in industries designated essential to the nation's defence.

HMAS Sydney is shown at anchor off Broome.
(Western Australian Museum, Murray Collection
– MHA 4503/92.)

During the so-called 'phony war', when the approach of real war became apparent, Australia had established government-owned munitions factories, which were employing three thousand men by 1939. Military aircraft were also being produced, the first being completed in March 1939.[1] There was to be a great expansion of these industries after Japan entered the conflict. With the men away fighting in the war, many women would be employed in these heavy industries.

When war broke out, the Royal Australian Navy (RAN) had two heavy cruisers, HMAS *Australia* and HMAS *Canberra,* and four light cruisers, HMAS *Adelaide,* HMAS *Sydney,* HMAS *Hobart* and HMAS *Perth*. *Hobart* and *Perth,* originally built for the Royal Navy (RN), were recommissioned into the RAN in 1938 and 1939. The second HMAS *Sydney* had also been intended for the RN, but was commissioned as a RAN vessel when launched in 1935. There was also a destroyer fleet consisting of *Stuart, Vampire, Vendetta, Voyager* and *Waterhen;* two escort sloops, *Swan* and *Yarra;* and a newly commissioned boom-defence vessel, *Kookaburra*. *Perth* had not yet left Britain for Australia when the war began, and at the request of the British Admiralty it was sent to the West Indies to help protect British interests there. The RAN had no submarines at this time, as the O-class submarines had been returned to the RN.

In October 1939, the RAN's destroyer fleet, with the cruiser *Hobart,* sailed to the support of the RN. At first they were ordered to Singapore, but then were diverted to the Mediterranean to protect Allied supply lines. By Christmas the fleet was at Malta, where they were joined in May 1940 by the cruisers *Australia, Canberra,* and *Sydney. Adelaide* remained in Australian waters, but it was an old vessel and the country was virtually undefended. New ships, particularly minesweepers, were soon ordered, but the RAN was forced to rely on requisitioned civilian vessels. These ranged in size from passenger liners to pearling luggers.[2]

Most of the men who rushed to join up as volunteers were enlisting for overseas duty in the 2nd AIF, but the government felt that more men were needed in the militia to defend Australia. In October 1939, therefore, a limited form of conscription was introduced whereby men over twenty-one years of age were called up for three months' training. Australian airmen were also being recruited to serve with Britain's Royal Air Force (RAF), which had been in action against the German navy since the day after war was declared. By the end of 1939, the Empire Air Training Scheme had been set up to provide a supply of trained Australian, Canadian and Rhodesian[3] air crews for service in Britain and Europe. Many of these airmen were to play important roles during the Battle of Britain in September 1940. From January 1940 some 500 men joined the Royal Australian Naval Volunteer Reserve and went overseas to serve in RN ships.

The 6th, 7th and 9th AIF divisions were sent to the Middle East and North Africa, where they would be involved in protecting British and Allied territories. By the 1930s Italy had control of a large area of north-east Africa, including Libya on the Mediterranean coast, and most of Eritrea and Somalia on the eastern side of the continent. In 1936 Italy had also conquered Abyssinia (now Ethiopia). Although they did not enter the war until June 1940, the Italians were in a position to threaten not only the important Middle Eastern oilfields, but also the vital trade route through the Mediterranean Sea and the Suez Canal. The 8th division was sent to Malaya (Malaysia). Most of the men would die in action during the first weeks of the war with Japan, or become prisoners of the Japanese when Singapore fell in 1942.

By the end of May 1940, the German army was advancing rapidly across Europe. Poland, the invasion of which brought Britain and the Commonwealth countries into the war, had fallen within a few weeks and would be divided up between Germany and her then Russian ally, the Union of Soviet Socialist Republics (USSR). Denmark and Norway were invaded in April 1940, followed in May by France, Belgium, Luxembourg and the Netherlands. The Netherlands surrendered in mid May, after a Dutch government in exile was set up in Britain. Some Dutch forces continued to fight with the Allies, including the submarines based in the Dutch East Indies.

As the enemy advanced across France, the British were forced back into a small part of the north-eastern coast. Between 27 May and 3 June, in one of the legendary feats of courage by ordinary British people, some 340,000 troops were evacuated from the small port of Dunkirk by a motley flotilla of small ships. Belgium fell at the end of the month, and Norway surrendered on 10 June. By that time German forces had pushed well into France, taking Paris on 14 June, and the French government was forced to retreat to Bordeaux. Then, with more than half the country under German control, France surrendered on 25 June. Some French people escaped to Britain, including Charles de Gaulle, who became leader of the Free French Forces.

In Britain, an invasion was expected at any time, and Hitler really was planning one. Civilians, mainly children, were evacuated from areas thought to be at risk, such as obvious military targets and coastal areas facing Europe. Men deemed to be enemy aliens, many of them refugees from Nazi Germany, were rounded up and interned. Although the terrible days of the Blitz were yet to come, the population was already feeling the effects of the war. Britain relied on imports of food and raw materials from overseas, and because German attacks on shipping were preventing essential supplies reaching the country, rationing was introduced in January 1940. Everyone was issued with a ration book containing coupons that were needed to buy food such as meat, butter or sugar. Petrol and everyday needs like paper were also rationed. Rationing was to become even more restrictive as the war progressed.

Hitler had been forced to postpone his invasion, but in August 1940 the British faced worse than food shortages. Airfields and industrial centres were the earliest targets of German bombing, but from 23 August London and other major cities were regularly attacked. During the first couple of months of intense bombing, known as the Battle of Britain, the RAF put up an effective defence, but there was a terrible toll, with 544 airmen lost between 10 July and 31 October. Many of these men were Australians.

When Italy entered the war, Australian navy vessels were involved in actions in the Mediterranean Sea, and it was there that, on 17 July 1940, HMAS *Sydney* sank the Italian cruiser *Bartolomeo Colleoni.* During the following month, the Italians occupied British Somaliland in north-east Africa. When the British were forced to retreat to Aden, HMAS *Hobart* supervised the withdrawal. The Italians were then able to move into Egypt in September, and the following month invaded Greece. The Australian 6th AIF division was part of the British forces that arrived in March 1941 to help defend the country. By the end of April, however, Greece was overrun and the Allied troops withdrew to the island of Crete. After a month of bitter fighting the enemy had gained the upper hand there as well, so Crete was also abandoned at the end of May, with heavy Allied losses.[4]

Meanwhile the Allies had been having some success against the Italians in North Africa. The Italians were forced to retreat in Egypt and the Australians took Bardia, capturing thousands of

Italian prisoners. Then Tobruk fell to British and Australian troops on 22 January. Germany was sending reinforcements, however, in the form of Rommel's Afrika Corps. This efficient and well-armed force arrived in February 1941 and soon began to turn the tide against the Allies. By 14 April the Afrika Corps was at Tobruk to begin a long siege that was not relieved until December.

During these first two years of the war, the lives of people at home in Australia began to be affected by increasingly intrusive economic and security measures, and for the families of those fighting overseas there was the ever-present fear of receiving an official telegram telling them their loved one was dead or missing in action. Nevertheless, for many Australians the war remained something happening far away, in Europe, Africa, the Atlantic and the Mediterranean.

By 1941, however, there were growing signs that war might not stay safely on the other side of the world. During the 1930s the rise of Nazi and fascist militarism in Europe had been mirrored in Asia by the Japanese imperial variety, and there was growing concern for the stability of the region. Ethnocentric prejudice and ignorance of Asian society may have aggravated people's fears, but the Japanese aggression of the 1930s was not just something in the imagination of nervous Australians. Japan invaded Manchuria in 1931 and pressed on into northern China in 1937. Most of northern and eastern China was occupied until 1945. This ruthless invasion of Chinese territory should have been recognised by the rest of the world as the prelude to greater expansionism.

The United States, for one, had seen Japan, a World War I ally, as a potential enemy throughout the inter-war period. Espionage and code-breaking expertise was focused on Japan, and the United States was soon able to access military and diplomatic information. The ability to read Japanese codes was to play a crucial role during the coming conflict, but US naval strategy was hampered by an outdated view that anticipated one conclusive naval battle rather than the drawn-out campaign that eventuated.[5]

Meanwhile, many were unaware that the war with Germany had already invaded Australia's 'moat', with a number of merchant vessels being lost in the seas around Australia. Then, in November 1941, Australians were shocked into a new awareness of their danger when HMAS *Sydney* was lost, with all hands, after a clash with the German raider HSC *Kormoran* just off the undefended Western Australian coast. Two weeks later the war was to become truly worldwide, and the new battlegrounds were right on Australia's doorstep.

IMPORTANT DATES

'39	3 September	World War II begins.
'40	15 February	Hitler orders unrestricted submarine warfare.
	10 May	Germany invades Luxembourg, Belgium, Holland and France.
	13 May	Winston Churchill makes his famous 'blood, sweat and tears' speech. A Dutch government in exile is set up in London.
	28 May	Belgium surrenders.
	10 June	Italy enters the war. Norway surrenders.
	25 June	France surrenders.
	10 July	The Battle of Britain begins.
	22 September	The Japanese occupy Vietnam and establish bases in French Indochina.

'41	10 April	Siege of Tobruk begins. Australian and British forces had taken the town on 21 January.
	24 April	British and Australian forces leave Greece for Crete.
	8 September	Siege of Leningrad in Russia begins.
	3 October	Mahatma Gandhi promotes passive resistance against British rule in India.
	19 November	HMAS Sydney is lost off the Western Australian coast.

	7/8 December	(8 December Australian/Asian time) Japan invades Thailand and British Malaya before attacking US forces at Pearl Harbor, Guam and Wake Island; later that day, attacks are made on the Philippines, Hong Kong and Singapore.
	9 December	Japanese sink HMS Prince of Wales and HMS Repulse.
	10 December	The Japanese bomb Manila.
	29–30 December	US submarines withdraw from the Philippines and go to Java in the Dutch East Indies (Indonesia).
'42	1/2 January	The Japanese enter Manila.
	11–12 January	Japan invades the Dutch East Indies.

	20 January	HMAS Deloraine sinks Japanese submarine I-124 near Darwin. The Japanese invade Bali and Timor.
	23 January	The Allied base at Lae in New Guinea is bombed. Battle of Rabaul begins.
	15 February	The fall of Singapore. Allied forces surrender to Japanese.
	17 February	Japanese submarines I-2 and I-3 begin patrolling off Western Australian coast.
	19 February	Japanese bomb Darwin for the first time.
	3 March	Broome is bombed. USS Holland arrives at Fremantle, Western Australia, with the first US submarines.
	15 March	USS Holland and five submarines arrive at Albany, Western Australia.

	9 April	Japanese naval attacks on British base at Trincomalee in Ceylon (Sri Lanka). HMS Hermes and HMAS Vampire are sunk east of Ceylon.
	17 April	Dutch and British forces in Sumatra surrender to the Japanese. General Douglas MacArthur arrives in Australia.
	4–8 May	The Battle of the Coral Sea.
	4–7 June	The Battle of Midway.
	8 June	Japanese submarines shell Sydney and Newcastle in NSW.
	20 July	In New Guinea, the Kokoda Track campaign begins. Australian troops oppose a Japanese advance over the Owen Stanley Range.
	7 August	Guadalcanal campaign begins.

	9 August	Pro-independence riots in India; Gandhi is arrested.
	26 August	The Battle of Milne Bay begins; ends 5 September with the first outright defeat of Japanese land forces. Threat to Australia eases.
	12–15 November	Battle of Guadalcanal.
	31 December	17,513 tons of enemy shipping claimed to have been sunk by US Western Patrol submarines in the previous six months.
'43	1 January	Only eight submarines remain based at Fremantle, owing to reinforcement of Brisbane base in latter months of 1942.
	28 January	Japanese shell Port Gregory, north of Geraldton.
	7–8 February	Japanese evacuate Guadalcanal.

	2–5 March	Battle of the Bismarck Sea.
	6 May	US base at Exmouth Gulf declared operational. On 27 May it is downgraded to refuelling station after being bombed.
	14 May	Hospital ship Centaur torpedoed off Cape Moreton, Queensland.
'44	4 March	Japan begins an invasion attempt on India. Invasion attempt not foiled until 31 May and Japanese routed in August.
	6 June	Allied invasion of Normandy begins.
	19–20 June	Battle of the Philippine Sea.
	10 August	Japanese defeated in New Guinea. US troops liberate Guam.

	4 September	HMS Maidstone arrives at Fremantle from Ceylon, followed by submarines of the British 8th Submarine Flotilla.
	23 October	Battle of Leyte Gulf, Phillipines.
	31 December	Over fifty submarines are based at Fremantle.
'45	3 February	US forces enter Manilla.
	19–26 February	US landings on Iwo Jima
	20 March	USN submarine fleet headquarters transfers to Subic Bay, Phillipines, when Rear Admiral Fife leaves Fremantle on board USS Hardhead.
	1 April	US troops land on Okinawa.

	11 April	HMS Adamant and 4th Flotilla replace Maidstone and 8th Flotilla at Fremantle. Rear Admiral Fife arrives at Subic Bay.
	11 May	Australians attack Wewak in New Guinea.
	21 June	Japanese defeated in Okinawa.
	1 July	Australians land at Balikpapan, Borneo.
	4 July	Philippines liberated.
	6 August	Hiroshima destroyed by atomic bomb delivered by a US plane. First use of nuclear weapons in warfare.
	9 August	Second US nuclear attack on Japan. Nagasaki destroyed by atomic bomb.
	14 August	Japan accepts surrender terms.

	15 August	Ceasefire order transmitted to Allied forces. Allies celebrate victory over Japan as VJ Day.
	2 September	Formal signing of surrender takes place aboard USS Missouri.

HMS Repulse entering Fremantle Harbour, 27 February 1924. The loss of the Repulse, together with the Prince Of Wales, on 10 December 1941 was keenly felt in Western Australia by a populace who fondly remembered her visit in 1924 with HMS Hood, another shocking war loss. (Western Australian Museum, courtesy Richard McKenna – MHK D14/664).

CHAPTER FOUR

Japan Enters the War

In 1939, Australia was an isolated outpost of European culture with a small population and a long, poorly defended coastline. Because of this historical and geographical fact, there was a longstanding fear of invasion by ethnically alien forces. To the majority of Australians, it was only the umbrella of British imperial power, represented by the 'impregnable' fortress at Singapore, that ensured the nation's security.

Britain, meanwhile, was preoccupied with developments in Europe and the threat of Nazi Germany. Despite its dominion status in the new British Commonwealth of Nations, Australia seems to have been seen as a source of men and primary produce for the war effort, or, at best, as an important imperial territory to be defended. It certainly seems that in those last days of the British Empire, the British government did not see Australia as an independent sovereign nation. Furthermore, the British High Command firmly believed that the base at Singapore, the foundation stone of British power in the Far East, was secure against attack.

Some Australians, however, were becoming aware that both Britain's ability to defend Australia and its commitment to do so were weakening. With increasing evidence of Japan's expansionist intentions, they began to look to the United States of America, hoping it would make some move to defend its own interests in the Pacific region.

The US had seen Japan as a threat to its interests ever since she took over some of Germany's Pacific possessions after World War I. So despite maintaining an isolationist foreign policy, American naval planning and intelligence gathering concentrated on this potential conflict, and the naval fleet began to be built up during the 1930s. Some strategic moves were made to defend bases in the Pacific, but the US seems to have relied on its naval power to deter direct Japanese aggression. Like Britain, the US had underestimated the Japanese.

Taking advantage of the American stance, the Japanese planned a quick war to gain control of the South-East Asian and western Pacific region. The mechanisms of international diplomacy were successfully manipulated to stave off open conflict while Japan gathered strength for the attack. An important part of the plan was to prevent a counterattack by the United States Pacific Fleet, based at Pearl Harbor in Hawaii.

In the early hours of 7 December 1941, while still technically at peace with Britain and the United States, Japan launched surprise attacks on the United States naval base at Pearl Harbor in Hawaii. Slightly earlier that morning, which was 8 December on the west side of the international dateline, the Japanese invasion of British Malaya had begun. Despite resistance by the RAF, and British, Australian and Indian troops, the enemy could not be driven off. The American base at Manila in the Philippines, and the British bases at Hong Kong and Shanghai were also attacked that day. Two days later two British battleships, the *Prince of Wales* and the *Repulse,* were sunk. Suddenly, Australia's allies in the Indian and South Pacific Oceans were in retreat. John Curtin, the Australian prime minister, warned Australians to prepare themselves for the possibility of invasion.[1]

The build-up of American naval strength had really only begun to take effect in 1940, so it was fortunate for the Allies that the attack on Pearl Harbor was not as effective as the

Japanese had hoped. Land-based repair facilities were still operable, and no aircraft carriers were lost. Despite the subsequent loss of the Philippines, the United States Navy in the Pacific was still able to operate, and the unprovoked attack meant that the US was now fully committed to the war. Without this support Australia and New Zealand would have been completely isolated.

At first, however, the US was fighting on the run, while the Japanese, following up their advantage, had a string of successes. Two days after Pearl Harbor, they again bombed Manila and the nearby US naval base at Cavite. This was followed on 22 December by a successful invasion, landing on the archipelago's second largest island, Mindanao. The same day, the US base at Wake Island collapsed.[2] Meanwhile, Japanese submarines began patrolling the west coast of mainland USA. During the last two weeks of December they are thought to have been responsible for the loss of about ten Allied vessels in those waters.[3]

At the outbreak of war with Japan, the American naval presence in the Pacific region consisted of the Pacific Fleet, based at Pearl Harbor, and the recently established Asiatic Fleet, based at Manila. The Pacific Fleet included all US battleships and carriers in the Pacific, while the Asiatic Fleet had only three cruisers and supporting destroyers. It did, however, include 29 submarines, made up of 23 of the larger Fleet-class and six of the obsolescent S-class, together with the specially designed submarine tender USS *Holland.* There was also an old submarine tender, the USS *Canopus;* a small rescue vessel, USS *Pigeon;* and a modern merchant ship, the *Otus,* which was in the process of being converted to a submarine tender. The Pacific Fleet at Pearl Harbor had only 13 submarines and the support vessel USS *Pelias.*

On 10 December, when Manila was bombed, the submarines had to withdraw. They operated for a while from *Canopus* and the tunnels at Corregidor, the island fortress at the entrance to Manila Bay. On 31 December 1941 Manila was evacuated, and the following day the Japanese entered the city. The Asiatic Fleet submarines escaped and Corregidor continued to hold out until 6 May 1942.

The submarine fleet was soon forced to retreat further by the rapid Japanese advance, and a decision was made to split the fleet. Some boats were to be based at Surabaya, in Java, while the others went to Darwin with *Holland* and *Otus. Canopus* and *Pigeon* remained behind and were lost when Bataan and Corregidor fell. The fleet was now scattered, with the administrative headquarters at Darwin but operations being directed from Surabaya.

Java was then part of the Dutch East Indies, so Dutch submarines were also operating in the region. The Royal Netherlands Navy had based successive classes of submarines in the Dutch East Indies since World War I. Most of these were the K-boats, which were purpose-built for service in the tropical waters around the Dutch colonies. The smaller O-class submarines were intended for use in European waters.

When Holland fell in May 1940, some of the home-based Dutch

submarines had escaped to British ports and continued to operate with the British Royal Navy. At the outbreak of war with Japan, 15 Dutch submarines were based in the East Indies and these immediately became involved in defending their own bases and Singapore. During December 1941 they sank five Japanese ships, but losses were heavy. *K XVI, K XVII, O 16* and *O 20* were lost, while the *K XII* was badly damaged.[4]

As the war rapidly approached Australia's north coast, John Curtin issued his New Year message to the people of Australia, warning them that 'every citizen must place himself, his private and business affairs, his entire mode of living on a war footing'. Going on to discuss the government's foreign policy, he made it clear that it would take an international effort to stop the Japanese advance, and that 'Australia looks to America' as the 'keystone' of such an effort. Though often seen as a rather subservient plea to the United States to rescue Australia, the document also referred to cooperation with British, Chinese, Dutch and Russian forces, and called on Australians to make an all-out effort.[5]

With the threat of invasion looming, the lives of Australians were to change radically. Within days of the Japanese attack on Pearl Harbor, the Federal Cabinet, although stopping short of conscripting men to serve overseas, had introduced a partial mobilisation. It was also announced that, to release more men for active service, 1,600 women were to be enlisted in the Australian Women's Army Service.[6] It was not long before the mobilisation of the whole available workforce was announced. Those with skills required for the war effort could not enlist in the forces but were bound to use their expertise where it was needed.

The Japanese were very soon on the advance in the Dutch East Indies and on 3 February, Surabaya, the Dutch naval base at the eastern end of Java, suffered its first air attack. When it became obvious that the Javanese bases could not be held, the operational headquarters of the United States Navy's Asiatic Fleet was evacuated to Australia.[7]

Like the Americans, the British were also in retreat. By 11 January 1942, Malaya was practically in Japanese hands, and Japanese forces were advancing on Singapore. Within a fortnight they were pushing into Burma and had landed in Borneo, and at Rabaul in New Britain, about 500 kilometres from the coast of New Guinea and only 1,000 kilometres from Cape York, at the northern tip of Queensland. From Rabaul they were able to bomb Allied targets in New Guinea, and the base at Lae had to be evacuated after it was bombed on 23 January.[8] Meanwhile the Imperial Japanese Navy was already targeting the approaches to Darwin on Australia's northern coast. In mid January four Japanese submarines, *I-121, I-122, I-123* and *I-124,* were laying mines in the vicinity of the Torres and Clarence Straits.

On 20 January 1942 a Japanese submarine attacked an American navy tanker in Beagle Gulf, not far from Darwin. The Australian corvette *Deloraine,*accompanied by three Allied aircraft, went out to find and destroy the enemy vessel. About hundred kilometres out of Darwin, *Deloraine* itself came under attack. The corvette immediately retaliated. When the damaged submarine surfaced, a depth charge from the corvette and bombs dropped by one of the USAF aircraft sent it to the bottom, apparently out of action. When oil and bubbles were seen floating on the water some three kilometres away the presence of another submarine was suspected. *Deloraine* used up all its depth charges attacking the new target, after which the RAN corvettes, *Katoomba* and *Lithgow,* and the USN destroyers, *Alden* and *Edsall,* joined in the hunt. The submarine sunk by *Deloraine* has been identified as the *I-124,* which was the only Japanese submarine lost in the area at that time, but other Japanese submarines may have been involved and escaped undamaged.[9]

The Australian-built corvette HMAS Deloraine, which sank the Japanese submarine I-124 just 100km from Darwin in January 1924. (Western Australian Museum, McKenna Collection, courtesy of Bruce Farrington – MHK D14/161.)

At the end of January, Malaya was evacuated and British and Empire forces retreated to the fortress at Singapore, which was believed to be unassailable. On 15 February 1942, only a week after the start of the Japanese assault, the impossible happened. Singapore fell.

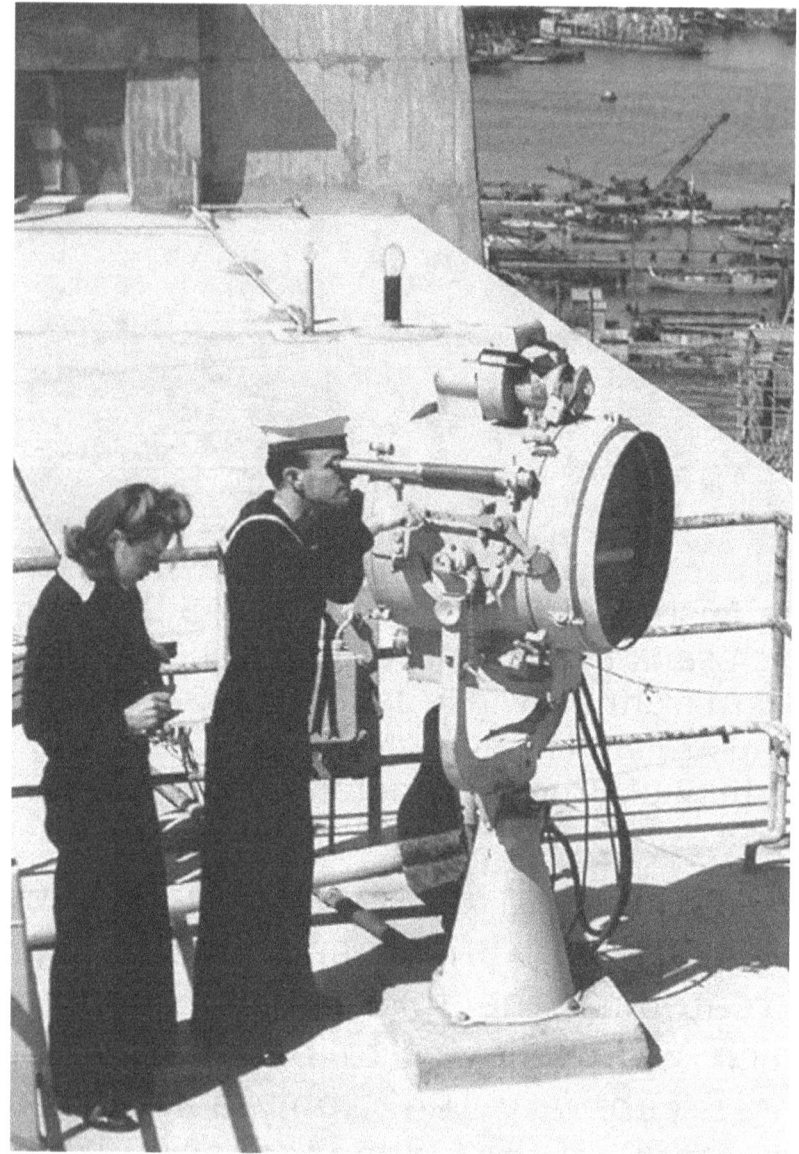

A signal station was built on top of the Fremantle grain silos, partly staffed by members of the Women's Royal Australian Naval Service (WRANS), as part of the 'Fortress Fremantle' defensive installations. (Western Australian Museum, courtesy Fremantle City Library – MHD 0088/78.)

CHAPTER FIVE

Australia Prepares for Invasion

Post-war Australia tended to see the response of the Australian Government and public as over-reaction and panic, but given the information available at the time it was not unreasonable. As American, Dutch and British bases had been unable to withstand the Japanese advance, it was only sensible to face the possibility that the trend would continue. After all, it was a new experience for white Australians to face a threat of invasion. The isolation that had previously kept war at a distance now meant vulnerability, and the small population clustered in southern cities could not be mobilised to protect the long, uninhabited coastline.

Australia had not been sitting back waiting to be rescued by the United States, however. Those Royal Australian Navy vessels not involved in the war in Europe were fighting against the

Japanese beside British, Dutch and American ships. Unfortunately the small fleet was to be drastically depleted when HMAS *Perth* and HMAS *Yarra* were both lost in battle, on 28 February and 4 March respectively.[1]

The Australian army had been in action at Rabaul, New Britain, and in Malaya and Singapore, with heavy casualties. Almost 15,000 Australian servicemen and nurses were captured when Singapore fell. The 6th, 7th and 9th AIF divisions were still fighting in the Middle East, and those soldiers left at home were mostly new, untrained troops, or poorly trained and equipped militia. 'The Australian Army in Australia stood at twenty-eight brigades, mainly recently mobilised and partly trained militia with only one of these (13 Infantry Brigade) in WA to defend over a third of the continent.'[2] If an invasion had come at that time, the prospects of holding the whole country were minimal, and contingency plans for a fallback position were no doubt the basis for the belief in something called the Brisbane Line.

Darwin harbour in the aftermath of the first Japanese attack. The American freighter Meigs can be seen on fire and sinking. (Western Australian Museum, Murray Collection – MHA 4591/23.)

It was not long before an attack was made on Australian soil. On 19 February 1942, only four days after the fall of Singapore, the Japanese bombed Darwin. Interestingly, reports that the northern port had been bombed appeared in two eastern states newspapers in early January, prompting the chief publicity censor to forbid publication of sensational reports from enemy sources unless officially confirmed.[3]

This time it was the real thing. The attacks were carried out by 54 land-based bombers and 188 attack aircraft launched from Japanese aircraft carriers in the Timor Sea. Just before 10am the heavy bombers led the first attack on the town and harbour, then dive-bombers, escorted by Zero fighters, targeted shipping in the harbour, and both the military and civil airfields. This attack lasted about forty minutes, but enemy planes were back an hour later, bombing the RAAF base at Parap.

In the interests of security and the maintenance of morale, the losses were minimised in published reports. The *West Australian* of 23 February 1942 published a government communiqué concerning the raid. No mention was made of casualties, but it was reported that there had been no vital damage to service installations and that 'some damage had been done to shipping'. Quite an understatement! Some 243 people died in that first attack, including eight at the post office, while between three and four hundred were wounded.[4]

The town was devastated, with most civil and military facilities destroyed. Eight ships, including the United States Navy destroyer *Peary,* were sunk in the harbour. Fifteen more ships were damaged and 20 aircraft were destroyed. The explosions, and oil spilled from wrecked ships, had caused damaging fires, and the harbour was strewn with the burnt remains of vessels, wharves and men.

Many of the dead were never found. By 3 March the police had buried 72 bodies, many unidentified. On 10 March it was reported that two decaying corpses had been found near the quarantine station. The same report stated that 'many more bodies are apparently in the swamp but owing to the number of crocodiles now in the swamp it is considered recovery of the bodies will unnecessarily endanger human life'.[5]

During March Darwin was again attacked, as were Broome and Wyndham in Western Australia, Katherine in the Northern Territory, and

Townsville in Queensland. At Broome, 70 people are known to have died and 24 aircraft were destroyed, fifteen of them flying boats. Many of those killed were women and children, refugees from the Dutch East Indies who must have thought they had finally reached safety. Bombing raids on Darwin, which suffered more than sixty attacks, and the north-west ports continued until late 1943.

What even the Australian authorities apparently did not know was that seaplanes launched from the Japanese submarine *I-25* made reconnaissance flights over Sydney, Melbourne and Hobart between 17 February and 1 March, while another two Japanese submarines, *I-2* and *I-3,* were operating off the Western Australian coast. They began their patrol some 480 kilometres north-west of North West Cape, then sailed south along the coast and operated off Shark Bay and Fremantle until early March.[6]

A brief look at the contemporary press shows that, even without this knowledge, Australian civilians had reason to expect that they would soon be fighting for their homes and lives. During the last week of February 1942, the *West Australian* published several reports on the bombing of Darwin, and also reported that the Japanese were advancing in Bali, Java and Burma. Singapore, Malaya and Timor, some five hundred kilometres from Western Australia's coast, were already in their hands, and Port Moresby, on the southern coast of New Guinea, was under attack. A report from London quoted 'Japanese sources' which advocated 'the entire Japanisation of Australia',[7] and broadcasts from Vichy France claimed that Japanese warships were already operating to the south of Australia, which may have been true.

On 20 February, a *New York Sun* columnist made it clear that US observers saw Australia as the last bastion of resistance to the Japanese:

> We have to assume ... that the Dutch East Indies and Burma will sooner or later fall, now that Singapore is gone ... Australia now offers the principal hope and prospect of stopping Japan. Only Australia remains to serve as a

base in the South Pacific, only Australia can challenge Japan's hegemony ... And only the United States remains to hold Australia.[8]

The British, still under attack at home and struggling to retain control of Burma, were virtually out of the war in the region, while the Dutch were fighting a rearguard action in Java, destroying oil installations and other facilities as they retreated. The United States of America was still something of an unknown quantity. It possessed enormous economic power, but had taken an isolationist approach to the war until openly attacked by Japan, and, strange as it seems now, its forces were relatively untried in warfare. Nevertheless, the Americans were Australia's last hope.

By 24 February, the minister for labour was advocating a scorched-earth policy 'if an invader succeeded in forcing us to retire to the inland'.[9] That this was not just scaremongering rhetoric is shown by the report, eleven days later, of contingency plans indeed being formulated that would allow such a policy to be implemented. Cars, trucks, motorcycles and pushbikes were to be destroyed, while small boats, and their possible destruction, were the subject of 'a complete plan'. The report went on to say that at the appropriate time 'the military authorities will give the State officials the signal for starting the scorched earth policy'.[10]

In Western Australia, a total and permanent blackout was imposed on the coastal areas between Woodman Point and Trigg, and all direction signs within one hundred and sixty kilometres of the coast were to be removed. Air raid precautions were put in place, and plans were made for the evacuation of certain areas.[11] Some schools were to be closed 'in conformity with the policy of removing scholars from possible target areas'. Those closed at Fremantle were Fremantle Boys' School, Princess May Girls' and Infants' School, and the state school in South Terrace. Private colleges began to evacuate their students to inland centres.[12]

United States Navy sailors marching in Wellington Street, Perth, on America Day, 14 June 1943. (West Australian Newspapers – War 2806.)

For the anxious, news-starved public, the suppression of the results of Japanese raids on the northern ports could not have been reassuring, and may have made the situation seem more serious than it really was. Evacuees' tales and eyewitness accounts showed that considerable damage had been done and people had died. These accounts also suggested that information about installations in Darwin was available to the enemy airmen, who 'did not waste bombs on unimportant targets'.[13] Fear of the enemy learning how to penetrate Australia's inadequate defences was very real during these grim months. Espionage being a reality of war, fear of enemy agents was not unreasonable and had to be taken seriously by government and military leaders. With the lack of reliable news, the emphasis on security encouraged the growth of rumours and an atmosphere of fear and mistrust. No doubt some people were affected by 'spy fever' and developed an unreasoning suspicion of foreigners. At the official level, this could lead to unfair treatment of aliens, including naturalised Australians, many of whom were interned.

What was not widely reported in the press, and which might have allayed some of the anxiety, was the fact that large numbers of American servicemen had arrived in Australia, with more on the way. These included the nucleus of Fremantle's submarine fleet, which began to arrive on 3 March. Australia had already taken on its role as the base in the South Pacific from which the Allied forces were to challenge Japan's hegemony in the region.

It was not before time. By the end of April, Japan was in control of British Malaya, Singapore, the Dutch East Indies and Timor, which placed the enemy very close to Australia's north-west coast. This proximity, an obvious threat to Australia, was to last throughout the war, as this territory was not recaptured until mid 1945. Two of the most important United States naval bases, at Guam and Wake Island, were also in enemy hands, as were most of the Philippine islands. The Japanese now had access to some of the world's best supplies of raw materials, including oil-rich areas of the Dutch East Indies. Of particular concern to Australia was the enemy's southerly push through New Guinea.

The 19 February attack on Darwin had only been the beginning of Japan's harassment of Australia's northern settlements. In March, Broome, Wyndham and Port Hedland on Western

Australia's north-west coast were bombed. Darwin was also attacked again, as was the inland town of Katherine.

During that month, the flamboyant General Douglas MacArthur arrived in Australia, setting up his headquarters in Melbourne. From 30 March, the Pacific was divided into two areas of command. MacArthur became Supreme Commander of Allied Forces in the South West Pacific Area, which included Australia, New Guinea, the Dutch East Indies and the Philippines. Admiral Nimitz commanded the rest of the Pacific Ocean Area.[14] It was MacArthur, however, who for many Australians symbolised the strength and arrogance of the American war machine.

> The American role in the defence of Australia was significant, but it came slowly and with the terms which larger countries impose on smaller ones. Not until April 1942 was General MacArthur appointed Supreme Commander for the South West Pacific, based in Australia. He arrived in Australia in characteristically regal fashion with

a large entourage, setting himself up in the best quarters in grand hotels. However, he brought more in the way of ego than troops in the first instance. The crucial early American role was in naval defence.[15]

The United States submarines at Fremantle were an important part of that naval defence, but the Allied navies faced a formidable task in trying to regain control of the south-west Pacific and the eastern part of the Indian Ocean. The Japanese seemed unstoppable. During March they had moved into the Indian Ocean, sinking 28 Allied ships in the Bay of Bengal, and bombing the British naval base at Trincomalee in Ceylon (now Sri Lanka) on 5 April. By the end of April, the Japanese forces had already achieved what even their own planners expected would take a whole year and cost them a third of their naval strength. Their naval losses were minimal, however, and soon replaced by newly commissioned vessels.[16]

It was not until May 1942, with the Battle of the Coral Sea, that the Allies began to turn the tide in the Pacific Ocean. This battle is generally seen as marking a turning point in the war with Japan, but for most Australians the news was overshadowed by reports that on 31 May three Japanese miniature submarines had made a daring, if unsuccessful, attack on Sydney Harbour. The small craft were launched from mother submarines lurking only 57 kilometres off Sydney Heads. The Japanese also intensified their attacks on shipping off the east coast of Australia during June and July. Six coastal vessels were sunk, while another six ships were attacked but managed to survive.[17]

The Battle of the Coral Sea was followed in June by another Allied success, the Battle of Midway, when Japanese naval power was weakened and an attempt to capture more territory thwarted. Their presence in Borneo, Malaya, the Dutch East Indies and Timor, however, remained a threat to Australia.[18] As if to remind the Australian public of this fact, just after midnight on 8 June, Japanese submarines approached the New South

Wales coast and shelled Sydney and Newcastle.

Australians could not know that the Japanese had already decided that invasion of Australia was not feasible at that stage of the war. It had, however, been considered.

Japanese naval planners were, nevertheless, under no delusion that the war had been won. They estimated that by the middle of 1943 the American Navy would be strong enough to challenge both Japan and the long logistic lines of the Pacific Ocean ... Miyo, who was air plans officer on the Naval General staff, reasoned that a counterattack would be launched from Australia ... Tomioka favoured the direct method of invading Australia and seizing all that continent's northern ports.

The Army vetoed any such ambitious plan. It would take ten divisions, the Army estimated ... Tomioka believed five divisions could do the job, but a check on resources soon convinced him that there was insufficient shipping available to lift even that many divisions to Australia and support their operations.[19]

Unaware of this decision, the government and people of Australia had to remain on the alert. In mid 1942, when an invasion was still expected, a special commando group, the North Australia Observer Unit (NAOU), had been formed to patrol the sparsely populated north of Australia. Nicknamed the Nackeroos, the NAOU was made up of 550 volunteer bushmen equipped with radios, horses, donkeys, vehicles and small vessels. Fortunately they were never called on to confront the Japanese army, but there were reports of suspected Japanese landings, possibly by submarine crews, and possible espionage. These reports could not be ignored.[20]

The epic cattle drive that inspired the post-war film, *The Overlanders,* took place in the latter part of 1942. Amid fears that the important meatworks at Wyndham in Western Australia's north-west might be bombed, drovers undertook the evacuation of the region's cattle herds. Some of the cattle were brought south in Western Australia, but most were driven overland to Queensland. The operation, the longest cattle-droving exercise in Australia's history, was completed by January 1943.[21]

THE PORT OF FREMANTLE

The Japanese entry into the war had a dramatic effect on the activities of the Port of Fremantle. In the early months of 1942, Fremantle became a haven for refugees fleeing the war zone. The harbour was packed with navy and merchant vessels, with sometimes as many as four moored side by side at each berth, while up to thirty other ships could be waiting in Gage Roads to get into the port.[1]

Though the Fremantle Harbour Trust (FHT) continued to handle berthing and loading facilities at the port as usual, harbour entrance control, harbour patrol, underwater detection, surface detection radar and net defences were the responsibility of the RAN.[2] Under national security regulations the wharves had been closed since June 1940, and now barbed-wire barriers and sentries appeared, and special entry permits were required. FHT patrol staff and a military guard took care of wharf security until 29 June 1942, when the Commonwealth government appointed special peace officers to man entrances to the wharves.[3]

The everyday work of the port had to continue, however. Besides the inconvenience of working with the wartime restrictions, the loss of shipping tonnage, either sunk or requisitioned by the forces, had a serious impact on the work of all Australian ports during the war, hindering the work of harbour pilots and waterside labourers who were called upon to deal with 'old decrepit ships brought back into service because of the shortage of shipping capacity, and raw crews who could not handle the gear'.[4]

From May 1942, the RAN used the FHT's old visual signal station on the top of Cantonment Hill at the south end of the Fremantle traffic bridge, but in June 1944 the operation was transferred to a signal station set up on the top of the Australian Wheat Board's wheat silo at North Fremantle.[5] Two USN warrant officers and two enlisted men were employed at the signal station in 1944.[6]

(top) North Wharf, Fremantle, at the end of World War II. (Western Australian Museum, courtesy J. V. Parker – MHA 4561/6.) (Bottom) Aerial view of the mouth of Fremantle Harbour 1944, looking south. Allied submarines are visible at Berths 1 & 2, North Wharf, as is the submarine slipway at the base of South Mole. (Western Australian Museum – MHP 0073A/04.)

The USN's degaussing facilities for submarines, used by the submarine repair unit, were also made available to the British and Dutch submarines, while the RAN maintained degaussing facilities for surface ships.[7] Degaussing is a process that gives some protection against magnetic mines, by counteracting a ship's magnetic field.[8]

A USN warrant officer with the title 'operations officer for service force subordinate command vessels' looked after berthing, pilotage, tugs, cranes and launch services for USN vessels, and liaised with the Australian military and civilian authorities. The USN used a floating pontoon bridge section for mooring their small boats.

Work had started on the 2,000-ton slipway at Victoria Quay in late 1940. It was originally designed to be 225.5 metres long and have a telescopic cradle with a draft of 3.05 metres, but submarines required support at closer centres and a flatter cradle line, so the slipway was lengthened during construction and changes were made to the specifications. When finished, the overall length of the slipway was 288.95 metres, with some 181 metres below water.[9] It still could not fully accommodate the Fleet-type submarines, so repair work was done with only part of the submarine hauled out of the water. Divers were used for underwater work. The slipway was ready by September 1942 and the merchant ship *Chungking* was the first vessel to be slipped. The Slipway was to remain in use until 1998.

(top) The Dutch submarine Tijgerhaai on the Fremantle slips, 2 July 1946. (Bottom) On 22 September 1942, the merchant ship Chungking was the first vessel to use the Fremantle slipway. (Western Australian Museum, Murray Collection – MHA 4504/76A.)

CHAPTER SIX

The US Submarines come to Fremantle

As the Allied resistance in the Dutch East Indies crumbled, it was soon obvious that the hard-pressed US submarines would need bases in mainland Australia. The original plan was to use Darwin as the major base, but the northern port suffered from a number of disadvantages, including poor road communications, a high tidal range and the vulnerability of its approaches to enemy mine-laying. At that time, although it was the largest port on the north coast of Australia, Darwin was just a large outback town, an enormous distance from the nation's major population centres.

Fortunately, when the port was bombed on 19 February 1942 the submarine tenders USS *Holland* and USS *Otus* were not there. With the Javanese bases increasingly under attack, the tenders had been sent to Tjilatjap, on the south coast of Java, to evacuate the Asiatic Fleet submarine force staff to Australia.[1]

Darwin was no longer safe, so *Holland,* accompanied by the destroyer-tender *Black Hawk,* sailed for Exmouth Gulf, which was being considered as an alternative base to Darwin. Rear Admiral Purnell, who arrived at the gulf by air on 28 February, decided that the area was unsuitable and sailed for Fremantle on board the *Holland,* with two submarines, *Snapper* and *Sculpin,* as escort. *Black Hawk* and the submarine *Stingray* stayed at Exmouth Gulf to service incoming submarines bound for Fremantle.[2] Corwin Mendenhall, who was on the *Sculpin,* recalled coming back from a patrol out of Surabaya and being sent down to Exmouth to join *Holland.*

> ...we were only there for a few hours however, and then that's when the *Holland,* the *Sculpin,* and the *Snapper* got underway and headed down to Fremantle. So the *Sculpin* and the *Snapper* were put out each on the bow of the *Holland,*

and we were their escorts. We were running along sounding our sonar and doing all that sort of thing, and zig-zagging and we thought that it was kind of superfluous to think of a submarine escorting a big ship down to Fremantle, but that's the way it went ... We got to Fremantle and found out again we were going to be there one week, and we were going out on patrol again.[3]

United States submarines at North Wharf at the end of World War II. A submarine tender (possibly USS Anthedon) is at the wharf. (West Australian Newspapers – War 906.)

On 3 March 1942 they arrived at Fremantle. Over the next two days, five more submarines, *Sargo, Seadragon, Stingray, Sturgeon* and *Tarpon,* joined them.[4] Unfortunately, communications between the Allied forces were not operating at a very efficient level. As

Sargo approached Fremantle, an RAAF Lockheed Hudson aircraft was searching for an enemy submarine reported to be in the area. Its crew, not having been notified of the approach of the US submarines, took *Sargo* for an enemy craft and bombed it. The submarine suffered considerable damage to its conning tower, and both periscopes were wrecked.

It is not really surprising that the RAAF was looking for a Japanese submarine. It is most likely that as the American submarines headed south they were passed by the Japanese *I-2* and *I-3* returning northward after their patrols off the Western Australian coast. The *S-40* reported sighting a Japanese submarine between Exmouth Gulf and Fremantle on 6 March.[5]

The battle-weary US submarines had been in action since 8 December, so Fremantle was a welcome haven, but there was no certainty they would be staying. Two days after the first submarines arrived, however, the commander of the US naval forces, South West Pacific Area formally notified Australian authorities that the Asiatic

Fleet submarines would be operating from Fremantle. Twenty-five survived their hazardous patrols during the retreat from Java, and twelve of these had reached Fremantle by 10 March, when *Otus,* still only partly converted to a submarine tender, also arrived.[6]

The first commander of the new base was Captain John Wilkes, who had the task of establishing a secure haven from which the submarines could be sent out to harass enemy shipping. It seems that the first premises used by Wilkes at Fremantle was at 7 High Street, but he later moved to Dalgety's building in Queen Victoria Street.[7]

In Perth, Captain Wilkes reestablished submarine headquarters. After Soerabaja [sic], the city's telephones, radio station, office space and other accommodations seemed an embarrassment of riches. Driven from pillar to post, the force had at last found sanctuary.[8]

As soon as the support vessels arrived at Fremantle, work had started on repairing and servicing the submarines. There were no existing facilities for submarines at the port, however, and even those for surface vessels were incapable of handling the sudden influx of shipping.

> In the ... month after Singapore had fallen, vessels crowded with refugees arrived at Fremantle, taxing accommodation to the utmost in the inner harbour, whilst as many as 30 took up anchorage in Gage Roads ... Altogether, some 75 vessels were using the inner and outer harbours at one and the same time, and in the fortnight ending 20th March, a total of 103 vessels, Naval and merchant, and mainly seeking refuge, arrived at the port.[9]

Two USN supply ships had already arrived, and more equipment became available when shiploads of equipment and other stores intended for Japanese-held ports in the Philippines and the Dutch East Indies were diverted to Fremantle. Two wheat-loading sheds on North Wharf were leased for workshops, and repair work went on 24 hours a day. After repairs, the submarines were tested in Cockburn Sound.

Work on the 2,000-ton Fremantle slipway at the west end of Victoria Quay had started in 1940, but it was found that its design would need modification so it could be used for slipping submarines. The slipway was lengthened and changes were made to the cradle before it was opened for use in September 1942. It was in constant use during the war years, servicing both naval and merchant vessels.[10]

At first the situation was very tense, with a Japanese invasion on the north coast of Australia expected at any time, and the possibility that Fremantle itself could come under attack. With the arrival of the second tender, it was possible to protect the fleet by dispersing it, so USS *Holland* and five of the submarines were sent to Albany. They left on 15 March, escorted by the destroyer USS *Pope* and accompanied by the seaplane tender USS *Childs*.[11] The Albany harbour-master's logbook records the arrival of *Holland, Childs* and a number of unidentified submarines on 17 March.[12] The

Albany quarantine station was taken over and used as barracks, and once the fleet had settled in, some of the men who had gone to Albany with the *Holland* travelled back to Fremantle by train to assist with the work of setting up the base.[13]

On 11 March, aerial attacks by Australian and United States bombers dispersed a Japanese invasion force believed to be heading for Port Moresby. Eight days later, the progress of Japanese forces moving through New Guinea was halted by further Allied attacks, but the situation remained extremely grave. On 23 March the Japanese had occupied the Andaman Islands in the Bay of Bengal, giving them a valuable base from which to attack Indian Ocean targets. With the surrender of Dutch and British forces in Sumatra on 17 April, the Japanese were in control of the whole Malay Archipelago. This gave them access to valuable oil supplies, as well as naval and air bases from which to harass Allied shipping moving between the Pacific and Indian Oceans.[14]

By the end of March, 22 United States submarines had reached Fremantle. These were: *Pickerel, Pike, Porpoise, Sailfish, Salmon, Sargo, Saury, Sculpin, Seadragon, Searaven, Skipjack, Snapper, Spearfish, Stingray, Sturgeon, Swordfish, Tarpon, S-37, S-38, S-39, S-40* and *S-41.* Another three arrived in early April. Three submarines, *Shark, Perch,* and *S-36,* had been lost.[15]

Three Dutch submarines had also come to Fremantle to serve with the Americans. On 7 March, Batavia (now Jakarta), capital of the Dutch East Indies, was taken over by the Japanese, and three days later the Dutch base at Surabaya also fell into their hands. The islands would not be completely subjugated until April, but the Dutch submarine bases had to be abandoned. Of the submarines working from these bases, *K VII, K X, K XIII* and *K XVIII* were lost, *K XIV, K XI, K XV* and *O 19* went to Ceylon (Sri Lanka), and *K VIII, K IX* and *K XII* came to Fremantle.[16]

For the first month or so, the submarine fleet, which had been in retreat almost from the beginning, was occupied in repairing damage, setting up the bases, assessing its losses and generally licking its wounds. As soon as the submarines could be made ready, however, they were sent into action. At first they were sent mainly to patrol the seas to the north of Darwin, where the Japanese were expected to attempt a landing. Otherwise, the fleet's operational policy was aimed at attacking the enemy supply lines, in particular to intercept oil supplies from the newly conquered areas. The submarines were also involved in supplying and evacuating Bataan and Corregidor in the Phillipines.

A number of air raid shelters were erected on Perth streets. These shelters, in Murray Street near the corner with Forrest Place, are being demolished in November 1944. (West Australian Newspapers – War 130.)

The first to leave was *Snapper*, which sailed on 6 March for Indonesian waters, but was diverted to the Philippines to deliver food and ammunition to Corregidor and pick up 27 evacuees. *Sculpin* departed Fremantle on 13 March for the Molucca Sea, off the Celebes, and *Sturgeon* left on 15 March to patrol the Makassar Strait area. The following day *Stingray* sailed for the Celebes and Java Seas, and on 18 March *Seadragon* set off for the coast of Indochina, but it was also diverted to take supplies to Corregidor.

Spearfish departed on 27 March for the Philippines and *Tarpon* left on 28 March, but *Tarpon* was transferred to Pearl Harbor at the end of the patrol. *Searaven* sailed on 2 April to patrol near Timor, where it rescued 32 RAAF men, but a fire on board caused a complete breakdown so *Snapper*, returning from its March patrol, towed the crippled submarine back to Fremantle.

With the combined efforts of the United States and Australian authorities, the physical structure of a naval base had been quickly established at Fremantle. The USN's Public Works Department, made up of six officers, two warrant officers, 87 enlisted men and 23 civilians, was responsible for maintaining the base.[17] The provision of shore-based storage and workshop facilities was a first priority, and a number of local buildings were leased, including several warehouses and two of the large cargo storage sheds on North Wharf. These buildings usually required modifications to provide living quarters, office space and other special areas. The work was done by local government agencies or private firms rather than by US military construction squadrons, as was the case at many other American bases. When such work was required, the USN's Public Works Officer forwarded a requisition to the Allied Works Council, and the Commonwealth Department of the Interior called tenders.[18] The local firms demonstrated efficiency and adaptability in coping with the various kinds of work needed.

The Dutch submarines had been in the thick of the fighting and arrived in a very bad condition, with no spares, stores or repair facilities, so they could not be immediately used for normal operations. These were old vessels and difficult to keep seaworthy. It was decided that the *K VIII* could not be repaired, so it was decommissioned on 8 May 1942 before being sold for scrap and partially stripped of its machinery. The main electro-motor supplied DC power to ships on the Fremantle slipway for many years. *K VIII* was finally abandoned in Jervoise Bay, south of Fremantle, where some of the remains still lie.[19]

The *K XII* was also in a bad condition but not beyond repair, so it was sent to Sydney for a refit, returning to Fremantle in September 1942 after a successful mission. For the next two years the submarine was in constant service carrying out special missions in the occupied islands. The *K IX* was transferred to the RAN to be used for anti-submarine training. It left Fremantle in April for Sydney, and was later damaged during the Japanese midget submarine raid on Sydney Harbour. *K IX* was finally lost off New South Wales after the war while on its way to be scrapped. The Dutch K-class vessels, though manned by Dutch submariners, operated under United States command.[20]

The United States Navy submarine Tautog, which operated out of Fremantle between June 1942 and May 1943. (Western Australian Museum, courtesy William Pouleris – MHA 4561/32).

The USN's five S-class submarines were not suited to carry out the long patrols from Fremantle, so they were transferred to Brisbane where a second base was being established, leaving the twenty long-range Fleet-class boats based at Fremantle. Neither of the submarine tenders could be spared to go with them, so the supply ship *Goldstar* was sent as a makeshift tender. As the submarines were by this time in need of more comprehensive maintenance than could be supplied at Fremantle, all needed to return to Pearl Harbor over the following months to be overhauled. *Tarpon* was the first to go, after which two went at a time. As they left, they were to be replaced by two of the same class. *Porpoise* left on 26 April for the East Indies, and *Pike* sailed on 19 April, patrolling north of the Palau Islands and off Wake Island on its way to Hawaii.

The arrival of the Allied submarines at Fremantle had not been reported in the press, and only those closely concerned with the harbour or with security were really aware of their presence. American and Dutch submariners on leave were seen about the city, but the movements of their vessels were not supposed to be discussed with chance acquaintances. With thousands of US personnel from other branches of the services pouring into Australia, the significance of the submariners' presence went unnoticed.

THE SUBMARINES AT ALBANY

When the American submarines arrived at Fremantle on 3 March 1942, there was a real fear of an attack by Japanese forces. To prevent the possibility of losing the fleet, it was decided to split it into two sections. The submarine tender USS *Holland* and five submarines were sent to Albany, where they arrived on 17 March.

No warning had been given to the Australian Army gunners at the Albany forts, who were quite alarmed to see a large vessel and several submarines entering the harbour. Much to their relief, they soon identified *Holland's* flag as the Stars and Stripes of the United States of America.

Holland was stationed at Albany until July 1942, when it was relieved by the *Pelias,* which stayed at the port until October. During this time, 31 submarines visited the port. Most of them were refitted by the submarine tenders' technical staff, assisted by the crews. The submarines were tied up at the Albany jetty and the jetty at the quarantine station, which was used for rest and recreation.

The USN took over a number of buildings in the town. Wesfarmers Building, at the bottom of York Street, housed the periscope shop, and the periscopes were brought there by rail from the deepwater jetty. Steam trains from Perth brought torpedoes and other supplies, and transported servicemen on leave to and from the capital.

Then, in March 1944, when a Japanese attack on Fremantle was feared, the two submarine tenders, *Pelias* and *Otus,* were sent to Albany for safety. They left Albany after less than a week, when the scare proved to have been a false alarm.

Many of the submariners made lasting friendships with local people, and some travelled to Albany from Perth to spend their leave with Albany friends. A number of local girls married US servicemen. USN veteran Homer White, who married a local girl and returned to live at Albany, served on USS *Holland.* He recalled the friendly small-town service provided by the local businesses, visits to local farms, kangaroo shooting trips and other entertainments.

Submarines remembered as visiting Albany

Gar
Grampus
Grayback
Grenadier
Gudgeon
Permit
Pickerel
Pike
Porpoise
S-38
S-39

S-41
Sailfish
Salmon
Sargo
Saury
Sculpin
Seadragon
Seal
Searaven

Seawolf
Skipjack

Snapper
Spearfish
Stingray
Sturgeon
Swordfish
Tambor
Tarpon
Tautog
Thresher

Sailors working on the guns of a British submarine in Fremantle port. (Western Australian Museum, courtesy West Australian Newspapers – MHP 0147/24.)

CHAPTER SEVEN

1942: Submarines on the Offensive

With the final surrender of Corregidor in early May, the Fremantle submarines were no longer needed to supply the forces there and could concentrate their efforts on attacking Japan's supply lines. Japan needed plentiful supplies of raw materials to maintain military production, and in conquering the islands of the Malay Barrier (a national line from the Malayan Peninisula, through the southern-most islands of the Dutch East Indies) gained access to important primary resources; in particular, the oilfields of Borneo, Java and Sumatra. It was vital to prevent these materials reaching Japan, so in the second half of the year the submarines began to penetrate further north into the South China Sea and along the coast of Indochina to harass Japan's supply lines.

A strong merchant marine was vital to the economy and war-making potential of the island nation of Japan. Its ships imported oil, iron ore, coal, bauxite, rubber, and foodstuffs; they exported arms, ammunition, aircraft, and soldiers to reinforce captured possessions. When submarines succeeded in stopping this commerce, Japan was doomed.[1]

The tide had already begun to turn in the Pacific War. Early in May 1942, a combined United States and Australian fleet struck the main body of the Japanese fleet in the Battle of the Coral Sea. Though it could not be called an Allied victory, for the first time since they entered the war, the Japanese suffered severe losses.

During May, Rear Admiral Charles Lockwood arrived at Fremantle to replace Captain John Wilkes as commander of the Fremantle base. He set up his headquarters at the Colonial Mutual Life Insurance building in Perth and began to prepare the fleet to take the offensive against the Japanese.

He began by installing in Fremantle such drivers as Commander John M. Will—a matériel and maintenance officer, tough and exacting, who could find a pump in the bottom of an Australian gold mine on Thursday and have it inside a submarine before the weekend.[2]

Nine submarines left Fremantle on patrol during May, patrolling mainly in the South China Sea and Indonesian waters.[3] *Salmon* accounted for two large enemy vessels: the *Asahi* (11,441 tons) and the *Ganges Maru* (4,382 tons) off the south coast of Java. *Permit* went hunting enemy vessels off Makassar, Celebes Island and Balikpapan in Borneo. On 12 May, *Seal* sailed for the Indochina coast, and *Seawolf* left for the Philippines, where it sank the *Nampo Maru*. *Swordfish* sailed on 15 May and sank two cargo ships, in the South China Sea and Gulf of Siam (Thailand), while *Saury* departed on 7 May for Timor, the Flores Sea and the eastern Celebes coast. *Stingray*, which had been withdrawn from Fremantle, left on 27 May to patrol the Davao Gulf and Guam areas on its way to Pearl

Harbor. *Snapper* sailed on 28 May to patrol the Flores Sea, Makassar Strait and the western Celebes Sea, and on 29 May *Sculpin* departed for the South China Sea.

Fremantle harbour from North Fremantle, 3 August 1943, showing a US submarine on the slipway. (Western Australian Museum, Murray Collection – MHA 4503/20.)

The Battle of Midway, on 3 June, marked another milestone in the Allies' slow advance in the war against Japan. When a large fleet of Japanese warships, aircraft carriers and troop transports were sent to capture the US naval and air base at Midway Island, the defence was immediate and very effective. Bombers from the base, reinforced by the arrival of part of the American Pacific Fleet, forced the invaders to withdraw. Enormous damage was inflicted on the Japanese fleet, including the loss of four aircraft carriers.

Submarine support for the battles of the Coral Sea and Midway came mainly from Brisbane and Pearl Harbor. The Fremantle submarines were patrolling further to the west and experiencing a disappointing lack of success in sinking enemy vessels. The submarine commanders blamed the Mark XIV torpedoes with which the submarines were equipped. They seemed to be running too deep and passing underneath targets and, at times, exploding prematurely. After receiving several of these reports Rear Admiral Lockwood contacted the United States Navy Bureau of Ordnance. As they refused to accept the possibility that the torpedoes could be running too deep, he decided to conduct his own experiments.

The tests were carried out at Frenchmans Bay, Albany, on 20 June 1942, under the direction of James Fife, who was later to take command of the Fremantle base. A fishing net borrowed from a local fisherman was lowered to a suitable depth and three torpedoes were fired by the *Skipjack.* The torpedoes were found to have holed the net at an average of 3.35 metres lower than the level at which they had been set to run. Lockwood's report to the Bureau of Ordnance received short shrift, but he followed it up with another test on 18 July, using another submarine, the *Saury.* This produced similar results. Partly as a result of these experiments the Bureau of Ordnance conducted its own tests. Fife's results were confirmed and modifications were made to correct the fault.

Nevertheless, controversy over the premature explosion of the torpedoes continued. The fault was thought to be in the magnetic exploder, which was supposed to be set off by the magnetic field created by the target vessel's hull.

The following year, when Lockwood, then a vice admiral, was in command at Pearl Harbor he was able to arrange a series of tests which proved that the fault was in the exploder mechanism itself. Meanwhile, experiments continuing in the United States were to bring the more efficient Mark XVIII electric torpedoes into use towards the end of the following year.[4]

In June, *Gar, Grampus, Grayback* and *Tautog* arrived to replace the submarines that had been withdrawn. United States Navy veteran, Andy Anderson, who later migrated to Western Australia, was on board the *Gar* when it arrived at Fremantle on 8 June 1942. After three days *Gar* left for Albany with half the crew, who were to help overhaul the submarine. Anderson served on *Gar* during four patrols out of Fremantle before transferring to the *Cabrilla* in October 1943.[5]

By the first weeks of July 1942, the Western Australian fleet was made up of twenty of the long-range Fleet-class submarines, with fifteen at Fremantle and five at Albany. During July and August, *Permit* and *Pickerel* were transferred to Pearl Harbor and their replacements, *Thresher, Gudgeon, Grenadier* and *Tambor,* arrived in August and September. *Pickerel* departed on 10 July and patrolled in the vicinity of Guam and Saipan on her way to Pearl Harbor.

United States Navy surface forces in Western Australia at this time consisted of the submarine tenders *Holland* and *Otus;* the cruiser *Phoenix;* the seaplane tenders *William B. Preston, Childs* and *Heron;* and four small vessels, *Lark, Lanakai, Isabel* and *Whippoorwill.* On 23 July 1942 the submarine tender *Pelias* arrived at Albany from Melbourne to replace USS *Holland.*[6]

Former US submariner William Pouleris, later a resident of Western Australia, arrived at Albany aboard the *Gudgeon* just before *Holland* left. *Gudgeon* was badly in need of repairs after surviving 60 depth charges during its patrol from Pearl Harbor. Pouleris was transferred to the *Pelias's* submarine relief crew and stayed with the vessel until after it moved to Fremantle in October.[7]

When USS *Holland* returned to Fremantle, USS *Otus* could return to the United States for its conversion to be completed.[8] On 27 July, Commander Keith of the USN informed the manager of the Fremantle Harbour Trust that *Holland* would replace *Otus* at No.4 berth on North Wharf. He also asked permission to erect three collapsible sheds as sleeping quarters for the crews of submarines that were being overhauled by the repair ship. These buildings were erected at the rear of No.3 berth.[9]

The Allies had begun to fight back from the desperate position of early 1942, but the danger to Australia was still very real, with the Japanese based in the northern part of New Guinea and aiming to gain control of Port Moresby on the south coast. Their invasion plans had been foiled by the Allied success in the Battle of the Coral Sea in May, so they began to push southward over the rugged Owen Stanley Mountains where, from 23 July to November 1942, defending Australian troops found themselves locked into the grueling series of battles known as the Kokoda

Track campaign. On 25 August an attack was made on the Australian base at Milne Bay, at the eastern end of the island. The Japanese planned to use the base for air and sea support of their forces fighting along the Kokoda Track, but were driven off by a predominantly Australian infantry force.[10]

Meanwhile, further out in the Pacific the US had begun its campaign to recapture Japanese-held islands. On 7 August 1942, United States marines landed on Guadalcanal in the Solomon Islands in an attempt to regain control of the group, and the American navy was involved in reinforcing the land troops. During the remainder of the year a number of fierce clashes took place, both on land and at sea. It was during this campaign that the Australian navy lost HMAS *Canberra*.

From August to November 1942, while the USN fleet was involved in the Guadalcanal campaign, the number of submarines based in Western Australia was drastically reduced. The inferior S-class submarines were being gradually withdrawn from Brisbane and replaced with Fleet-class boats, so the Western

Australian fleet was depleted to supply these reinforcements. In July, August, September and October twelve submarines—*Grampus, Grayback, Gudgeon, Sailfish, Sargo, Saury, Sculpin, Seadragon, Snapper, Spearfish, Sturgeon* and *Swordfish*—left for Brisbane, and for a short time the major force was actually based there.

Nevertheless, *Thresher* arrived at Fremantle on 15 August, and in September the commander-in-chief advised that submarine maintenance at Fremantle should be planned on the assumption that 30 Fleet-class submarines would eventually be assigned to the South West Pacific Area. Fremantle was allocated one complete shore-based repair unit, Navy 137, which arrived early the following year. The setting up of maintenance facilities had progressed so efficiently that in February 1943 estimates of equipment required to complete the program were reduced. Work on the Fremantle slipway had been completed, with the design modified to allow the large Fleet-class submarines to be docked.

By the end of November, after *Skipjack, Seawolf, Salmon* and *Seal* were shifted from the South West Pacific Area command to Pearl Harbor, only six of the original 20 submarines remained at Western Australian bases. The United States Navy surface force based on the west coast was also depleted when, towards the end of October, *Pelias* returned to Fremantle from Albany and *Holland* sailed for the United States, via Melbourne, where damage to its rudder was repaired.

In December, *Grayling* and *Trout* arrived to join *Gar, Grenadier, Searaven, Thresher, Tambor* and *Tautog,* bringing the number up to eight. *Searaven,* the only one left of the original Asiatic Fleet which arrived in March 1942, transferred to Pearl Harbor at the end of its December patrol, sinking a 5,693-ton ship on the way.

Tautog left on 15 December 1942 for the Java Sea and waters around Ambon, Timor, and the Celebes islands. During its patrol, the submarine sank two enemy vessels: the *Banshu Maru No.2* and the *Hasshu Maru. Thresher* sailed from Fremantle on 16 December.

Encountering an enemy convoy off Surabaya on Christmas Day, the submarine sank one ship and damaged another, then four days later sank the 3,000-ton *Haichan Maru. Tambor,* which also sailed in December, two days after *Thresher,* attacked a Japanese destroyer on 1 January 1943, but it missed and was bombarded with eighteen depth charges.

A total score of 17,513 tons of enemy shipping was claimed by Western Patrol submarines during the second half of the year, though some claims were subsequently disallowed.[11]

The anti-submarine boom at the entrance to the harbour can be seen in the distance in this view of Fremantle harbour from the slipway. (Royal Australian Navy Public Affairs, HMAS Stirling.)

PREMISES USED BY THE UNITED STATES NAVY

Old Fremantle Asylum and Old Women's Home, Cnr Finnerty Street and Ord Streets, Fremantle	21 officers, 35 enlisted men and 60 civilians were employed in the Naval Supply Depot administration office. They looked after lend-lease accounting, purchasing, contracting and general provisions for all American ships and navy activities, housing and billeting of American servicemen and civilian employees. In 1944 the depot temporarily took over organising and handling supplies for Allied Military Services (Australian, British and Dutch).
Dalgety's Warehouse, Queen Victoria Street, Fremantle	
Will's Warehouse, South Street, Fremantle	14 enlisted men and 18 civilians were employed.
Wool Sheds Numbers 6 and 7, Shuffrey Street, Fremantle	Five enlisted men handled all ordnance spares and landing force gear.

Woolworths Storehouse, Henry and Phillimore Streets, Fremantle	Four enlisted men and two civilians were employed.
Tarpot Warehouse, Swan Street, North Fremantle	Four enlisted men were in charge of bulk storage for all warehouses.
Essex Street Warehouse, Essex Street, Fremantle	Essex Street, Fremantle
Port Garage Warehouse, Canning Highway, Fremantle	One enlisted man handled all types of gas cylinders.
Lysaght's Warehouse, Pakenham Street, Fremantle	Four enlisted men and three civilians handled storage of advance base material and cordage.
Cadd's Warehouse, Beach Street, Fremantle	Eight enlisted men were in charge various classes of stores.
Scott St Warehouse, Scott Street, Fremantle	Four enlisted men and two civilians looked after various classes of stores.
Harper's Warehouse, Marine Terrace, Fremantle	Six enlisted men and one civilian were in charge of various classes of stores.
Gibson Park Warehouse, Holland and Chudleigh Streets, Fremantle	Ten enlisted men and one civilian handled various classes of stores.
Carpenter Shop, Scott Street, Fremantle	Six enlisted men and 15 civilians.
Claremont Drill Hall, 139 Stirling Highway, Claremont	Unstaffed storage for bulk materials.

New warehouse constructed for USN, Stirling Road, Claremont	Two enlisted men in charge of bulk storage of clothing and small stores.
Wyola Hall, Stirling Road, Claremont	One enlisted man (when required) handled overflow from the above.
Open storage areas	Several lots in Fremantle, some adjoining the warehouses.
Cold storage facilities	Facilities available at Anchorage Butchers, South Fremantle, Richmond Brewery and Fremantle Cold Storage.
Ammunition storage	USN magazine at Spring Hill (4,000 tons); Subiaco torpedo depot (storage and maintenance of torpedoes for arming the submarines); armory and gas chamber at the receiving barracks, Fremantle.

Source: USN Base Facilities Report; Southwest Pacific Area.

The US Shipping and Receiving Section operated out of the Lysaght Building in Pakenham Street. (Western Australian Museum – MHA 4564/8.)

(top) Dalgety's warehouse in Queen Victoria Street, Fremantle, was used as storage and administrative offices by the US as its Naval Supply Depot. (Western Australian Museum – MHA 4564/15.) (Bottom) The US Navy established a receiving barracks in the former asylum and old women's home in Finnerty Street. Now the Fremantle Arts Centre. (Western Australian Museum – MHA 1619.)

CHAPTER EIGHT

1943: The Fremantle Submarines at War

At the beginning of 1943 only eight Fleet-class submarines were operating out of the Fremantle submarine base, compared to 12 with Task Force 72 at Brisbane, but six of the eight set out on patrol during the first two months.[1] The first to leave was *Grenadier,* which sailed on 1 January and sank three small vessels before returning to Fremantle on 20 February. *Grayling* left on 7 January for Philippine waters, sinking a cargo ship and a schooner during its patrol. *Thresher* returned from its previous patrol on 10 January, and sailed again on the 25th. After making an unsuccessful attack on a Japanese submarine, *Thresher* reconnoitred Christmas Island, taking photographs of facilities and gun emplacements there, then sank two Japanese transports and the 5,232-ton tanker *Toen Maru* in the Flores Sea before returning to Fremantle on 10 March.

Gar, Tambor and *Tautog* returned from patrol in January, but were soon ready to return to action. *Gar* set out on patrol on 9 February, and *Tambor* left on the 18th to carry out a special mission in the Philippines. On 5 March, the submarine landed a small navy party on southern Mindanao. *Tautog* left on 24 February for the Java Sea and Makassar Strait area, where it accounted for a destroyer, a freighter and three small vessels. *Gudgeon,* which had gone to Brisbane in late 1942, returned on 18 February after completing two special missions. Six commandos were landed on Mindanao in the Philippines, and 28 men were rescued from Timor and transported to Fremantle.[2]

The base was soon to have a new commander. In January 1943, Rear Admiral English, commander of the Pacific Fleet submarines, died in an air crash. In the resulting reshuffle Lockwood was promoted to vice admiral and given command of the base at Pearl Harbor. He left Fremantle during February. His replacement, Rear Admiral

Ralph Christie, arrived some time later and moved into Lockwood's quarters, known as 'Bend of the Road'.[3]

Fremantle's small fleet of submarines continued to enjoy some success. *Gudgeon,* leaving port on 13 March, accounted for some 15,000 tons of enemy shipping during its short patrol. Encountering a convoy on the 22nd, it sank the *Meigen Maru* (5,434-tons), damaged two other ships and added a 9,997-ton tanker, the *Toko Maru,* to its score before returning to Fremantle on 6 April. On 9 April *Grayling,* which had departed on 18 March for its patrol area off the coast of Borneo, sank a cargo ship and damaged four other vessels. *Trout* left Fremantle on 22 March to lay mines north of Borneo, and also sank two trawlers before returning on 3 May.

Sadly, *Grenadier,* which left on 20 March, was lost in the Malacca Straits in April. During the previous night the submarine had sighted two enemy ships so it prepared to make a dawn attack. As *Grenadier* closed in for a surface attack, however, a Japanese plane suddenly appeared. They went into a crash dive, but at a depth of 36.5 to

39.6 metres the submarine was violently rocked by two bomb blasts. Power and light failed, and a fire broke out inside the submarine. The *Grenadier* lay on the bottom for thirteen hours while the crew tried to repair the damage. They were able to surface after dark but the submarine was irreparably damaged. The stern was twisted out of shape, and shafts, torpedo tubes, hatches and valves were warped and rendered useless. They rigged a makeshift sail, hoping to sail the crippled submarine in close to the shore to scuttle it where there was a chance of escaping into the jungle, but there was no wind, so the men were forced to abandon ship and sink the submarine in open waters. Picked up by a Japanese merchant ship and taken to Penang, they suffered brutal treatment as prisoners of the Japanese. Four men died in captivity, but 71, including the skipper John Fitzgerald, survived. Fitzgerald, who underwent severe torture, was awarded the Navy Cross.[4]

Meanwhile, the other submarines were keeping busy, and the short time it took to ready them for action between patrols reflects the efficiency of the maintenance facilities at the base. Three submarines, *Gar, Grayling* and *Tambor,* were put on the Fremantle slips for painting during April and May.[5]

During April 1943, the *West Australian* published more news of successful US submarine operations against enemy supply lines from Indochina to the South Pacific. One of the victims claimed was a Japanese submarine. Of course, neither the submarines nor their bases were identified.[6]

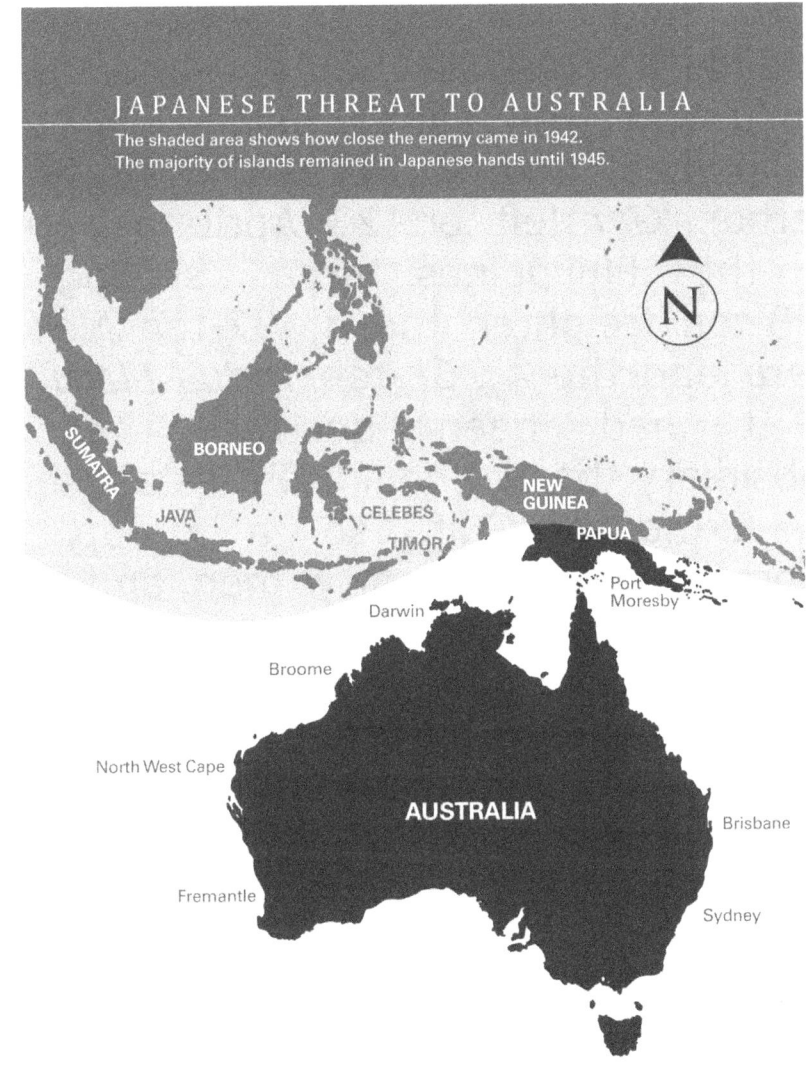

Thresher left Fremantle on 4 April for an uneventful patrol, and *Gudgeon,* which had been withdrawn from the Fremantle fleet, sailed on 15 April to patrol the Flores Sea area. It sank a 17,526-ton transport, the *Kamakura*

Maru, and two smaller vessels, then landed six guerilla fighters and their equipment on Panay Island in the Philippines, before proceeding to Pearl Harbor. *Gar* left on 23 April to patrol in the Philippines area, sinking a 703-ton freighter, the 3,197-ton *Meikai Maru* and the 4,361-ton *Indus Maru.*

It had been decided that a subsidiary base should be established at Exmouth Gulf, so a group of submariners, about fifty men and five officers, was sent to 'Potshot', as the base was called, to work with Australian soldiers building basic facilities such as airstrips and accommodation.[7] On 9 March 1943 USS *Otus* returned to Fremantle from the United States. With a second submarine tender now available, *Pelias* was sent to Potshot, arriving there on 4 May. Two days later, the Exmouth Gulf base was declared operational, but the area was exposed to north-west gales and a heavy swell, making the servicing of submarines impossible. To make matters worse, the Japanese soon discovered something important was going on at the gulf, and the base was bombed twice during the month.

It was soon obvious that the attempt to establish a base there had been a mistake and the project was abandoned. On 27 May, *Pelias* returned to Fremantle, and Potshot was downgraded to a fuelling station. The tanker *Ondina* was stationed there for oil storage until tanks, capable of storing 8,000 tonnes, were built ashore. This allowed submarines to call in and take on fuel and supplies before heading off on a second leg of their patrol. Time actively spent on war patrol could be considerably lengthened, by making these 'double-barrelled' patrols, using either this base or Darwin. The communications and radar stations, as well as American and Australian anti-aircraft batteries, continued to operate at the gulf. The submarine tender *Otus* was now no longer required and left Fremantle for Sydney during July.[8]

On 7 May, *Tambor* departed for the coast of Indochina, where it sank a cargo ship, the *Eiski Maru*. *Tautog* was withdrawn from Fremantle at this time.

Sailing on 11 May to patrol in the Flores, Molucca and Celebes seas, the submarine sank two cargo ships, the *Shinei Maru* and the 4,474-ton *Meiten Maru*, before ending its patrol at Pearl Harbor. *Grayling* set out on 18 May for the waters off north-west Borneo, where it damaged a freighter and two smaller ships before returning to port on 6 July. *Trout*, which left Fremantle on 27 May, carried out a special mission in the Philippines and sank two vessels, the tanker *Sanraku Maru* and the *Isuzu Maru*. USS *Griffin* arrived in May as the tender for the Squadron 12 submarines that had been assigned to Fremantle. They were to arrive over the following months.

With the loss of *Grenadier* and the withdrawal from Fremantle of *Gudgeon* and *Tautog*, submarine numbers had shrunk during the first half of 1943. According to Daily Intelligence Summaries, Task Force 71 was reduced to only six submarines by the end of June. *Grayling, Tambor* and *Trout* were out on patrol, while *Gar* and *Thresher* had just returned to port. Included in the six was *Finback*, which arrived on

26 June, but it seems not to have been a replacement as this contemporary source suggests,[9] just temporarily at Fremantle to refit.[10]

As the Allies advanced in the Pacific the importance of the submarine base at Brisbane diminished. Japan, however, was increasing its tanker fleet by some thirty percent to tap oil supplies from the conquered East Indies. As Fremantle-based submarines were ideally situated to slip north through the Malay Barrier and interfere with this traffic, the Fremantle fleet was built up again, at the expense of Brisbane, in the second half of the year.

As the war moved up the Solomons chain and westward into New Guinea, the boats were reapportioned in favor of Fremantle, and when the total number of Australia-based submarines was increased to 30 late in the year, Fremantle was allocated 22 and Brisbane the rest.[11]

After USS *Otus* left for Sydney on 2 July, American surface vessels attached to the base were the submarine tenders *Pelias* and *Griffin;*

submarine rescue vessel *Chanticleer;* seaplane tenders *William B. Preston, Heron* and *Childs;* the small vessels *Whippoorwill, Isabel* and *Lark;* patrol vessels *YP 286* and *YP 288;* and the submarine chaser *SC-739.*[12]

Finback left Fremantle on 18 July 1943. Patrolling along the Java coast, it sank two cargo ships and inflicted damage on others on the way to Pearl Harbor. *Thresher* was also withdrawn and left in late June, sinking a tanker and the 5,274-ton passenger-freighter *Yoneyama Maru* in the Makassar Strait, and delivering ammunition and stores to Filipino guerillas on Negros Island.

During August, *Gar* and *Trout,* which had both been on the slips on 1 August,[13] were withdrawn, returning to the US for overhauls after their patrols. *Gar* left on the 8th for Timor and the Makassar Strait, and *Trout,* which sailed on 12 August to patrol off the Philippines, sank a Japanese submarine, the *I-182,* the freighter *Ryotoku Maru* and a transport, *Yamashiro Maru.* A small Japanese vessel was also sunk, its crew taken prisoner, and charts and other documents recovered.

The fleet suffered another loss in August. USS *Grayling* had departed from Fremantle in July to undertake special missions in conjunction with its patrol. The submarine made two separate visits to Panay Island in the Philippines, delivering supplies to guerilla groups on 31 July and 23 August. Then, on 27 August, it reported sinking a 5,500-ton vessel, the *Meizan Maru*. After that report, there was silence. *Grayling* and her brave men were gone, and nothing was ever to be heard of them.

The Dutch submarine *O 21* arrived in August after a special mission, and another Dutch submarine, the *K XII*, was on the Fremantle slips during that month. This submarine appears to have been involved in ASDIC trials during this period. ASDIC, also known as sonar, was an underwater detection system that utilised soundwaves. Dutch submarine veteran Pieter Andriessen, who later migrated to Western Australia, recalled that when not engaged in special missions the Dutch submarines attached to the US fleet carried out patrols under similar conditions to the American submarines, often refuelling at Darwin for double-barrelled patrols.[14]

Kingfish, which left on its fifth war patrol on 24 September, had been the first of the replacement submarines to reach Fremantle, and more came in September and October. *Billfish* and *Bowfin* arrived on 10 October, and *Bonefish* on the 21st. Of the submarines that left Brisbane for Fremantle during September and October, however, only these and *Bluefish, Cod, Crevalle, Narwhal, Pompon, Puffer* and *Rasher* arrived safely. *Capelin* and *Cisco,* from Submarine Squadron 16, never reached Fremantle. *Cisco* was lost towards the end of September, somewhere between Darwin and the Sulu Sea. *Capelin,* after calling at Darwin for repairs, disappeared in the Makassar Strait. *Rasher* and *Pompon* arrived in November, and *Crevalle, Cod* and *Narwhal* in December. The patrol made by the *Narwhal,* a large older-type submarine, included a special mission to the Philippines, where it evacuated 31 adults and a baby. *Bonefish* left on

22 November and sank a cargo ship, the *Suez Maru* (4,646-tons), in the Flores Sea, and a passenger-cargo vessel, *Nichiryo Maru,* off the Celebes coast.

Rear Admiral Ralph Christie joined the US submarine Bowfin for the second leg of its third war patrol. He is seen with Lieutenant John Bertrand (left) on watch. (Courtesy Commander J Bertrand.)

Bowfin returned to Fremantle in triumph at the end of its second war patrol. Commanding Officer Walter Griffith is at centre front. (Courtesy Commander J Bertrand.)

Towards the end of 1943 the US submarines began hunting in three-boat 'wolf packs', and sometimes submarines operated in pairs. *Bowfin* and *Billfish*, two of the submarines that arrived in October, had tried working in partnership and sank three ships on their way to Fremantle. Leaving on 1 November for their next patrol, they again cooperated and *Bowfin* sank ten vessels.

On the voyage out, *Bowfin* encountered five schooners travelling together and sank three of them. They were probably carrying goods for the Japanese, but, with women and children aboard, some of the crew questioned the necessity of destroying such apparently innocent craft. *Bowfin* sank another schooner and holed two tankers before joining up with *Billfish* on 20 November. The weather was bad and it was difficult to maintain contact. On 26 November *Bowfin* accidentally surfaced in the middle of a Japanese convoy. Not only did the submarine escape but it also sank a 5,000-ton tanker and two freighters. On 1 December it sank a 9,900-ton tanker and a 5,400-ton transport. *Bowfin's* skipper, Walt Griffith, was awarded the Navy Cross by base commander Christie, who 'wined and dined the wardroom in spectacular fashion at Bend of the Road'.[15]

By the end of 1943 submarine numbers at Fremantle exceeded those at Brisbane. *Tinosa* arrived from Pearl Harbor and reported for duty during December. *Kingfish,* which returned on

14 November, was withdrawn from Fremantle, departing on 16 December for the South China Sea, where it sank three tankers before continuing to Pearl Harbor. The Dutch submarine *O 21*, which had suffered engine damage on its last patrol, departed in December for the UK.

The Fremantle submarines had played an important part in limiting Japan's access to the rich resources of her conquests during 1943. The introduction during the year of the electric torpedo, Mark XVIII, which left no wake and could be set to run at very shallow depths, would have increased their level of success.[16] In the second half of the year the submarines were concentrating on attacking the oil traffic from Borneo and Sumatra. 'Nearly 50 enemy ships were sunk by the Fremantle force between June and December, and a dozen of these were oil tankers.'[17]

Besides their role in cutting supply lines in Indonesian waters and the South China Sea, Fremantle-based US submarines were heavily involved in special missions to the Philippines during the year, while the Dutch boats handled missions to the Dutch East Indies. During 1943, the majority of patrols made by the Fremantle-based submarines were to the South China Sea and by the end of the year they had accounted for 244,487 tons of enemy shipping.[18]

THE SUBMARINE REPAIR UNIT AT NORTH WHARF

The USN set up its submarine repair facility at the Fremantle Harbour Trust's No.1 Grain Shed on North Wharf, Fremantle, after October 1943. Barracks for the submarine crews were built behind the shed.[1]

American submariners relaxing on the beach at North Fremantle in 1944. (Western Australian Museum, courtesy C. Elder – MHA 4592/10.)

In September 1944, the Submarine Repair Unit Navy 137 on North Wharf was described as a shore-based facility attached to Task Force 71. It provided the same service as a submarine tender, including spare parts. It also provided a motor vehicle pool for its own use and for other vessels of the task group.

A prefabricated building 12.2 metres by 30 metres housed the fleet schools as well as workshops for the ship fitters, sheet metal workers, pattern-makers, blacksmiths, carpenters and electricians. There were also workshops for machining, optical work, radio and sound, and photography. The Western Australian State Engineering Works, Midland Railway workshops, or other local engineering works were called on to do engineering work beyond the capabilities of the Submarine Repair Unit.

The unit, which employed an average of 32 officers and 575 enlisted men, was capable of refitting four submarines at the same time, though usually the number was kept to three. The Fremantle slipway was used for slipping the submarines until the arrival of the USN floating dry dock, *ARD 10,* in March 1944. The *ARD 10* was moored at the eastern end of the harbour. Australian civilians, led by foreman Bill Archibald, were employed on the floating dry dock.

A surface ship-repair activity, also attached to Task Force 71, was responsible for the repair and upkeep of USN surface vessels. Local ship-repair facilities were also available for USN use. In 1944 Commander, 7th Fleet, USN reported: 'By use of the Western Australian Government Shop and employees, and civilian contractors, all work on ships up to 3,000 tons can be handled – steam turbine, reciprocator engine and diesel'[2]

One of the United States Navy submarines in the floating dock ARD 10. William Archibald, who was in charge of the civilian work force is seen at right wearing a hat. (Western Australian Museum, courtesy W. Archibald – MHA 4531/3.)

Wartime crowds, Hay Street, Perth. (Western Australian Museum, courtesy Lynne Cairns – MHA 4561/08.)

CHAPTER NINE

Meanwhile, on the Home Front

By the time the Americans arrived in Australia in 1942 a large proportion of the adult male population had been fighting overseas for two years, the civilian population was not yet fully organised to support the war effort, and the public works programs that had stalled during the Great Depression were still unfinished. The Americans, ignorant of Australia's history, had little understanding of the economic sacrifices required to supply several divisions of fighting men from such a small population. By contrast the United States, by staying out of the war until the end of 1941, had been able to increase its industrial power while the European nations were busily destroying each other's industries. The United States was set to expand its markets as those of the European colonial powers were shrinking.

America sought to weaken imperial preference and to extend American markets at the expense of Britain during the war. Under Lend Lease, an American-originated scheme to fund wartime production, Australia exported much primary produce to the US and imported secondary industry materials; in simple terms, from 1941-42 to 1944-45 over 40 per cent of Australian imports came from the US.[1]

Although American opportunism no doubt played a part, these figures also reflect the drying up of British sources of imports. This factor also encouraged growth in local production.

Australian heavy industries such as steel-making, shipbuilding, engineering works and foundries were soon put completely onto a war footing. Shipbuilding was one of the major requirements, and Australian shipyards built more than 250 service vessels between 1939 and 1945, including three Tribal-class destroyers, two Grimsby-class sloops, three Bar-class boom defence vessels, six River-class frigates and 60 Bathurst-class minesweepers, popularly referred to as 'corvettes'.[2]

The other vessels ranged in size from small workboats to 300-ton wooden vessels, 70 of which were built. A number of these were built in Western Australia. Local shipyards, and even companies not normally involved in the industry, were contracted to build timber vessels. Builders like A.T. Brine and Company, who constructed the boom defence buildings at Victoria Quay, were building 12-metre workboats, and timber milling companies like Millars and Bunnings were involved in building larger vessels, some of which were used by Z-Force commandos.

Engines for some of the navy's 'corvettes' were built at the Western Australian Government Railways workshops at Midland Junction, and between 1939 and the end of 1945 the engineering workers there also built 15 new locomotives designed by staff members and eight new engines for rebuilt locomotives. They also assembled 14 locomotives imported from Britain.[3]

Australian Government and private companies were also producing fighting aircraft throughout the war. These included 212 Mosquitoes, 364 Bristol Beaufighters, 700 Bristol Beaufort bombers, more than 700 Wirraways, and over one thousand Tiger Moths. Several new designs were also being developed in Australia.[4]

One of the boom defence buildings constructed during World War II by A.T. Brine and Company. (Western Australian Museum – MHA 4564/25.)

This 318-ton steel vessel was built at Fremantle during World War II. (Western Australian Museum, Murray Collection – MHA 4504/78A.)

These achievements highlight the extent of Australia's contribution to its own defence. But it was not achieved without a great deal of effort. Demand for essential war supplies placed great pressure on the civilian workforce, and women were recruited into occupations previously closed to them. When the 'pool of unemployed female labour dried up', workers were transferred from non-essential industries. In early 1944, so urgently were essential supplies needed on the home front that 39,000 Australian servicemen were transferred back to the civilian workforce.[5]

Much of the increased demand was for provisioning American forces in Australia.

The arrival of tens of thousands of American troops placed a great strain on limited resources and substantially reduced the availability of goods for civilian use. To the end of August 1943 Australia had provided the United States forces with eight million articles of clothing and 146,298 tons of food.[6]

By June 1942 there were 88,000 American servicemen in Australia, and the number rose to 250,000 by early 1943.[7] The United States Government supplied many of their needs, but essential everyday supplies were provided by Australia as reciprocal Lend-Lease. Lend-Lease can perhaps best be described as a bartering system, designed to facilitate the transfer of goods and services between Allied forces and governments. Under its provisions, each nation supplied materials when needed on the understanding that the cost would be offset by the return of equivalent value in goods and services.

One of the steel barges built by the State Electricity Works at North Fremantle during World War II. (Western Australian Museum, courtesy L. Rourke – MHA 4577/23.)

When goods or services are supplied to the Commonwealth by the US under Lend-Lease arrangements, Australia does not incur any specific debit expressed in monetary values. Neither does the Commonwealth debit the US Government with the cost of furnishing the American forces with goods and services as reciprocal Lend-Lease ... each country kept its own records of what it supplied to the other in so far as it was possible to do this.[8]

Under the agreement, Australia was responsible for providing major infrastructure, such as ports, airfields, hospitals and transport facilities, as well as food and other basic provisions, while the US supplied military equipment like aircraft, vehicles and communications technology. A major Australian responsibility was the supply of food for the American forces, and when Australian civilians were coping with rationing and the food supplied to Australian servicemen was limited to basics, the quality and quantity of food demanded by the American services became a cause for resentment. The Americans contributed a greater amount in money terms through Lend-Lease, but Australians contributed 17 per cent more per head of population.[9]

In 1942 most of Australia, and particularly the vulnerable north, was sparsely populated, with few roads or other facilities, so it was no easy task to house the American thousands and provide the necessary infrastructure required to make Australia a defensible base from which the Allied forces could win back the lost territories. Airfields, highways, barracks, munitions factories, hospitals and other facilities were soon under construction all over the country, particularly in the north. The largest military complex was in Queensland.

The work was usually done by Australian and American troops or by the Civil Construction Corps, the labour force of the Allied Works Council, made up of men who were not young or fit enough for military service, and some who had experience in the building trades. By mid 1943 some 53,000 men were employed. There was also the Civil Alien Auxiliary Corps, made up of about four thousand young foreigners who were not considered as a threat to national security. In Perth and Fremantle, however, local government departments or private contractors often did construction work. The availability of this work gave a boost to the local economy.

There was no New Year's Day holiday for Australia's workers on 1

January 1943, though many took the day off anyway. By this time 715,000 men and women were serving in the armed forces, and, of the rest of Australia's 7,000,000 population, many were too young or too old to join the workforce. With the need to boost production well above the peacetime level, the lives of the working population were controlled by the manpower regulations. People no longer checked the newspaper advertisements when looking for a job but went to the Ministry for War Organisation of Industry, to be sent wherever they were needed. Employees were not allowed to change jobs, or employers in 'protected' industries to sack workers, without the approval of the manpower officials.[10]

Women were recruited into organisations like the Women's Land Army, which sent them out to work on farms where they did whatever work was needed. Other women worked at the munitions factory at Welshpool, near the railway crossing. Established in August 1942, it produced small-arms ammunition and fuses. Several smaller factories were opened in other suburbs, and in late 1943 a factory was set up at Kalgoorlie that manufactured 40-millimetre Bofors anti-aircraft shells.[11]

Women workers at the Welshpool munitions factory receive a visit from Premier Sir James Mitchell during World War II. (West Australian Newspapers – War 1856.)

At the outbreak of the war with Japan ... 3,600 women were in the Defence Services, 71,200 were in Government, Semi-government, munitions, shipbuilding, aircraft works and defence work in factories ... By June 1943 there were 190,000 women in direct war work and, altogether, 840,000 women occupied ... enlistment in the women's services had grown to 16,243 WAAAF, 18,210 AWAS, 1,408 WRANS and 8,846 nursing services. As well, by September of that year, the Women's Land Army had 2,205 women in the field.[12]

Much has been written about the opportunities that the war provided for women to move into the workforce, and indeed they proved they could do anything the men could do. But class differences dictated, to some extent, the kind of work women did, with those from working class families concentrated in the more boring and lowly paid jobs. Those in the important war industries did get better pay, but working long hours (shiftwork, with a six-day week, plus overtime) in noisy, dirty or even dangerous conditions to produce munitions, engines or aircraft, was no picnic. What with the bleak war news and most of the young men away fighting, there was little glamour or romance in the lives of most young women. So, when young American men appeared on the streets of Australia's towns and cities wearing smartly tailored uniforms and sounding like Hollywood heroes, romance bloomed.

It was not only the girls who welcomed the American servicemen, however. Australian men and women from all walks of life opened their homes to the visitors, who were not only seen by many as the saviours of Australia, but also just as boys far from home, very much like their own sons, brothers and husbands who were fighting overseas. With so many Australian men away, however, the large numbers of United States personnel soon overwhelmed the remaining male population. Australian servicemen resented the ease with which the Americans' free-spending use of their higher pay seemed to impress Australian women. They were also annoyed by the vastly different quality of food, clothing and leisure facilities supplied for the two services, and the tendency of some taxi drivers, shopkeepers and hotelkeepers to exploit the Americans' spending habits at the expense of other clients. This mercenary attitude was echoed by the behaviour of some girls. The American servicemen had access to goods such as nylons and chocolates, which were impossible for most Australians to obtain.

Perhaps the worst kind of provocation was the brash manner of some Americans who belittled Australia's efforts in the war. American servicemen were warned against this attitude in a booklet published by the US War and Navy Department:

> You aren't in Australia to save a helpless people ... their soldiers, in this war and the last, have built up a great fighting record. For three years now, they've fought on nearly every battle front of the war; they've suffered heavy losses in Crete, Libya, Greece, and Malaya; and they're still in there pitching ... You might remember this story when you get into an argument about 'who's going to win the war': Not so long ago in a Sydney bar, an American soldier turned to an Australian next to him and said: 'Well, Aussie, you can go home now. We've come over to save you. 'The Aussie cracked back: 'Have

you? I thought you were a refugee from Pearl Harbor.'[13]

Occasionally the simmering resentment erupted in violent brawls. The most notorious clash occurred in Brisbane in November 1942. As was to be expected, this received a restricted coverage in the press. The report in the *West Australian* of 2 November did not identify the 400 'soldiers' and 'military police' involved as belonging to the American, New Zealand or Australian services. There seems to have been a particular enmity between the New Zealanders and the Americans. These two groups were involved in a brawl in Fremantle later in the war, in which two New Zealanders died.[14] A member of the Voluntary Aid Detachment who was nursing at Hollywood Hospital recalls:

> ...both sides used broken beer bottles, and broken glasses, along with their fists, to inflict the most horrifying injuries on each other. All theatre staff were recalled ... We had patients with heads laid open, eyes gouged out, horrible jagged stomach and abdomen wounds—all

requiring surgery ...—yes, we were very busy that night.[15]

These clashes were, however, the exception rather than the rule. The experiences of the Fremantle submariners reflect more positive interaction, with most remembering the kindly hospitality of Australian families, and many making long-lasting friendships. For many Australians, even if they did not quite see the Americans as saviours, the comforting presence of 'Uncle Sam' and his men outweighed any minor irritations.

During the first half of 1943 the war news was becoming less alarming for the Australian public, as the Allies continued their dogged fight back from the weak position of early 1942. In early March, a Japanese attempt to bring in large numbers of reinforcements was foiled when eight transports were sunk during the Battle of the Bismarck Sea, and Japanese naval leadership was weakened in April when Admiral Yamamoto, commander-in-chief of the Imperial Japanese Navy, died when his aircraft was shot down.

Meanwhile Australian and American forces were on the offensive in the Solomon Islands, while in New Guinea, the Australians had routed the enemy in the Kokoda Track campaign by November 1942. In January, the Japanese were driven out of Gona and Buna at the north end of the track. On 9 February they also withdrew from Guadalcanal, bringing the long campaign there to an end. In the islands north of Australia, however, they still held most of the territory they had captured.[16]

In March 1943, though they had actually arrived at Fremantle in February, Prime Minister John Curtin announced that the 9th AIF division, which had established a distinguished record in battle in North Africa, had returned to Australia.[17] In 1942, when Australia's chances looked very grim, Curtin had insisted that the 9th be sent home, despite opposition from Churchill and Roosevelt. These seasoned troops were to play an important role at Lae later in 1943.

There was also a heartening improvement in the war against

Germany. The RAF was penetrating into the German heartland to bomb Berlin and industrial targets. In May 1943, using a specially designed 'bouncing bomb', they demolished the Moehne and Eder Dams in the Ruhr Valley, causing widespread damage. In North Africa, the Allied victory in the Second Battle of El Alamein in late 1942 had put an end to Germany's hopes of occupying Egypt and controlling the Suez Canal, and Rommel's troops had been forced to retreat to Tunisia, where the Axis forces surrendered on 13 May. In Russia, the siege of Stalingrad had been relieved in February, with the German army routed by Soviet forces and the Russian weather.

Though the likelihood of a Japanese invasion of Australia had diminished, it could not be completely ruled out, as northern Australia was very much within the reach of the enemy and still subject to Japanese air attacks, which continued throughout most of 1943. Darwin was bombed in March, May, June, August and November, raising the score to 64 Japanese air raids since February 1942. In all, there had been a total of 97 raids on northern Australian targets, from Exmouth Gulf in Western Australia to Townsville in Queensland. In September 1943, several people were killed when the remote Kalumburu Mission in northern Western Australia was bombed.[18]

People in the southern part of Western Australia still had no reason for complacency either. The Japanese submarine I-165 cruised, unhindered, down the west coast during January 1943 and on the 28th shelled the small coastal town of Port Gregory, 75 kilometres north of Geraldton, apparently its original target.[19] Later in the year the searchlight unit working at Swanbourne spotted a Japanese reconnaissance plane in broad daylight and tracked its course by radar.[20] There were other reported sightings of strange aircraft and even what was believed by some to be a Japanese midget submarine.[21] Z-Force midget submarines, based at Careening Bay, may have been responsible for such reports, as their presence was shrouded in secrecy. When one of the small submersible boats sank in Cockburn

Sound, it drifted ashore and was discovered by fishermen, who thought it was a torpedo. The damaged craft was retrieved and buried at the Byford ammunition depot.[22]

Japanese submarines continued to be a menace to Allied shipping in Australian waters. Twelve merchant navy vessels were lost during 1943, most off the east coast of New South Wales, and, in some cases, less than 160 kilometres from the major cities. In the most notorious of these incidents, the hospital ship *Centaur,* a former Blue Funnel liner, was torpedoed off the Queensland coast on 14 May, with the loss of 268 lives, but many lesser tragedies remained unreported. On 11 April, for instance, 32 out of a total of 42 crewmen were lost when the Yugoslav ship *Recina* was torpedoed off Cape Howe, Victoria.

Dutch officers and sailors, Submarine Naval Base, Crawley Bay, Nedlands. (Western Australian Museum, courtesy the Royal Australian Navy – MHA 4561/24.)

CHAPTER TEN

A Submariner's Life

Most people would not be suited to life on board a submarine, even today with the comforts provided by modern technology. Imagine being on a long patrol in the tropics during World War II: overcrowded conditions, little water, little or no air conditioning, and the ever-present fear of being blown up, drowned or trapped in the depths inside a disabled submarine. Submariners see themselves as belonging to an elite, and they must, indeed, be people with a special kind of personality, able to remain calm and carry out their duties in extremely stressful situations. Just to live together in such restricted and uncomfortable conditions would have required a great deal of patience and tolerance.

The large USN boats were built for use in the tropics and so were equipped with air conditioning. They also had some facilities for distilling water, but the supply was restricted. The air conditioning did not always work properly either. As Corwin Mendenhall, who served in *Sculpin,* recalls in his *Submarine Diary:*

> Sculpin's air conditioning was not at all efficient, particularly in the humid tropical climate. Showers were closed to conserve water. We depended on the exhaust heat of the diesel engines to distil whatever water was made, and the water was more important for the battery and for cooking than for cleaning people. The boat took on even more of that peculiar submarine smell of diesel fuel, cigarette smoke, cooking odors, paint, and human aroma.[1]

Mendenhall goes on to explain how, when the air inside the submarine was particularly foul after running submerged all day, it was possible to use the diesel engines, which needed a supply of oxygen, to suck fresh air through the boat. The forward torpedo room escape hatches were opened, as were all the compartment doors between the forward torpedo and engine rooms. When one of the engines was started, it 'sucked a hurricane of air through the boat, purging the foul air'.[2]

The British submarines were not only smaller, but had been intended for use in the northern Atlantic and the North Sea. Consequently they lacked air conditioning and other facilities available on the American boats. Veteran British submariners described conditions on board these submarines as very trying. Tempers occasionally became frayed, particularly in the tropics, where sweat rashes, prickly heat and boils plagued the men. It was very humid when they were submerged, and everyone was dripping with perspiration. In these conditions they often stripped to a pair of briefs or a towel around the waist. As they were unable to distil water, it was rationed. The tanks were filled before leaving harbour and that water had to last for the whole patrol, so there were no showers.

Living accommodation was not very comfortable, either. There was very little room for meals or relaxation, very few bunks for sleeping and nowhere to go when off watch, except to the mess, or an empty bunk, if one could be found.

Only the captain had his own cabin, which was very small. Ordinary sailors and even some officers had to share bunks. Watches were continuous—two hours on and four hours off—and often the men had to take turns in the bunks, with the person coming off watch climbing into the bunk vacated by the person going on watch. The recently vacated bunk was often sodden with perspiration. With such shortage of room, extra food supplies were stored wherever they could be squeezed in during the outward leg of the patrol.

The hot, noisy and cramped diesel engine room of a submarine. (Western Australian Museum – MHA 4557/35A)

Nevertheless, life in submarines was good, considering the cramped conditions. Officers and ratings ate the same food, out of the same galley, and shared much the same conditions. Perhaps that is why submarine crews are more tolerant. They had to get on and work together as a team or else they were quickly drafted out of the service. Discipline was also less restrictive than in other branches of the navies, and relations between the ranks, from captain on down, were less formal. Each man's life depended on the cooperation of the group, and the skill and judgment of the skipper.

The usual complement on a British T-class was 60 to 65 men, with 48 men on the S-class boats. There could be up to 18 extras if the submarine was transporting a commando party. The normal length of patrols in the British submarines was 28 days for S-class and 35 days for T-class. They often exceeded these limits, however. HMS *Telemachus* made a patrol of 48 days, *Sirdar* went for 49 days, and *Tantalus* made the longest patrol of the war by a British submarine (56 days, including 37 in the patrol area).[3]

The American Gar, Salmon, Sargo and Tambor classes carried a complement of five or six officers and 54 enlisted men, and the Porpoise class had five officers and 49 enlisted men. The newer Gato and Balao classes were manned by up to ten officers and 70 enlisted men. The smaller, and older,

S-class submarines carried four officers and 34 to 39 enlisted men, while the large Narwhal class had a complement of 89.[4] Space was even more restricted when the submarines were called upon to evacuate people from behind enemy lines.

The Dutch who were under US command had the same supplies as the Americans. 'The Yanks supplied us with everything, even fresh milk and fruit in Gage Roads before we were in port.'[5] The old K-class vessels had been built for use in the tropics, but were obsolete and in poor condition by the time they reached Australia. The O-class submarines, like the British boats, were not intended for use in this region.

Submarine crewmen had to be multi-skilled so that each man could do several jobs, and even in port they were kept busy looking after their boat when not on leave.

The interior of the forward torpedo room of the Dutch submarine O.21. (Western Australian Museum, courtesy W. Broertjes – MHA 4592/18.)

So we got settled down to harbour routine again, cleaning, repairing and renewing where necessary. The P.O. Tel. [petty officer telegraphist] went on leave so I was in charge of everything W/T [wireless telegraphy]. The transmitter wanted dishing up, a B28 was out of action, corrections had piled up, the machines wanted cleaning, stores to draw, aerials to take down, renew and replace. So, there was not much time to stand around with my fingers up my bottom.[6]

The submarine tender staff, assisted by the crews, carried out maintenance of the American submarines until the Submarine Repair Unit was set up at North Wharf, and then the specialists connected to the unit were responsible for repair and maintenance work. The submarines' spare crews worked with technical staff from the mother ships to maintain and service the British submarines.

While in port, if not on leave the American submariners slept in barracks at the Submarine Repair Unit on North Wharf, and the British stayed on board their depot ships. When they went on leave, the Americans were able to stay at local houses and hotels that had been taken over by US forces as rest camps. For officers there were several houses and hotels in the affluent suburbs, while most of the hotels for enlisted men were in the city. The crews of Dutch submarines attached to the United States command could also use the American hotels. Pieter Andriessen stayed at one of them, the

Hyde Park Hotel, when he first arrived on *K XV* in February 1944. The Dutch were given an allowance to pay for their accommodation and he later stayed at a private house. Later in the war the Royal Netherlands Navy took over barracks at the University of Western Australia that had been built for the US Navy's Air Wing 10.[7]

A US Navy truck carting a load of beer from the Swan Brewery to the Chief Officers' Club, 1943. (Western Australian Museum, courtesy C. Elder – MHA 4592/8.)

The Liberty Train on which submariners travelled to Perth on leave. (Western Australian Museum, courtesy V. Parker – MHA 4561/4.)

Many submariners, however, quickly found friendly local families to stay with, and if a man had a local girlfriend he was more likely to spend his leave time with her family. This was the experience of most men from the three Allied navies who married local girls and eventually returned to live in Australia. Many also spent time as guests of farming families and experienced life in the Australian bush.

Ben and Scott Russell, two US submariners from Michigan, were travelling down to the base at Albany when one of their comrades fell ill and had to get off at Katanning. The Russell brothers stayed with him and struck up a conversation with Arthur Sargent in the Royal Exchange Hotel. They were invited to stay at his farm at Boongadoo, 55 kilometres northeast of town, and came back to visit the family on several occasions. One of Arthur's daughters and her husband kept in touch with them after the war, and a number of visits were exchanged over the years.[8]

None of the USN rest camps were in Fremantle itself, so the men usually traveled directly to Perth to enjoy their leave. At first transport was provided by a special US Navy bus (a covered truck), but later most caught a Western Australian Government Railways train to the city. Sometimes a group would walk down to one of the North Fremantle hotels and share a taxi for the trip into Perth.[9] The Americans, better paid than their British and Australian counterparts, generally had plenty of money to spend and some taxi drivers took advantage of them. To the chagrin of Australian servicemen and civilians, they often ignored other potential customers in favour of the big-spending 'Yanks'.

The British submariners were more likely to use the train. RN veteran Alf Jobson, who served in HMS *Thorough,* described his first leave in April 1945:

> ...most of the crew and myself headed for North Fremantle railway station, for the trip to Perth. Noticed the railway tracks were narrow gauge. Then along came a funny little black steam engine, with eight dog box carriages. Ten matelots crammed into one compartment. The trip to Perth took 50 minutes ... as the train left the West Perth station, most of the matelots in the compartment rushed to the left hand windows. As a new chum, I was keen to have a look. To my surprise, the train was moving slowly close to the fence in Roe Street. Quite a number of the prostitutes were leaning on the front fence of their brothels. They were showing quite an amount of bare flesh.[10]

There were plenty of more respectable entertainments for the sailors, however. Young Alf and his mate, like many of the submariners, chose to take up the invitation to stay with a local family. Many people opened their homes to servicemen on leave, but the city also had a lot to offer. Edwin Young, in diary entries addressed to his young wife back in England, was quite impressed:

> There are 6 or 7 cinemas and as many good canteens and hostels—one, Phyllis Dean's will offer a dinner of soup, three course eats and sweet with cake or coffee afters, for absolutely nothing to RN ratings and if you have all night leave they will give you a clean white!! sheeted, pillowed, soft bed, also free.[11]

As well as the good food and clean beds, the Phyllis Dean Service Club and Hostel on the corner of Murray and Queen Streets offered hot baths and showers, which would have been a real luxury for the submariners returning from their long, uncomfortable patrols. Other places in Perth that offered accommodation were run by organisations such as the YMCA and Toc H. At Fremantle the Missions to Seamen and the British Sailor's Society ran similar hostels.

Of course, one of the main attractions for many of the sex-starved young men was the presence of lots of girls. There were plenty of places for young couples to meet, with dances and other entertainments, and servicemen's clubs run by organisations such as the American Red Cross, which ran the social club known as the Swan Dive in one of the local boating club sheds on the Swan River at the foot of Barrack Street.

Typically, war brought about changes in social attitudes. With the fear of invasion, and possibly annihilation, hanging over them, young people snatched what happiness was within their reach. For many of the Australian girls who dated Allied servicemen it was a chance for a bit of fun, to relieve the drudgery and anxiety of their wartime lives, and to entertain the visitors. But relationships ranged from this casual sharing of entertainment to more serious attachments. Naturally there were a few 'gold-diggers' among the women, as well as irresponsible men prepared to exploit the local women, but the majority were simply normal young people living in abnormal times.

Even Australian sailors tended to be seen as promiscuous, with 'a girl in every port', so parents would have viewed a daughter's involvement with an Allied sailor with some apprehension. The British were probably seen as safer than Americans, due to the established ties between the two countries and their smaller numbers. The Dutch were in the minority so possibly did not represent such a threat.

Royal Navy sailors enjoying a meal at the Phyllis Dean Hostel, March 1945. (West Australian Newspapers – War 2897.)

Casual relationships at that time did not necessarily lead to sex, as premarital sex was not acknowledged, let alone accepted, and the visitors also came from societies that respected 'nice girls'. But in the stressful wartime atmosphere, many young people threw off pre-war restrictions. Also, unlike today, information about contraception and protection from sexually transmitted diseases was not generally available, though servicemen had access to special 'prophylactic stations' which supplied the so-called 'Blue Light Outfits' containing a condom and tubes of anti-VD preparations. The instructions for their use seem to have been designed, as one soldier later recalled, 'to scare people off sex for life'.[12] The main purpose, of course, was to protect the men from sexually transmitted diseases and not necessarily to protect the women with whom they had sex, who were, by definition, 'bad girls'.

> It is quite clear that unless infected women in areas occupied by the military are rendered non-contagious there will be a large number of V.D. infections ... brothels should be placed out of bounds and all known clandestine prostitutes deported ... It seems fairly certain that many soldiers miss the decent female society which they are accustomed to at home. In all probability the presence of members of the women's services would have a beneficial effect.[13]

Of course, in that era, these members of the women's services would be dismissed from the service if they became pregnant. All the girls who went out with the Allied servicemen were extremely vulnerable, as it was quite possible that a young man might not return. Unexpected orders might send him away without warning, or he could be killed in action or become a prisoner of war. So, like Mary Blind, the Perth girl whose new husband was lost off *Crevalle* a few weeks after their wedding,[14] many girls were left heartbroken through no fault of their sweethearts.

That the intentions of many of the young men were 'honourable' is reflected in the number of young couples who decided to marry, despite the war and the obstacles put in their way by concerned parents and the rules of the Allied navies. The American armed forces, in particular, had stringent requirements that had to be met by the young couple. The bride, for instance, had to undergo a blood test and prove that she had no criminal record. Some of the couples decided to wait for peace, and either married in Australia or in the groom's homeland after the war. Most of the young women went to live overseas, but a few of the couples returned to Australia.

Wives of American servicemen left for the United States during late 1945 and 1946, some travelling to the eastern states by train to board ships at Sydney, others sailing from Fremantle on the *Fred C Ainsworth,* the only US bride ship to sail from Fremantle. Wives of British and Dutch servicemen sailed for England on the British aircraft carrier *Victorious* in July 1946. Many of the girls going to Holland were unable to speak Dutch when they arrived in their new country.

Horse riding was a popular activity among American submariners on leave. (Western

Australian Museum, courtesy J.V. Parker – MHA 4561/3.)

US submariner Claudie Elder and his Australian bride, Teresa, with a family group at her aunt's Bunbury home in 1945. (Western Australian Museum, courtesy C. Elder (MA 4592/3.)

I arrived at the Hague at 7a.m. and was taken by Army jeep to my destination in the south of Holland. My husband was supposed to be in Holland when I arrived, but ... he arrived 10 months later. My Mother and Father-in-law couldn't speak or understand English, and my sister and brother-in-law could only speak a little 'school' English. Anyway I was received with open arms and we soon got to understand each other ... When my baby was due, I was taken by taxi to the hospital, where the doctor didn't speak English.[15]

WAR TIME MARRIAGES

War places an enormous amount of stress on society. People find themselves living under quite abnormal conditions, often separated from their families and friends, and from any certainty as to the probable course their future lives will take. But men and women feel a need for stable relationships, so it is not really strange that people from different backgrounds can form lasting attachments, despite cultural differences, parental objections, and the intervention of governments and the military establishment. A number of the men from the submarines and submarine tenders stationed at Fremantle during the war met and married local girls. In nearly all cases, the bride left Australia to live in her husband's country, but some of the couples returned to live in Western Australia. Here are some of their stories:

Kath and William (Bill) Pouleris met in the spring of 1942. His submarine returned to the United States for repairs, but they continued to date after he returned to Fremantle and they got engaged in May 1944. They were married by special licence on 12 July 1945, but did not receive their official 'permission to marry' until 3pm on their wedding day. Fortunately the registry office stayed open until 5pm to issue the licence so they could be married at 6pm. Bill left on another war patrol and had been at sea three weeks when the war finished. He returned to the United States, and his bride followed in July 1946.

Kathleen and William Pouleris. (Western Australian Museum – MHA 4593/11.)

Homer White, who served on the submarine tender USS Holland, married Ethel Hassell, whose parents had a farm at Warriup, near Albany. They met at the Allied Service Club in Albany shortly after the tender arrived at the port in March 1942, got engaged in July and were married in August. Ethel travelled to the United States after the war, but the couple returned, with their two children, in 1947. Homer was in business in Albany as a watchmaker and jeweller for 32 years.

Claudie and Teresa Elder met in 1943 at the Sawyers Valley Hotel. Claudie had arrived in Fremantle on the US submarine Kingfish and Teresa worked at the munitions factory in Welshpool. Shortly afterwards he transferred to permanent shore patrol, and after going out together for about twelve months the young couple were married on 19 August 1944. Claudie left on the USS Clytie in September 1945 and Teresa followed in early 1946, on the *Fred C Ainsworth.*

Merle and Derek Drayson. (Western Australian Museum – MHA 4531/30.)

Merle and Derek Drayson met at a YMCA dance in October 1944. He was a petty officer on HMS Maidstone, the depot ship for the 8th Submarine Flotilla. They got engaged in February 1945. In April the Maidstone left Fremantle for service in the Pacific, but returned to Fremantle at the end of the war. Derek went home to England with the Maidstone, but returned to take his discharge in Australia and they were married in January 1949.

Claudie and Teresa Elder.

Franz Dohmen, from the Dutch submarine *K XV*, met his wife Sylvia in 1944 at the Embassy Ballroom. His submarine was based in Fremantle and undergoing repairs at the time. They were married in February 1946 and Sylvia sailed to Holland via England on the British aircraft carrier *Victorious* in July 1946.

Isaac (Gerry) and Miriam Goldman met in November 1944 at an engagement party for another RN sailor and a local girl. Gerry was a member of the relieving crew of the depot ship HMS *Maidstone*. He had previously served on the submarine *Porpoise* when it took the Operation Rimau commandos into action in September 1944. They were married on 21 March 1945 at the old synagogue in Brisbane Street, Perth. He didn't return to Britain, but was demobilised in Australia in 1946.

(top) Miriam and Gerry Goldman. (Western Australian Museum – MHA 4592/31.) (Bottom)

Joy and Ary Jongejan. (Western Australian Museum – MHA 4531/21.)

Dutch submariner Ary Jongejan met his wife Joy on Wednesday, 4 April 1945. He had just arrived on the *O 24* from Scotland. It was love at first sight and he proposed that night. The next day he bought the wedding ring, which was the custom in Holland (worn on the right hand for the engagement and passed to the left hand at the wedding). Joy wasn't happy with this, so next day Ary bought the engagement ring. On Saturday they went to Christ Church, Claremont, and arranged their wedding for 7 June, but *O 24* was damaged during its next patrol and went to Darwin for repairs. It then went back on patrol and Ary didn't get back to Fremantle until 21 July. They were married a week later. Despite the speed of their courtship, they were still happily married fifty years later.

Alf and Audrey Jobson met in April 1945 at her home in Mount Lawley. His submarine, HMS *Thorough,* had just arrived, and the crews were given the opportunity of spending their leave with

Western Australian families. Alf and a friend stayed at Audrey's home, and from then on he spent every leave with the family. Alf returned to Britain after the war, but came back to Fremantle in September 1947 and they were married on 10 April 1948.

Audrey and Alf Jobson. (Western Australian Museum – MHA 4531/34.)

Elaine and Alan Porter met toward the end of the war at the Phyllis Dean Hostel canteen, where she was doing voluntary work. Alan served on HMS *Trump,* based at Fremantle during the latter part of 1945. He was demobilised in Britain in 1946, and because of the need to further his engineering studies in London the romance was continued by correspondence. They were reunited in London in 1949 and married in Perth in 1950.

Trot of British submarines in Fremantle. View between two boats with more submarines in distance. (Royal Australian Navy Public Relations, HMAS Stirling – MHA 4568/08.)

CHAPTER ELEVEN

Early 1944: The Allies Fight Back

By the beginning of 1944 the Japanese-controlled area of the Pacific had begun to shrink as Allied forces gradually won back island bases. The enemy still held a large part of China and South-East Asia, however, and all the islands forming the barrier between the Pacific and Indian Oceans. They were also still firmly entrenched in the western part of New Guinea, although the Australian 9th Division and their American allies were forcing them to retreat. In Europe, progress was being made against Germany in the Soviet Union and Italy, but it was slow and wasteful of lives on both sides. Britain continued to suffer from bombing raids on its cities, and Allied bombing was devastating German-held industrial centres in Europe.[1]

When the year started, the US Navy had sixteen Task Force 71 submarines based at Fremantle. Ten of these were on patrol and six in port. *Bowfin,* which departed on the 8th to patrol the Java, Banda and Flores Seas, called in at Darwin for more torpedoes after sinking the 4,308-ton *Shoyu Maru* and damaging its escorts. Rear Admiral Christie was at Darwin, and joined the submarine for the remainder of its patrol, mainly to examine torpedo performance in person.[2] USS *Cod* departed on 11 January for the South China Sea and the seas off Java and the Halmaheras (east of the Celebes).

In February the Japanese admiral, Koga, moved his main fleet base from Truk in the Caroline Islands to Tawi-Tawi, Davao and Singapore, to be nearer oil supplies and to avoid USN aircraft-carrier strikes. This brought the main Japanese fleet within the area of Fremantle submarine command, so the Fremantle force was strengthened while the numbers at the Brisbane base were reduced.[3]

During the first months of the year, numbers began to build up as the new arrivals reported for duty. *Angler, Flasher, Haddo, Hake* and *Hoe* from

Squadron 20, and *Jack* from Squadron 12, transferred to Fremantle at the end of their patrols. During February, *Haddo* arrived on the 4th, *Hake* on the 20th and *Flasher* on the 29th. *Angler,* which had to return to Midway for repairs, did not arrive until April. Squadron 16's tender, *Orion,* also arrived from Brisbane.[4] The newly arrived submarines were soon ready to set out once more on their dangerous patrols. *Puffer* left for the South China Sea on 4 February and *Pompon,* which had arrived in November 1943, departed on 22 February, transferring to Pearl Harbor at the end of its patrol. The Fremantle slipway was kept busy, with *Ray* and *Bluefish* being painted in late January, and six other USN submarines on the slips in February.[5]

The Dutch submarines *K XIV* and *K XV* had arrived at Fremantle early in the year to take over the role of *K XII,* which was withdrawn from front-line service and later went to Sydney. The two submarines, and their crews, had spent about nine months in the United States from the end of 1942, while their obsolete sonar detection system was replaced with ASDIC (sonar) and radar. They were then sent to Scotland, where their crews were trained to use the new equipment, before coming to Fremantle via Colombo. Dutch submariners Pieter Andriessen and Franz Dohmen, who later migrated to Western Australia, served on *K XV,* which spent much of the war behind enemy lines, landing and evacuating commandos or refugees. The crews had undergone special training for this work at Colombo.[6]

The United States Navy's floating dock, the *ARD 10,* arrived at Fremantle on 3 March 1944, having been towed from San Francisco by the American tug *Yuma.* The *ARD 10* measured 150 metres long and nearly 22 metres wide, and was capable of accommodating the largest submarines. With the assistance of *Yuma,* the local tugs *Wyola* and *Uco,* and the USS *Chanticleer,* the dock was carefully manoeuvred into the harbour and moored at the eastern end, near the Fremantle railway bridge.[7] A number of Australian civilians were employed by the USN to work on the floating dock.[8] The Fremantle slipway continued to be used for slipping American submarines for painting.[9]

Although the Allies had been consistently pushing the Japanese back since the decisive successes of late 1942 and early 1943, the danger of attack had not been eliminated. As an important base, Fremantle was an obvious target. In March 1944, Allied code breakers picked up information which suggested that the Japanese were planning an attack on the port, so Rear Admiral Christie directed the submarine *Haddo,* which had left Fremantle on 29 February, to look for signs of a Japanese convoy moving southward through Lombok Strait.

The United States Navy submarine Nautilus in the floating dock ARD 10. (Western Australian Museum, courtesy W. Archibald – MHA 4531/4.)

The rescue vessel USS Chanticleer was based at Fremantle during 1943 and 1944. (Western Australian Museum, courtesy W. Archibald – MHA 4531/6.)

When *Haddo's* report seemed to confirm the information, fears of a Japanese surprise raid on the base were taken seriously, though a cyclone developing off Australia's north-west coast hindered attempts to verify whether Fremantle was the target. The Australian forces were informed and army units stationed in Western Australia were moved to strategic areas. Aircraft were brought hurriedly from the east and north of Australia to Exmouth Gulf and Fremantle. An American heavy-bomber group was moved from New Guinea to a Northern Territory base, ready to be brought down to Cunderdin to the east of Perth, while RAAF Spitfires and Beaufighters joined Dutch Mitchell bombers and Kittyhawks at Exmouth Gulf. Transport planes also arrived in the west, bringing supplies and support staff.[10]

Meanwhile, the floating dock was moved to Cockburn Sound, the submarine tenders were sent to Albany, and even the submarines undergoing refits—except for *Crevalle,* which could not be made ready—were ordered to sea to intercept the approaching Japanese carriers. Dutch submarine veteran Pieter Andriessen remembered the submariners being recalled from leave by an announcement over the radio, and having to get on board their vessels as quickly as possible.

The Dutch submarines formed a cordon outside Rottnest, and *Flasher, Hoe, Robalo, Hake* and *Redfin,* the American submarines hurriedly sent out from Fremantle, were further out, near Geraldton. Submarines already on patrol were diverted to guard the northern approaches. *Bonefish,* returning from patrol with 13 torpedoes but little food, took on sheep carcases at Exmouth Gulf before standing out to sea to watch for the enemy, where the crew suffered the combined effects of a tropical cyclone and a diet of mutton, which was intensely disliked by most Americans!

By this time, with increasing reports of Allied successes over the previous two years, fears of a Japanese invasion had receded and people were beginning to breathe easier. This sudden flurry of activity—servicemen called back to duty, an exodus of vessels from the harbour and extra planes arriving—must have set the rumour mills working in Perth and Fremantle. Fortunately it was all a false alarm and the expected raid did not eventuate.[11]

The Squadron 12 submarines that had been transferred to Western Australia began to arrive in March, April and May. *Hoe* had arrived on 5 March, followed on the 13th by *Jack,* which had sunk four tankers of more than 5,000 tons during its patrol from Pearl Harbor. *Redfin* left on its second war patrol on 19 March, followed on 4 April by

Crevalle, *Flasher* and *Hoe*. Twelve submarines were slipped and painted at the Fremantle slipway during March and April.[12] It was about this time that camouflage colours were introduced for the American submarines. Until this time they were painted all black, as in peacetime.[13] Fourteen US submarines departed Fremantle on patrol in April. *Gunnel* and *Lapon* reported for duty during that month, while *Haddo* returned from patrol on the 22th.

During April 1944, Allied code breakers reported that a Japanese convoy carrying reinforcements to New Guinea had left Shanghai. USS *Jack*, which left Fremantle on 6 April, intercepted the convoy on the 26th, near Manila. Despite the presence of a Japanese submarine, and attacks from the air, *Jack* stalked the convoy. That night the American submarine attacked, sinking a 5,425-ton transport, the *Yoshida Maru I*, and damaging other vessels. The Japanese convoy put in to Manila, continuing its voyage about a week later. In the Celebes Sea it was intercepted by *Gurnard*, en route from Pearl Harbor to Fremantle. Even though extra escort ships had joined the convoy in Manila, and *Gurnard* was bombarded with depth charges, the submarine sank three of the large transports: *Tenshinzan Maru* (6,886 tons), *Taijima Maru* (6,995 tons) and *Aden Maru* (5,824 tons). The convoy, vital to Japan's plans, lost nearly half of the 40,000 troops it was transporting to New Guinea. *Gurnard* sank another 10,090-ton tanker before arriving in Fremantle on 11 June.[14]

The submarine tender *Griffin* arrived on 8 May to replace *Pelias,* which departed for Pearl Harbor on the 14th.[15] *Harder, Paddle* and *Pargo* arrived in May, and on 26 May *Harder* and *Redfin* sailed for the Celebes Sea to patrol waters around the Japanese fleet anchorage at Tawi-Tawi. *Harder* sank two Japanese destroyers in the heavily patrolled Sibutu passage between Tawi Tawi and North Borneo, then picked up six British coast watchers from the north-east coast of Borneo before resuming its patrol. The submarine then sank another destroyer and damaged two more before reconnoitring the enemy base on 11

June. The information sent to headquarters was very important in the preparations for the Battle of the Philippine Sea.

Early in May, when the United States aircraft carrier *Saratoga* arrived at Fremantle, Rear Admiral Christie suggested that it should be sent to attack enemy anti-submarine shore batteries at Lombok Strait, one of the Fremantle submarines' important routes, and facilities at the port of Surabaya. The carrier had just returned from bombarding Sabang Island, to the north of Indonesia, in company with ships of the British and Free French navies.[16] This also became a combined operation, with the British navy sending the flagship of its Eastern Fleet, HMS *Queen Elizabeth,* accompanied by the battleship *Valiant,* the battle cruiser *Renown,* the aircraft carrier *Illustrious,* the cruisers *London* and *Suffolk,* and the Free French battleship *Richelieu.* Eight Fremantle submarines, *Angler, Bluefish, Cabrilla, Flasher, Gunnel, Puffer, Rasher* and *Raton,* were involved in supporting the air strikes on Surabaya on 17 May. Aircraft from the two carriers demolished Surabaya's important refineries and engineering works, but five Japanese submarines in the dockyards escaped.

The eight submarines achieved little, but *Lapon,* on a normal patrol off Indochina, sank two large Japanese freighters with a combined tonnage of 11,100 tons on 24 May. Three days later, however, *Lapon* almost sank *Raton* when it was mistaken for a Japanese I-class submarine.[17]

By mid-year, Allied forces were gradually gaining the upper hand in Europe, though Britain was being bombarded day and night by the new German flying bombs. On 6 June, with the invasion of Normandy, Allied troops began to push into German-occupied territory. In Italy, the Allies liberated Rome and the front line moved inexorably northward, while on the eastern front the Russians were attacking Finnish defences to the north of Leningrad. In the Pacific, American forces struck a devastating blow at Japanese naval power during the Battle of the Philippine Sea in June 1944.[18]

The Fremantle submarines were not directly involved in the Battle of the Philippine Sea, but in the build-up to the inevitable confrontation the Japanese fleet gathered in waters patrolled by Fremantle submarines. During the four weeks before the battle, they sank five destroyers and two aircraft-carrier support ships.[19] In all, during the first six months of 1944 submarine patrols out of Fremantle accounted for some 156,488 tons of enemy shipping.[20]

All this submarine activity had a devastating impact on Japan. Now that wolf-packing had been formalised and perfected and the torpedoes fixed, Japan was losing an average fifty merchant ships a month ... There was no way the shipbuilding yards could keep pace. Imports—especially oil imports—fell off drastically. There was a critical shortage of escorts for the convoys, and mounting chaos in the ranks of Japanese merchant seamen. Many hundreds were shipwrecked and marooned in southern waters, unable to get home.[21]

Sadly, USS *Robalo,* which departed Fremantle on 22 June 1944 for the South China Sea, was lost during July. The submarine travelled through the Makassar and Balabac Straits to reach its patrol area, and its last report was received on 2 July. At that time *Robalo* was just east of Borneo and had sighted a Japanese *Fuso*-class battleship, accompanied by two destroyers and aircraft. Nothing more was heard of the submarine, and it was presumed lost. A message received through Philippines guerillas was to tell the tragic story of how the submarine had been sunk off Palawan Island, probably as a result of striking a mine. *Robalo* took all but four of the crew to the bottom with it. The survivors struggled ashore and fought their way through the jungle, but were soon captured by the Japanese. Some time later the four men were taken from the island aboard a Japanese destroyer and no more was heard of them.[22]

UNITED STATES NAVY ACCOMMODATION

Living Quarters

Navy 137 Receiving Barracks	9 officers and 670 enlisted men housed at the Old Asylum building, cnr Finnerty and Ord Streets, Fremantle. A new wing for enlisted men was later added to this building.
Naval Supply Depot	49 enlisted men were housed in various warehouses, and four officers at 24 The Esplanade, Peppermint Grove.
Submarine Repair Unit, Navy 137, North Wharf	60 officers and 884 enlisted men were accommodated at North Wharf.

Rest Camps

For officers:	For enlisted men:
72 The Avenue, Nedlands	House at 55 Bay View Terrace, Claremont

51 and 53 Birdwood Parade, Nedlands	Beach cottage at Waterman Bay
'Lucknow', 2 Queenslea Drive, Claremont	O'Mahony's cottage, Safety Bay
148 Forrest Street, Cottesloe	His Majesty's Hotel, Perth
Hotel Majestic, Applecross	Hotel Wentworth, Perth
Commercial Travellers Hotel (five transients)	King Edward Hotel, Perth
Palace Hotel, Perth (one transient)	Ocean Beach Hotel, Cottesloe
The Weld Club, Perth (two medical officers)	Victoria Park Hotel, Victoria Park
	Hyde Park Hotel, Perth
	Court Hotel, Perth[1]

The British submarine tender HMS Adamant and some of the Royal Navy submarines lying at North Wharf at the end of the war. The US Navy's floating dock can be seen in the distance. (West Australian Newspapers – War 897.)

CHAPTER TWELVE

Late 1944: British Submarines Arrive

By 30 June 1944, 31 US submarines were assigned to Fremantle, operating as Task Force 71. *Gunnel, Gurnard, Haddo, Hake, Harder, Hoe, Jack, Lapon, Mingo, Muskalunge, Paddle* and *Pargo* comprised Submarine Squadron 12, with *Griffin* as tender. *Puffer, Rasher, Cabrilla, Crevalle, Bluefish, Bonefish, Cod, Raton, Ray* and *Redfin* comprised Submarine Squadron 16, with *Orion* as tender. *Narwhal* and *Nautilus* were reserved for special duties; *Aspro, Sand Lance* and *Guitarro* were assigned on temporary duty; and *Angler, Robalo, Flasher* and *Flier* were Task Force 72 submarines detached to Task Force 71. In June, *Gurnard, Sand Lance* and *Aspro* arrived, followed by *Flier, Guitarro, Mingo* and *Muskalunge* in July. Twelve submarines departed on patrol during June, and the same number in July. The frigate *Corpus Christi* also arrived during July, and on 6 August the submarine tender *Orion* departed for Brisbane. During June, July and August, staff at the Fremantle slipway slipped and painted 12 American submarines, the Dutch submarine *K XII* and a submarine chaser.[1]

In the latter half of 1944, Allied forces in Europe were advancing on all fronts. By the end of August the enemy had been driven out of Russia, while part of France and most of Italy were in Allied hands. In the Pacific, the Japanese had finally been forced out of New Guinea, and US forces had regained control of Guam and Wake Island, edging nearer to the Philippines.[2]

As the naval war in the Northern Hemisphere began to wind down, submarines of the British Royal Navy came to Fremantle. Besides the immediate strategic advantages, a British presence in the region was an important move towards regaining control of the former empire. Singapore, Malaya and Hong Kong had been important British possessions until captured by the Japanese.

When Japan entered the war in December 1941, no RN submarines had been operating in Asian waters. Those based in Singapore and Hong Kong before 1939 had all been transferred to the United Kingdom and the Mediterranean. After the outbreak of war with Japan, seven Dutch submarines were placed under British command and these operated from Singapore until it fell, after which they went to Sri Lanka. In September 1943, eight British submarines were sent out from the Mediterranean, with the depot ship HMS *Adamant,* and based at Trincomalee in Sri Lanka. As the situation in the Mediterranean eased, more submarines were sent out with a second depot ship, HMS *Maidstone.*[3]

While at Trincomalee, the RN submarines' patrol area included the eastern part of the Bay of Bengal, the Malacca Straits and the north-west coast of Sumatra, allowing the US submarines to concentrate on the area to the north and east of Java and Sumatra. The Trincomalee submarines' role was to keep the Japanese from gaining access to the Indian Ocean, and to stop supplies reaching enemy forces. As the Japanese retreated during 1943 and 1944, Allied bases were established at Manus Island in the Bismarck Archipelago, and at Mios Woendi on Biak Island. With these bases to supply fuel, torpedoes and emergency repairs, the American submarines, with their long-range capabilities, were able to patrol even further north into Japanese-controlled waters, so part of the British fleet was transferred to Fremantle to patrol the area around Malaya and the East Indies.[4]

The British submarines were much smaller than those of the United States Navy, with no air conditioning, less endurance and a shorter range. Their normal patrols were 28 days for the S-class boats and 35 days for the T-class, but they extended their range as much as possible. Some made incredibly long patrols. The main problem was finding room to store enough provisions for these long trips. Living areas were often cluttered with stores, and even the engine room and torpedo storage areas were used. Sometimes they were provisioned at sea by the larger American Fleet-class submarines.[5]

The first British submarine to arrive at Fremantle was one of the old River-class boats, HMS *Clyde,* which arrived at the port on 29 July 1944.[6] It was not part of the new redeployment, however, having travelled to Exmouth Gulf from Trincomalee to undertake a special mission. The submarine began to malfunction, so it was sent to Fremantle for docking. The Fremantle slipway records show that the submarine was slipped for repairs and painting during August.[7] *Telemachus,* which arrived at Fremantle on 6 September, carried out *Clyde's* special mission, codenamed Operation Carpenter.[8]

Another RN submarine, HMS *Porpoise,* arrived on 10 August. It had been detached from the 4th Submarine Flotilla at Trincomalee in order to prepare for its role as transport for Operation Rimau, an ill-fated secret mission about to be undertaken by members of the Services Reconnaissance Department.

Of twelve US submarines that set out on patrol during August, two failed to return. USS *Flier,* which had come to Fremantle for a refit, sailed on 2 August for its patrol area off the coast of Indochina. On the 13th, while on patrol in the Balabac Strait, the submarine struck a mine. Like *Robalo,* the *Flier* had no warning. There was a violent explosion, and the submarine sank in less than a minute. A number of men had been on deck at the time, and 13 were able to escape into the ocean. Before the submarine disappeared into the depths, they heard the screams of their trapped shipmates as they were dragged down to their deaths. For some of the survivors, however, that watery death had just been postponed: only eight lucky men survived to reach Mantagula Island after fifteen hours in the water. Friendly indigenous people helped them reach a coast watcher, who was able to send out a radio message and arrange for them to be evacuated by *Redfin* on 31 August. The presence of a watchful Japanese ship near the rendezvous point made the rescue a dangerous exercise.[9] The wreck of USS *Flier* has recently been located in Balabac Strait.[10]

The other submarine lost that month was USS *Harder*, which was sunk off the coast of Luzon in the Philippines on 24 August. *Harder*, nicknamed 'Hit-em Harder', and its skipper Sam Dealey had an impressive record of five very successful patrols. The submarine, which had arrived in May, left Fremantle on 5 August with *Hake*, heading for the South China Sea where they were joined by *Haddo*. The three submarines operated as a wolf pack off the coast of Mindoro Island and Luzon in the Phillipines and were involved in several successful actions. By 23 August *Haddo* had used up all its torpedoes and departed, but *Harder* and *Hake* continued their patrol. Near Dasol Bay on the fateful day the two submarines sighted a Japanese minesweeper and a destroyer, and closed in. *Hake's* attack was foiled when the destroyer turned away, at which time *Harder's* periscope was sighted some 550 to 640 metres to the north. Attacked by the minesweeper, *Hake* was forced to dive deep and slip away, running silent. Sadly, when the submarine returned, only a ring of marker buoys showed where the gallant *Harder* had perished, taking all hands to their watery grave.[11]

The US submarine tender USS *Euryale* arrived at Fremantle on 28 August, followed by the British fleet's tender HMS *Maidstone,* which arrived on 5 September, escorted by HMS *Nigeria,*[12] and berthed alongside North Wharf. One of *Maidstone's* crew, Eric Theedom, seeing an old River-class submarine lying there, thought it was *Severn,* but it would seem to have been the *Clyde,* which slipped out of harbour on its way home to the United Kingdom almost as soon as the flotilla arrived.[13]

On 30 August, HMS *Spiteful* arrived at Fremantle harbour, followed during September by three more RN submarines: *Sea Rover, Telemachus* and *Sirdar.*[14] The rest of the 8th Submarine Flotilla, made up of ten Royal Navy and Royal Netherlands Navy submarines, joined the mother ship over the following month, at the end of their patrols in the Malacca Straits. These British and Dutch submarines, designated Task Group 71.1, were operationally under the command of Rear Admiral Christie as Commander Submarines 7th Fleet, so a staff officer, Commander Helbert, was appointed to liaise with the United States operational headquarters in Perth. This was necessary due to the different codes used by the two groups. Language differences also emerged as a problem, and not just in communication between English- and Dutch-speaking groups. An example is quoted in the British Admiralty's *Naval Staff History,* where the American message 'go [to] Onslow for fuel' was read by the British submarine commander as 'go on slow for fuel'.

The American fleet very nearly lost USS *Crevalle* near the Lombok Strait in September. The submarine surfaced after a routine dive, but the main ballast tank vents had been left open. As the air rushed out of the vents, it suddenly went into another dive. Howard Blind, who was on the bridge, apparently managed to free the hatch so it would close before he was swept into the water and drowned. The Western Australian girl he had just married received a posthumous Navy Cross. William J. Ruhe, who was an officer on *Crevalle* at the time, gives a moving account of the tragedy in *War in the Boats.*[15] Sixteen other US submarines left Fremantle on patrol during the month.

The Dutch submarines *O 19* and *Zwaardvisch* arrived during September. *Zwaardvisch,* which arrived on 6 September, left on the 26th to begin an impressive patrol in the Java Sea. It was the former British T-class submarine, *Talent,* transferred to the Netherlands Navy in 1943. The submarine was at sea when a warning came from the Allied code breakers that a German submarine, *U-168,* was on its way to Japan from Germany with important technical information on radar and submarine plans. The Dutch submarine was deployed to intercept and dispose of it. After sinking the U-boat, *Zwaardvisch* rescued the 20 survivors before going on to sink one of the Japanese navy's large Itsuku Shima-class minelayers.[16]

By September 1944, with the Japanese finally driven out of New Guinea, bases became available from which Allied bombers could attack enemy installations in the Philippines. General MacArthur was set to make good his promise to return and liberate the islands, and the campaign began in earnest in October with the Battle of Leyte Gulf in the Phillipines, when the Japanese navy was shattered by the loss of 24 of its warships.[17] American submarines, including some from Fremantle, were involved in the battle, attacking the oncoming Japanese and helping to cover the landing of troops.[18] The Fremantle submarines were also targeting Japan's oil supplies.

Meanwhile, the Fremantle operation was approaching a peak of activity in September and October, when a total of 38 boats—most in wolf-packs—joined patrols against the Japanese oil' pipeline' from Sumatra and Borneo and enemy attempts to shore up the defenses of the Philippines.[19]

On 6 November USS *Dace* arrived at Fremantle, bringing the crew of another American submarine, *Darter,* which had been lost after being bombed by an enemy plane. The two submarines were involved in the early stages of the Battle of Leyte Gulf.

It was during that month that the American fleet lost USS *Growler.* The submarine had arrived at Fremantle on 26 September and departed again on 20 October with *Hake.* They were joined by *Hardhead,* and on 8 November, while operating as a wolf pack, the three submarines attacked a small convoy south of Mindoro. *Growler* began the attack, while *Hake* and *Hardhead* approached from the opposite side of the target. The order to start the attack was the last that was heard from *Growler.* Those aboard *Hake* and *Hardhead* heard the sounds of a vicious torpedo and depth-charge attack coming from *Growler's* side of the convoy. After that, they heard no more. *Hake* and *Hardhead* searched for three days, but the gallant submarine was gone, lost with all hands.[20]

In November, the USN 7th Fleet was reorganised, with Task Force 72 being merged with Task Force 71. Units still operated from Brisbane and Darwin, but Fremantle now became the major base. Between 1 September and 14 November, 17 submarines, including four British and one Dutch boat, were painted at the Fremantle slipway.[21] Of the 20 US submarines leaving during October, seven ended their patrols at Pearl Harbor. On 8 October 1944, HMAS *Adelaide,* which had been based in Fremantle, mainly doing convoy and escort duties in the Indian Ocean since 1942, left Fremantle for Melbourne. USS *Hawkbill,* which had arrived on 18 October, departed on 15 November.

USS *Barbel* arrived in Fremantle on 7 December, and USS *Besugo,* which arrived two days later, set out for the South China Sea on Christmas Eve. The last of the British 8th Submarine Flotilla boats, HMS *Spirit* and HMS *Spark,* also arrived during December.[22] At 12.30am on 18 December, however, one of the British submarines was very nearly lost in a collision off Rottnest Island. HMS *Sea Rover* was returning from patrol when it was ordered to rendezvous with the Australian corvette HMAS *Bunbury* to the north-west of Rottnest. The *Bunbury* had arrived in Fremantle on 29 September for tactical exercises with Fremantle-based Allied submarines that were working up after refits and the repair of battle damage. It was a dark night, with a running sea, and neither vessel was showing any lights when both reached the rendezvous early. Suddenly, *Sea Rover* rammed into the corvette's port bow. The collision buckled the submarine's bows and forward casing, and punched two large holes in *Bunbury's* hull. Help was at hand, however, and the damaged vessels were quickly escorted into Fremantle. The submarine was slipped at Fremantle, where the mangled bow was cut away and replaced by a makeshift bow. Unable to dive or defend itself, *Sea Rover* sailed for the United Kingdom in January 1945, and reached home safely after a long and hazardous voyage. After being repaired, it served in the British navy for another four years before being decommissioned and scrapped.[23]

By the end of 1944, when American forces had retaken part of the Philippines and were starting to bomb Tokyo and other Japanese cities, Allied submarines were patrolling ever closer to Japan. During the year, enemy oil tankers had been the most important target for submarines, and Japan's tanker losses were severe. In the six months to 31 December, USN submarines operating from, or on their way to, Fremantle had sunk 110 ships, totalling 493,207 tons. Four Fremantle-based USN submarines—*Growler, Robalo, Flier* and *Harder*—were lost in 1944.

Holes in the minesweeper HMAS Bunbury following a collision with British submarine HMS Sea Rover off Fremantle 17 September 1944. (Western Australian Museum, courtesy Lynne Cairns–MHA 4531/11.)

Forty-one US submarines were based at Fremantle at the end of December, together with 13 British and four Dutch submarines. US surface vessels connected with the base at this time were the submarine tenders USS *Euryale* and USS *Anthedon* (which had arrived from the US on 17 November to replace USS *Griffin*), the frigate *Corpus Christi,* a submarine chaser and two minesweepers. There was also the rescue vessel, *Coucal* (which had replaced the *Chanticleer* in October), the patrol vessels *Isabel* and *Number 286,* and the floating dry dock USS *ARD 10.*[24]

TRENCHANT SINKS ASHIGARA

From the diary of Edwin Young:

June 8th – ... Sylvia, this is something!! ... I'll try to tell you what happened this forenoon. We've certainly got the jackpot.

The Royal Navy submarine Trenchant returning to Fremantle at the end of a mission. (Western Australian Museum, courtesy S. Davey – MHA 4533/21.)

Trenchant crew members display their 'Jolly Roger'. (Western Australian Museum, courtesy S. Davey – MHA 4533/18.)

A Japanese CRUISER, 10,000 tons of mangled steel and bodies at this moment lies in the mouth of the Banka Straits. WE SANK IT!!!! It was terrific. It is afternoon now and still the boat is full of voices and hands sinking over and over again the NACHI class cruiser that steamed out of the Banka Straits at 22 knots heading for the open sea. Let me tell it as it happened. I came off watch at 8 and at 20 mins past we were obeying the Tannoy——which said—'Diving Stations'—excitedly, it seemed. Upon closing up 'Dick' was busy studying a destroyer which seemed to be nipping around at speed just S.E. of us and at extreme range. Frequently he asked Ben to try various frequencies on the asdic set to see if the destroyer was transmitting and on each occasion of Ben saying 'No Sir!' he just said 'keep trying'. Then suddenly, as he was still watching we heard loud muffled explosions and guessed right, the 'Stygian' was being heavily depth-charged, about 12 bangs were counted. The destroyer then seemed to start back in the mouth of the straits, the Palembang river joins the Banka Straits just inside the entrance of the Straits. We stayed at diving stations for a further 25 mins. and then went to watch diving. The forenoon's sleep was disturbed at 0948 and we closed up again, the fellows didn't seem very enthusiastic about this repeated performance as we found it the same, 'Dick' at the periscope looking intently in the mouth of the Straits—BUT, with a difference—Target is 'Heavy Japanese Cruiser—looks like one of the Nachi class' eyes popped out, faces brightened, beards crackled as their owners grinned. 'Boy this is something'.

A CRUISER? Incredible ... The Captain was calm as he looked, thought, and gave orders for the attack ... She was zig-zagging and only the one destroyer in attendance. The climax as 'Dick' raised the for'ad periscope—'Stand by Tubes' I repeated parrot fashion as trained ... No.1 Tube—FIRE!! No.2 Tube—Fire!!

Just like clockwork, as I repeated each order I pulled the firing lever indicated ... 'Down Periscope' It was so quiet you could have heard a bomb drop. A sharp 'click' and from 'Dick' excitedly—A hit astern! Another! Another!—2 more—5 hits, his face was alive, it twisted, creased, smiled, laughed, was cocky-all at once. A spontaneous cheer rang out, we would have cheered every hit, only it happened too fast ... So we had punched 5 holes into the enemy...

Edwin Young, whose diary tells of the trials and triumphs of life in a British submarine. (Western Australian Museum, courtesy S. Davey – MHA 4533/17.)

Recovering a folboat crew by submarine. Commando operations in folboats were extremely hazardous, not just due to enemy threats. (Western Australian Museum, courtesy Fred Lawrence – MHP 0213/12.)

CHAPTER THIRTEEN

Clandestine Operations

The Fremantle submarines were often called on to slip silently among Japanese-held islands to the north of Australia to rescue civilians or servicemen trapped behind enemy lines, or to land or pick up commandos.

In March 1942, three of the eight submarines leaving the new base on patrol made special missions to Corregidor, delivering food and supplies, and evacuating servicemen and civilians. USS *Seadragon,* diverted from its patrol off Indochina, took a load of fuel and food to the island and evacuated 21 people. *Snapper* collected another 27 evacuees when it delivered 46 tons of food on 4 April. *Spearfish,* which left Fremantle on 29 March, was the last US submarine to visit the fortress before it surrendered.

USS *Swordfish,* which had evacuated the Philippines president and high commissioner from the besieged islands before arriving at Fremantle, left again on 1 April with orders to deliver provisions to Corregidor, but was too late to complete its mission.

Two other submarines that left port in April 1942 undertook special missions. One of these, USS *Searaven,* picked up a group of 31 RAAF personnel who had been stranded on Timor, but the submarine was damaged when a fire broke out and had to be towed back to Fremantle by *Snapper.* USS *Porpoise,* which left to patrol off the East Indies on 26 April, rescued five airmen off the enemy-held island of Ju before heading out across the Pacific to Pearl Harbor.[1]

The Dutch submarines were also involved in secret missions, mainly to Java. The first was in September 1942, when *K XII* transported Operation Mackerel, a three-man party of the Dutch secret service and landed them on the south groups of commandos, Operations Tiger and Tiger 1, and in February 1943 to deliver Operation Tiger 3. At this time, unsuccessful attempts were made to contact the Tiger 1 party.

In May 1943 the submarine returned to deliver two one-man operations, Tiger 4 and Tiger 5, and to attempt to contact commandos who had been working on the Javanese island of Goagoa. The Colombo-based Dutch submarines, *O 21, O 23* and *O 24,* were also dropping parties in Java during this period.[2]

The Royal Netherlands Navy's submarine 0.23 arrived at Fremantle in April 1945 and remained after the war. (West Australian Newspapers – War 2130.)

In March 1942, Special Operations Australia, or the Inter-Allied Services Department, was formed, modeled on Britain's Special Operation Executive. In May it became the Services Reconnaissance Department, and the Z Special Unit (Z-Force) was established.

These were the volunteers for hazardous operations who, in groups of sometimes only four or five and mostly never more than 25, were clandestinely inserted onto a Japanese held coast from New Guinea to Borneo, through Malaya to China, by submarine, flying boat, parachute or small boat.[3]

These men disappeared for several months at a time, and families were lucky to receive a brief message from the army office every three months, informing them that their loved one had, at some recent time, been reported to be alive and well.[4]

A Welman midget being raised from the water by gantry at Garden Island during World War II. (Royal Australian Navy Public Affairs, HMAS Stirling.)

In June, a Z-Force camp was set up at Cairns, Queensland, where the commandos were trained to work behind enemy lines. Another camp was to be established in Western Australia. As part of their training, the commandos learned to handle collapsible surface craft known as Folbots, or folboats. These were light, easily dismantled, canvas-covered craft originally designed for peacetime use by canoeists. The adaptability of the canoes made them ideal for clandestine operations.[5]

In June 1943, a Z-Force practice for an attack on Rabaul harbour highlighted the vulnerability of Australian ports. A ten-man Z-Force group paddled Folbots into Townsville harbour without being detected, and attached dummy limpet mines to a number of vessels, including two Australian destroyers.[6]

Operation Jaywick, however, was the real thing. Fourteen Z-Force commandos sailed the *Krait,* a former Japanese fishing boat, from the USN base at Exmouth Gulf on 2 September 1943 to carry out a daring attack on Singapore harbour. With a safe passage through Lombok Strait behind it, *Krait* slipped through the Java Sea and the Temiang Strait, and among the Riouw (Bintan) Islands just south of Singapore. The six men, with their gear and three Folbots, were put ashore on Pandjang Island. They were to rendezvous with *Krait* on Pompong Island at midnight on 1 October. On the night of 26 September, they entered Singapore harbour and successfully attached limpet mines to a number of Japanese ships, putting eight out of action. After three nights of paddling (hiding from the enemy during the day), the six men reached the rendezvous and were all safely aboard the *Krait* on 2 October.7 Sadly, as often happens in wartime, the success of the raid had serious repercussions for the people of Singapore and some of the foreign internees in Changi Gaol. Suspected by the Japanese of being involved, many suffered torture, or execution.[8]

In Western Australia, the Z-Force training camp was in Cockburn Sound, at Careening Bay, on Garden Island. Here the men were trained in various commando skills, including the use of Folbots and miniature submarines. Three types of miniature submarines were used in training. There seem to be no accounts of the larger types of submersible craft—the Welman and the Welfreighter—being used in missions out of Fremantle, but the two-man submersible boats, known as SBs or 'Sleeping Beauties', were to have been used in the tragic Operation Rimau.[9]

Z-Force also used a number of small surface vessels in its clandestine activities. The successful use of *Krait* in Operation Jaywick led to many of the other Z-Force craft being named after snakes. This 'Snake Flotilla' consisted of captured enemy boats, converted luggers and locally built, special-purpose vessels such as *Mother Snake* (300 tons), and *Grass Snake* and *River Snake* (each 80 tons).[10]

USS *Tambor* departed Fremantle on 18 February 1943 to carry out a special mission in the Philippine islands. On 5 March it landed a small navy party, a large amount of ammunition and $10,000 in currency on southern Mindanao. Then, in September, the six Z-Force commandos of Operation Python I left Fremantle in USS *Kingfish,* which landed them and their supplies at Labian Point on the east coast of British North Borneo on 6 October, before continuing its patrol. During the next five weeks the commandos fought their way through the thick jungle to find and clear a suitable site and set up a radio station. They made contact with an American agent already working with guerillas in the area, helped organise a coastwatch and intelligence network of partisans, and did other reconnaissance work.

Welman midget submarines stored in a nissen hut. (Royal Australian Navy Public Affairs, HMAS Stirling.)

Another Fremantle submarine, USS *Tinosa,* delivered a second group, codenamed Python II, on 20 January 1944 to reinforce the group, but things now began to go wrong. One man became lost in the jungle and was captured by the enemy, while another became ill. USS *Narwhal* was directed to deliver supplies and evacuate some of the men, but the first rendezvous failed. The submarine returned on 5 March and two men went on board, but the approach of enemy vessels caused the submarine to submerge and some of the valuable supplies were lost. From then on the situation deteriorated, with more men being captured and the others constantly harassed. Attempts by *Guitarro* and *Haddo* to rescue the commandos failed, but the survivors were safely evacuated on 8 June by *Harder*.[11]

The *Narwhal,* a larger USN submarine, had arrived during 1943, and it was followed, in July 1944, by its sister ship, the *Nautilus.* These older and slower boats were not suitable for general patrols, so they were used mainly for special missions. Their greater size allowed them to transport more supplies and larger groups of commandos or refugees. On one special mission to the Philippines, *Narwhal* transported 92 tons of ammunition and medical stores, as well as ten commandos. It was not so easy on the smaller submarines. In February 1944, USS *Angler,* expecting to pick up about twenty refugees from Panay in the Philippines, found 58 people waiting to be rescued after being stranded in the jungle for two years. They were packed into the forward and after torpedo rooms like sardines, and with all aboard on short rations, the submarine made its way back to Australia. During the voyage many of the crew and passengers became ill as a result of contamination of the water supply.[12]

Early in 1944, the Dutch submarines *K XIV* and *K XV,* which had been to the US and Britain for modifications and specialised training, carried out special missions on their way to Fremantle. *K XIV's* mission was to destroy petrol tanks in Emmahaven Harbour, Sumatra, and during its next patrol it carried out reconnaissance at Christmas Island. The *K XV* also reconnoitred and photographed Christmas Island from the sea on its way to Fremantle. The Japanese on the island spotted the *K XV* and opened fire, but the submarine escaped unharmed. In April, it landed Operation Prawn, a seven-man party of Dutch commandos, on the New Guinea coast near the Japanese naval base at Sorong.[13]

In May 1944, USS *Crevalle,* diverted from its patrol in the South China Sea, picked up 40 refugees from Negros Island in the Philippines. The refugees, including 17 children, were squeezed into the available space after food, guns and ammunition were handed over to the Filipino guerillas. Then *Crevalle* went back on patrol, so the refugees experienced what it was like to be trapped in a submarine being bombarded with bombs and depth charges. It seems that the women and children bore the ordeal stoically, but one of the male guerillas panicked and had to be physically subdued. *Crevalle* suffered considerable damage but made it safely back to Australia.[14]

The three types of midget submarines that Z-Force used in training at Garden Island. From front to back: Sleeping Beauty, Welman, Welfreighter. (Royal Australian Navy Public Affairs, HMAS Stirling.)

For a time, pairs of Z-Force commandos regularly went on routine patrols in Fremantle-based US submarines as part of what was codenamed Operation Politician. They were attached to Task Force 71 for operational purposes, and stood watch, helped with tasks such as decoding messages, and also boarded and searched native vessels while waiting for opportunities to do reconnaissance or use their limpet mines. When *Redfin* rescued the survivors of USS *Flier* on 30 August 1944, Z-Force men went aboard the native craft they arrived on, to make sure it was safe, before the submarine approached.

By this time, the British submarines had arrived and were also involved in special missions. Operation Rimau began when HMS *Porpoise* left Garden Island on 11 September 1944, bound for the Riouw (Bintan) Islands, near Singapore. On board were 23 Z-Force commandos under Lieutenant Colonel Ivan Lyon, who had led the successful Operation Jaywick. Also on board were 15 SBs. The plan was, once again, to enter Singapore harbour and use limpet mines to destroy some of the Japanese vessels there.

On 28 September, near Merapas Island, the commandos seized a 40-ton perahu named *Mustika.* The SBs and stores were taken aboard the vessel and its crew was transferred to *Porpoise,* which sailed for Australia on 1 October, leaving the commandos to carry out their secret mission. They were to be evacuated from the island on 8 November, or thirty days later if unable to make the first rendezvous.

A Sleeping Beauty submersible in action in a Scottish loch during 1944. (Royal Australian Navy Public Affairs, HMAS Stirling.)

Mustika sailed through the Temiang and Sugi Straits and, by 6 October, it was off Laban Island, about seventeen kilometres south-east of Singapore's Keppel Harbour. While waiting for darkness to launch the miniature submarines, they were alarmed by a Malay police patrol launch from Kasu Island. Unfortunately someone on board opened fire on the launch, destroying all hope of a surprise attack. The commandos scuttled the perahu with the top-secret SBs aboard, and escaped with the Folbots and a larger folding boat. They were not prepared to give up the mission, however, and seven of the men paddled their Folbots into Singapore harbour and sank at least three enemy ships with limpet mines. Meanwhile, HMS *Porpoise* arrived back in Fremantle on 11 October in need of repairs, so *Tantalus* was sent to rendezvous with the Operation Rimau party. It arrived 14 days late, to find no sign of the commandos. Tragically, none of the gallant force was to survive. It seems they met up on Soreh Island, where they clashed with the Japanese. Lyon and another man were killed and the rest dispersed to other islands. Some eluded the enemy for more than two months, but the 11 who survived the ordeal were captured. One of these men died in captivity, and the others were executed.[15]

A Z-Force commando wearing the watertight suit and breathing apparatus required for operating the Sleeping Beauty. (Royal Australian Navy Public Affairs, HMAS Stirling.)

Another newly arrived British submarine, HMS *Telemachus,* was sent to Exmouth Gulf to pick up the 18 commandos of Operation Carpenter 1 and deliver them to the south-east coast of Johore. When the submarine sailed on 14 September 1944, RN veteran Arnold Hole, who later settled in Western Australia, was a member of the crew. He recalled that all the spare torpedoes were removed to make room for extra bunks. The crowding was made worse by the need to carry six inflatable boats with outboard motors, and about twelve tons of stores and equipment. It must have been very difficult for the commandos, who were unused to the crowded, claustrophobic conditions, when the submarine was forced to remain submerged for 17 hours to avoid Japanese anti-submarine patrols. Though the men and essential equipment were successfully landed on 5 October, *Telemachus* was unable to contact them again, encountering watchful Japanese anti-submarine vessels and aircraft at the rendezvous site. It was apparent that the operation was compromised, and the submarine was forced to withdraw.[16]

USS *Bream* departed Fremantle on 19 December 1944 with two commandos aboard. About midnight on 7 January 1945, the two men paddled ashore in a Folbot to attack what appeared to be a Japanese wireless tower and fuel storage tanks, but turned out to be grain storage facilities. After an alarming run of mishaps they were picked up by the submarine at about 3.30am.

The British submarine Telemachus. (Western Australian Museum, courtesy A. Hole – MHA 4531/12.)

On 15 January 1945, USS *Pargo* left Fremantle to patrol off the coast of Indochina. The submarine was ordered to rendezvous with USS *Flounder* in the South China Sea. Two commandos were transferred from *Flounder,* their mission to investigate activities on Woody Island, south-west of Hainan Island and the Gulf of Tonkin. The men were able to check that, despite a French flag being flown, the island was under Japanese control and so the facilities were destroyed.[17]

In February 1945, the United States submarine *Tuna* picked up a group of commandos from Darwin for a mission, codenamed Operation Agas 1, in British North Borneo. It was a false start, however, and the men were transferred at sea to another USN submarine, USS *Bream.* There were several operations codenamed Agas (Malay for sandfly), but the others were parachuted in behind enemy lines. Jack Wong Sue, who was one of the Agas 1 commandos, tells of his experiences in his book, *Blood on Borneo.*[18]

USS *Bream* left Fremantle again in March on a second Operation Politician patrol, passing through Lombok Strait and into the Java Sea, where it sank two Japanese ships, damaged a third and survived being depth charged. That night the submarine approached to within 4,000 metres of where the rest of the enemy convoy was anchored, and the commandos set out to paddle their Folbot among the vessels and attach time-delay limpets. They were to rendezvous with *Bream* to the north-east, but the commandos' wireless was malfunctioning, and the Folbot was caught in a strong tide and drifted off course. The Japanese convoy was also on high alert after being attacked by a British submarine after *Bream's* attack. Unable to contact them, the submarine commander, McCallum, went on to the rendezvous point, but the two men were apparently captured and executed by the Japanese. *Bream* was damaged by depth charges and after that disastrous patrol the routine inclusion of the commandos ceased, though they still went on planned operations.

Meanwhile, two commandos had been assigned to USS *Bluegill,* which left Fremantle on 12 March. They failed in an attempt to blow up a railway at Cape Varella, Indochina (now Vietnam), but later boarded a tanker and troop carrier, the *Honan Maru,* which had been wrecked earlier by *Bluegill.* The commandos retrieved useful documents and blew up the vessel to prevent the Japanese salvaging the precious fuel. The two men joined *Bluegill* again on its next patrol, where among other adventures they helped capture an abandoned Japanese installation on an atoll.

Also leaving Fremantle in March 1945 was USS *Rock,* on its sixth patrol, with four commandos from Operation Starfish on board. They were to reconnoitre enemy coastal artillery emplacements at Cape Pandanan on the south-west tip of Geroeng Peninsula, Lesser Sunda Islands, then assist a four-man Z-Force demolition team whose mission was to destroy the guns. On the way north *Rock* rescued 15 survivors of a merchant vessel, the *Peter Silvester,* which had been sunk by a German U-boat; they had traveled 2,575 kilometres in a 7.9-metre sailing boat. *Rock* took them to Exmouth and resumed its patrol.

On 13 March the submarine reached Lombok Island. After a failed landing that day, the commandos managed to get ashore on the 14th. Despite their rubber boat being tossed violently against the cliffs, they got their supplies ashore and into a cave, where they hid the dinghy, motor and fuel. Unfortunately they were not able to complete their mission. By 14 April they had managed to establish a base camp and friendly relations with some of the local people, but one man was captured, along with their radio codebook. They were soon under attack, and only two escaped and were able to make contact with Australian headquarters. These two men continued to play hide and seek with the enemy until 2 May, when they were evacuated by a Catalina flying boat.

Another special Z-Force mission, Operation Platypus, left Fremantle in USS *Perch* on 12 March 1945. This was a nine-man team commanded by Major Don Stott and accompanied by two Borneo native guides. They were to reconnoitre the area around Balikpapan in Borneo, gathering intelligence and organising resistance as a prelude to the proposed invasion. On 20 March four men set off in two Folbots to reconnoitre. The plan was for them to return to the submarine the following night, when the whole group would land using inflatable boats and Folbots, but the first boat, with Major Stott and Captain McMillan on board, disappeared and they were never found. Sergeants Dooland and Horrocks, in the second boat, could not make radio contact with them, or with the submarine. They managed to get ashore but were unable to return to *Perch,* which waited around before going back to sea, returning the next night.

There was no sign of the first group, so after sinking an oil barge, *Perch* landed the rest of the Z-Force group. They made contact with friendly locals, but Japanese forces, attracted by the explosion of the oil barge, soon found the group's supplies, after which a local in Japanese pay betrayed them to the enemy. The commandos managed to escape, but lost most of their supplies. Eventually, with the help of friendly locals, they were reunited with Horrocks and Dooland, and all escaped to sea in a native fishing boat. On 3 May they were rescued by a Catalina flying boat.

Another two commandos, Chaffey and Campbell, left Fremantle aboard USS *Boarfish* in March 1945. On 9 April they took to the Folbots to gather useful information about enemy shipping in Tamquan Bay on the coast of Indochina. A week later they went ashore at Tourane Bay to blow up a train. After concealing their outboard motor and other equipment, they paddled to a spot below the railway and climbed up the steep cliff to reach their objective. They placed six pounds of plastic explosive under the track, with the detonator hidden in the trackside rubble. The two men finished the job hurriedly and slid down the cliff when they saw lights approaching. They had just managed to reach their Folbot when a slow-moving train appeared from the south. There was an enormous explosion, which threw the locomotive and several wagons off the track. Despite Japanese soldiers searching for the saboteurs, and the threat of an enemy patrol boat in the area, they were able to reach their hidden equipment and motor back out to sea to be picked up by *Boarfish*.[19]

These are just a few of the daring missions carried out by Allied commandos between 1942 and 1945. Some of those brave men just disappeared into the jungles, not to be heard of again, so their stories can never be told. Fremantle-based submarines had carried out over 100 special missions by the time the war came to an end.[20]

THE BRITISH MINIATURE SUBMARINES

Everyone has heard about the Japanese miniature submarines, but other nations were also using them during the war. Britain began developing a range of miniature submarines and submersibles in 1941. The first of these were ride-on 'human torpedoes' called Chariots. These were used in five European operations and one in South-East Asia, where Chariots launched from HMS *Trenchant* off Penang sank two Italian vessels. The two-man crews returned safely to the *Trenchant*.

The SB, or submersible boat, used by the Z-Force commandos, was another early development. They were motorised submersible canoes, rather than real submarines. Driven by electric motors, with storage batteries, they were 3.65 metres long. The operator, who wore a watertight suit and breathed via a form of scuba apparatus, controlled the craft with a joystick. A weakness in the design meant that the batteries had to be vented by a small nozzle on the foredeck, closed with a rubber band. Damage to this could cause the battery compartment to fill with water, sinking the craft and requiring the commando to escape from the open cockpit and surface. At full speed, the SB travelled at about 4.4 knots and could cruise for 48 kilometres at a slower speed. Limpet mines were carried on the foredeck.

The crew of the XE 4. Max Shean is second from the left. (Western Australian Museum, courtesy M. Shean – MHA 4589/15.)

In addition to the SBs, the Z-Force commandos at Garden Island in

Cockburn Sound were trained in the use of the larger Welman and Welfreighter submarines. The 5.26-metre Welman was a real miniature submarine, armed with an explosive charge that was magnetically attached to the hull of an enemy ship. The Welman had no periscope, however, and the operator could only see through armoured glass segments in its rudimentary conning tower. Welmans were used in a failed attack on the floating dock in Bergen Harbour, Norway, in November 1943.

The 11-metre Welfreighter was an improved version of the Welman that was propelled on the surface by a diesel engine and by two electric motors underwater. The Welfreighter was provided with a periscope, and could carry three crew and up to four commandos. Two Welfreighters were sent to Fremantle late in 1944 to be trialed by Z-Force, but do not appear to have ever gone into action.

By that time, the Royal Navy had also begun using the larger X-class submarines. They were designed to cut through anti-submarine nets and attack enemy ships in protected waters.

Displacing 30 tons when submerged, they were 15.6 metres long with a beam of 1.75 metres. They had a crew of four, and were driven on the surface by a 42-hp diesel and, when submerged, by a 30-hp electric motor. The X-Craft submarines were used in late 1943 to disable the German battleship *Tirpitz.*

Two X-Craft divers dressed for action. Max Shean at left. (Western Australian Museum, courtesy M. Shean – MHA 4589/11.

These were followed by the slightly larger XE-class designed for operations in the Far East. These were flush-decked and air-conditioned submarines and, like the X-Craft, had a flooding chamber so that crew members could leave and return after attaching limpet mines to a ship's hull, or after undertaking other operations.

In July 1945 the RN submarines *Spark* and *Stygian* sailed from Subic Bay in the Phillipines to join HMS *Bonaventure* at Brunei Bay, North Borneo. They left there on 26 July with midget submarines *XE 1* (Lieutenant J.E. Smart, RNVR) towed by *Spark,* and *XE 3* (Lieutenant I.E. Fraser, RNR) towed by *Stygian.* The midgets were taken to the eastern approach to Singapore Strait, from where they attacked Japanese heavy cruisers.

The XE4 at Sydney. (Western Australian Museum, courtesy M. Shean – MHA 4589/24.)

On 26 July, HMS *Spearhead* left from Brunei Bay with the *XE 4* in tow. In command of the *XE 4* was a Western Australian, Lieutenant Max Shean, RANVR, one of the many Australians serving with the British. The mission was to cut the submarine telegraph cables and so disrupt the enemy's communications. The midget submarine was towed to the approaches to Saigon and, at 9.20pm on 30 July, the towline was slipped and *Spearhead* withdrew to seaward to await its return.

Both the Saigon-Hong Kong and Saigon-Singapore cables were

successfully located on 31 July by sweeping with a towed grapnel. The divers cut the cables and brought back 30-centimetre lengths as evidence. Meanwhile, another XE-class miniature submarine, the *XE5,* was cutting the Hong Kong end of the cable. Max Shean recounts his exciting X-Craft experiences in his book, *Corvette and Submarine.*[1]

CHAPTER FOURTEEN

The War Comes to an End

By New Year 1945, the Allies were on the march through Europe. The Russian army was set to liberate the Polish capital, Warsaw, and the German homeland was under attack on the Western Front. In the Pacific, the Allies were gradually winning the war in the Philippines. On 24 February, American forces recaptured Manila after a three-week battle, which devastated much of the city, killed 6,500 US marines, most of the Japanese servicemen involved in the battle, and up to 100,000 Filipinos.[1]

The war in the Pacific, and the stealthy activities of Allied submarines, had, by this time, decimated Japanese shipping and the Allies were steadily gaining control of the oceans. As Japan's forces were driven back towards their homeland, Japanese merchant ships rarely ventured beyond the Sea of Japan and the Yellow Sea, so the Allied submarines' war of attrition against enemy supply lines began to wind down. They now concentrated on supporting amphibious landings on enemy territory and harassing shipping in Japanese waters. Submarines also played an important role in rescuing the crews of aircraft that had been forced down.[2]

Rear Admiral Christie had been replaced as commander of the Fremantle submarine base at the end of 1944, and his replacement, Rear Admiral James Fife, arrived early in the new year. At this time, more than fifty Allied submarines were based at the port, with maintenance being provided by shore facilities, the American tenders *Anthedon* and *Euryale,* and the British tender, HMS *Maidstone.* On 1 January a second frigate, the USS *Hutchinson,* arrived at Fremantle to join the *Corpus Christi.*[3]Technological advances were reflected in the submarines' equipment by the beginning of 1945. These included improved types of sonar and radar, a deck gun especially designed for submarines, night periscopes, and special photographic equipment.[4]

Several submarines were refitting at Fremantle at the start of the year. On 2 January 1945, USS *Blackfin* set out for the South China Sea, where it worked with *Besugo* and *Cobia,* both of which had left port in late 1944. USS *Hake* left on its final patrol on 12 January, and *Flounder,* which had sailed on the 7th but returned for repairs, departed on the 14th to lead a three-submarine wolf pack in the South China Sea. *Pargo* sailed on 15 January for the Indochina coast, and *Bergall* left on the 19th for lifeguard duty off Lombok Strait. USS *Pampanito* followed on 23 January to join *Guavina* in a partnership that led to the elimination of the cargo ship *Engen Maru* (6,968 tons) and the passenger-cargo ship *Eifuku Maru* (3,520 tons). *Bashaw* and *Flasher* left port on the 26th and 29th.

The Fremantle fleet suffered another tragic loss in February 1945. USS *Barbel,* which had, arrived during December, sailed from Fremantle on 5 January bound for the South China Sea. Later in January it received orders to join *Perch* and *Gabilan* for a patrol in the western approaches to Balabac Strait and the southern entrance to Palawan Passage, at the northern end of Borneo. On 3 February a radio message was received from the submarine to report that it was under attack by an enemy aircraft and being bombarded with depth charges. Nothing more was ever heard of *Barbel,* or her crew, and it was not until after the war that Japanese records confirmed there had been a successful aerial depth-charge attack on an American submarine on 4 February. One depth charge had struck the bridge. There were no survivors.

On 17 January a major catastrophe in Fremantle harbour was narrowly averted. A Panamanian-registered merchant vessel, the *Panamanian,* was berthed close to HMS *Maidstone* when it caught fire. It was a very hot summer day and the harbour was packed with shipping, including the three depot ships and 20 submarines (13 American, six British and one Dutch). The submarines and warships were packed with enough explosives and fuel to destroy the harbour, and probably part of the town.

The old American-built vessel *Panamanian* was loading wheat when a piece of sacking caught fire. One of the men threw it overboard, expecting the fire to be extinguished on contact with the water, but the surface of the water was covered with a thin film of oil, which quickly ignited, sending flames billowing up the vessel's side. Very soon the ship was on fire. Like most merchant vessels during the war, it was armed for defence, and the ammunition stored on board began to explode. Though it was quickly thrown overboard, the fire was already spreading along the wharf towards *Maidstone,* with its much larger load of torpedoes, ammunition and fuel.

The two USN submarine tenders were powered by diesel engines and quickly got under way and moved, with their submarines, out of the harbour to safety. *Maidstone's* steam engines, however, needed twenty-four hours to provide full power. By the time the vessel could be safely towed out of the harbour by two of the harbour tugs, paint on the hull had caught alight and smoke shrouded the bridge. Both military and civilian firefighters were called in to fight the fire. It was not until the following afternoon that the fire aboard the *Panamanian* was brought under control, and another six days before it was fully extinguished.[5]

USS *Hawkbill* left Fremantle on 5 February and slipped through Lombok Strait to patrol in the South China Sea, where it sank two submarine chasers, some small vessels and the 5,400-ton cargo ship *Daizen Maru*. USS *Blenny*, which sailed the same day, sank the tanker *Amato Maru* (10,238 tons). *Caiman* and *Cobia* departed on 18 February, the latter to patrol the Java Sea. On the 19th, *Sealion* sailed for the South China Sea, and *Baya* and *Hammerhead* left to patrol off Indochina (now Vietnam). *Becuna*, which also departed Fremantle in February for Indochina, sank the tanker *Nichiryu Maru*, but was then bombarded with 70 depth charges from the tanker's escort. Another submarine that departed at this time was *Sea Robin*, which sank four enemy vessels in the Java Sea. *Croaker* arrived at Fremantle on 12 February.

HMS *Storm* was repaired and painted on the Fremantle slipway towards the end of January. By February, several of the British submarines were due to return home for refits. *Sirdar,* which set out on its last patrol on 8 February, returned to Fremantle on 12 March with a fractured crankshaft in the starboard engine. With a surface escort in case its port engine also broke down, it set out in April for the British base in Sri Lanka. *Spirit* also left Fremantle after returning from its February patrol. HMS *Telemachus* left on its final war patrol out of Fremantle on 24 February. On 23 March, when it was patrolling in the west Java Sea, the crew was faced with a medical emergency when the engineer officer nearly severed his hand in an accident while working on the port engine. The submarine radioed for help and headed towards Darwin. In the Flores Sea, the injured man was transferred to an RAAF Catalina and *Telemachus* was able to complete its patrol, after which it returned to

Trincomalee. From there it went back to Britain for a refit.[6]

On 16 February the Dutch submarine *Zwaardvisch* was seriously damaged by an aerial attack in the Lombok Strait. It arrived at Fremantle on 3 March, escorted by USS *Charr.* Another Dutch submarine, the *K XI,* which had been operating out of Bombay, arrived at Fremantle in March. It was taken out of service in April and stripped on the Fremantle slipway. On 28 March 1946, the submarine sank in the harbour. It was raised and later scuttled west of Rottnest Island.[7]

Three of Britain's V-class submarines, *Virtue, Vox* and *Voracious,* visited Fremantle during February and March. They all served in the Far East, but they do not appear to have been based in Western Australia, so were probably en route to Subic Bay in the Philippines.

Some time after Rear Admiral Fife took over as Commander 7th Fleet Submarines, operational control was transferred to Subic Bay. The plans had been laid late in 1944. The submarine tender *Fulton* was sent there during

February 1945, and the work of constructing the base began. There seems to have been no formal date at which the operational headquarters was moved, but by March most of the staff, and the tender *Anthedon,* had been transferred from Fremantle. On 20 March 1945, the fleet command was transferred from Fremantle, when USS *Hardhead* left port on patrol with Rear Admiral Fife on board. The submarine performed a routine patrol, laying mines in the Gulf of Siam, and delivering mail and provisions to the Royal Navy's *Tudor* at a rendezvous at sea on 31 March, before going on to Subic Bay, where it arrived on 11 April. In April, command of all Allied submarines in the Pacific reverted to Vice Admiral Lockwood at Pearl Harbor, but Fife directed the operations of submarines in the South China Sea, Java Sea and Flores Sea from Subic Bay.

Despite the changes, Fremantle continued to function as a subsidiary base until after the close of hostilities. During April, the submarine tender USS *Clytie* arrived to replace *Euryale.* After this, there were no further changes in

United States submarine maintenance facilities at Fremantle and little change in other surface-craft strengths until the end of the war.

USS *Boarfish* departed Fremantle on 11 March to patrol in the South China Sea, and *Bluegill* left on patrol on 12 March, joining *Blackfin* and *Blueback* in a picket line along the coast of Indochina. On the 28th, *Bluegill* destroyed the 5,542-ton tanker *Honan Maru* and ended its patrol at Subic Bay. *Hardhead,* which also left during March, laid mines off Indochina and sank the cargo ship *Araosan Maru* on 6 April. Two of the American submarines that left in March were responsible for the destruction of a Japanese warship, the *Isuzu,* which was torpedoed by *Gabilan,* then sunk by *Charr,* on 7 April. Two weeks later USS *Besugo,* which had left Fremantle on 24 March, sank the German U-boat *U-183.*

Allied submarines made 15 patrols out of Fremantle in March, and 14 in April. In March, the British submarines went to the Flores and Java Seas, and to the Gulf of Siam, but in April they concentrated on the west Java Sea.

Most of the American submarines patrolled the South China Sea, with a smaller number going to the Java Sea.[8] USS *Hawkbill,* which left Fremantle on 5 February, returned on 6 April, having sunk a 5,400-ton cargo ship, the *Daizen Maru* during its patrol. *Bream,* which had left port on 7 March to patrol the shipping lanes between Balikpapan and Surabaya, suffered severe damage as a result of a depth charge attack, and returned to Fremantle for repairs on the 22nd. Both periscopes, the starboard shaft and both screws were replaced, and the torpedo tubes repaired. On 20 April the submarine set out on its sixth and final war patrol. USS *Blackfin,* on patrol out of Subic Bay, was severely damaged by depth charges and returned to Fremantle for repairs on 9 April. On 14 April, *Blower,* which had arrived at Fremantle on 19 March, set out on its second war patrol. *Blueback* returned from patrol on 17 April, *Chub* reached port the following day, and *Lamprey* arrived on 22 April.

April 1945 saw the replacement of HMS *Maidstone* and the S-class submarines of the Royal Navy's 8th Submarine Flotilla, by HMS *Adamant* and the T-class boats of the 4th Submarine Flotilla.[9] *Maidstone* left for Subic Bay, to be joined by the 8th Flotilla submarines at the end of their patrols. *Solent* and *Sleuth* left on 14 April, followed by *Supreme* a week later. *Sturdy,* which left on its patrol on the 19th, went to Ceylon, then back to Britain.

The British T-class submarines arrived to join their mother ship during the following weeks. British submariner Alf Jobson, who later migrated to Western Australia, arrived in HMS *Thorough* on Anzac Day, 25 April. Going on leave, the submariners were surprised to find all the shops and hotels closed.[10] *Thorough* left on 13 May with *Taciturn* and *Trenchant,* which had reached Fremantle on 5 May. Edwin Young, who was wireless telegraphist in HMS *Trenchant,* wrote in his diary:

> We left Fremantle in company with the 2 'T' boats, *Thorough* and *Taciturn* to patrol the enemy waters below Singapore and N of Java. The big snag seems to be going through

the Straits of LOMBOK ... The apparent fool-hardy attempt to go through the straits instead of around the coast means a saving of everything, time, fuel, food, water, precious engines, but leaves the lives—not considered so precious open to grave risks.[11]

Although it was a new experience for the crew of *Trenchant,* Fremantle submarines had been making the dangerous transit through Lombok Strait, and the other narrow passages between the Indonesian islands, throughout the war.

After the change in flotillas, there were ten British submarines based at Fremantle, with four Dutch submarines, *O 19, O 21, O 24* and *Zwaardvisch,* also under British command. Some Dutch submarines had arrived with the 8th Submarine Flotilla in September 1944 and more arrived with the 4th Flotilla in April 1945. *O 19* was transferred to the 4th, but after it was damaged during its April patrol the old submarine was taken off operational patrols and used for transporting stores. *Zwaardvisch* returned to Britain for a refit after it arrived back from its patrol on 9 May.[12] The British submarine *Selene* also arrived in May.

USS *Hawkbill* left on 5 May for its patrol area in the Gulf of Siam, followed, on the 7th, by *Blackfin,* which suffered engineering failures and had to cut short its patrol and head for Subic Bay. *Blueback* sailed on 12 May, followed by *Chub,* which was transferring to Subic Bay, on the 14th. *Blueback,* and *Lamprey,* which departed Fremantle on the 21th, joined in a successful coordinated gun attack on a 600-ton escort ship. *Baya* and *Cavalla* arrived later in the month.

On 8 May, the war in Europe was over, and in Australia VE-Day (Victory in Europe Day) was celebrated enthusiastically. For some families it meant the prospect of reunion with their loved ones, as there were many Australians still serving with the British forces, or who had been trapped in German prisoner-of-war camps. From the military point of view, the German surrender meant that the Allies could concentrate on quickly bringing the war with Japan to an end. Throughout the early months of 1945 they had continued to close in on the Japanese mainland. At the end of March the island of Iwo Jima, south of Japan, was taken at the expense of some 28,000 Japanese and American lives. The Allied advance continued during April and May, with the United States steadily reconquering the Philippines.

The loss of *Isuzu* in April and *Haguro* in May had left Japan with only one large warship in the Singapore region, the heavy cruiser *Ashigara.* On 8 June, the 12,700-ton *Ashigara* was sunk by the British submarine *Trenchant,* which left Fremantle on 13 May. Edwin Young gives an exciting account of this action in his diary (see section entitled "TRENCHANT SINKS ASHIGARA"). The submarine had already torpedoed a minesweeper before teaming up with HMS *Stygian* to stalk a Nachi-class cruiser, reported to be in the area by the United States submarines *Blueback* and *Chubb.* While *Stygian* decoyed the cruiser's destroyer escort, *Trenchant* moved in for the kill. After sinking the Japanese cruiser,

Trenchant went on to Subic Bay before returning to Fremantle on 24 July.[13]

USS *Lizardfish* arrived at Fremantle on 2 June, and left again on the 28th for the Java and South China Seas. *Baya* departed on 20 June, and *Hammerhead* and *Becuna,* which had returned to Fremantle in mid June, sailed on the 21st. *Cobia* and *Caiman* returned from patrol on 18 and 27 June respectively.

During June, the 24th Australian Brigade landed in North Borneo after a devastating USN and Allied air bombardment of the Japanese base at Brunei Bay. By the end of the month, the 9th Australian Division was in control of most of North Borneo. Then, on 1 July, following bombardment of the area by the US Navy and Air Force, and the RAAF, the Australian 7th Division made an amphibious landing at Balikpapan on the south-east of the island. By this time the Japanese navy was virtually beaten, with no warships left in the area to mount a defence. Borneo was in Allied hands by the end of July.[14]

Meanwhile, Fremantle-based US submarines continued to patrol the South China Sea, but there were few Japanese vessels left.

Fife's boats finally ran out of targets. During the waning days of the war, they roved the seas on the surface like destroyers, blasting away with deck guns at trawlers, sampans, and other small craft, most of them manned by natives, not Japanese.[15]

There was still a Japanese presence in the submarines' patrol areas to the immediate north of Australia, however. William Pouleris was on board USS *Kraken,* which left Fremantle on its last patrol on 29 July. He recalled the crew's feelings of shock and grief when they learned of the tragic loss of USS *Bullhead,* which had been working in the same wolf pack. The submarine had set out from Fremantle on 31 July. Her mission was to slip through Lombok Strait and patrol in the Java Sea in company with other US and British submarines. On 2 August, *Bullhead* delivered mail to the Dutch submarine *O 21,* and four days later a report was received confirming that the submarine had successfully transited the strait and reached its patrol area. After that, there was just silence. It was not until after the war that the sad tale of how *Bullhead* met its end was pieced together.

Japanese records show there was a successful aerial depth charge attack on an Allied submarine off the Bali coast near Lombok Strait on 6 August 1945. A gush of oil and air bubbles was seen as the submarine sank, taking its gallant crew to their deaths. It is thought that with the mountains closing in so close to the coast at that point the submarine would not have had sufficient radar warning of the plane's approach to take evasive action.[16]

USS *Croaker* sailed from Fremantle on 1 July for lifeguard duties in the South China Sea and off Hong Kong, returning to Subic Bay on 13 August. *Icefish* arrived on 4 July and sailed on 29 July for its fifth war patrol, which ended at Saipan (an island 190km north of Guam). *Blenny* and *Boarfish* left Fremantle on 5 July to form a coordinated attack group in the Java

Sea with *Chub,* which was now on patrol from Subic Bay. *Cobia* departed Fremantle on 18 July, *Caiman* on the 22nd, and *Blower* at the end of the month. Many of the submarines leaving Fremantle at this time transferred to Subic Bay at the end of their patrols, while some were still in their patrol areas when Japan capitulated on 15 August.

The British submarine *Sidon,* sent to Fremantle for repairs, left on 7 July to rejoin the 8th Flotilla at Subic Bay, and six of the 4th Flotilla boats left Fremantle during July. HMS *Tudor* left Fremantle on 9 July to patrol the Java coast west of Surabaya, arriving back on 11 August. HMS *Taurus* arrived at Fremantle in July, followed by *Totem* and *Turpin* in August. The Dutch submarine *O 21* was also on patrol from 7 July to 8 August.

The Dutch lost the *O 19* in July 1945, when it was accidentally run on a reef in the South China Sea. The mishap took place on the 8th. The following day, USS *Cod* arrived to try to extricate the Dutch submarine from its predicament. After two days of repeated attempts to get the submarine free, however, they had no success, so the crew was taken aboard the American submarine and *O 19* was scuttled.

Four British submarines: *Tiptoe, Trump, Taciturn* and *Thorough;* and seven USN boats: *Bugara, Capitaine, Cavalla, Chub, Cobia, Kraken* and *Loggerhead* were still on patrol when the atomic bomb blasts at Hiroshima and Nagasaki heralded the end of the war. The first use of nuclear weapons in war took place on 6 August 1945, and after a second attack on the 9th, Japan surrendered on the 15th. The American submarines *Besugo, Blower, Brill, Cabrilla, Charr* and *Cod;* the British submarines *Stubborn, Tiptoe* and *Trenchant;* and the Dutch submarine *O 21* were still in port and their crews were able to take part in the victory celebrations. *Bumper* arrived on the day of the ceasefire. The formal signing of the Japanese surrender took place on board USS *Missouri* on 2 September 1945.

The United States Navy submarine Bugara was operating out of Fremantle in the final stages of the war. (West Australian Newspapers – War 4698.)

The Fremantle-based submarines' contribution to the Allied victory was, as David Creed says, 'out of all proportion to the number of boats engaged'.[17] The most impressive score was made by *Flasher,* which sank 104,564 tons of enemy shipping, but more than half the 354 United States submarine patrols which left Fremantle were successful, accounting for Japanese oil tankers totalling 409,761 tons, as well as 54 escort vessels. Two Fremantle-based American submarines were lost during war patrols in 1945, bringing the total number of US submarines lost while on patrols out of Fremantle during World War II to eight.

The British submarines based at Fremantle, and those Dutch submarines attached to the RN, accounted for approximately two per cent of Japanese shipping lost to submarines. They were also heavily involved in special missions. The total sinkings by British submarines from Ceylon (Sri Lanka), Fremantle and Subic Bay was 29 ships or 65,000 tons. The most successful patrol by the Fremantle-based British submarines was that made by *Trenchant*.[18] No British submarines were lost while operating out of Fremantle, though the *Terrapin,* crippled by depth charges off Java and escorted back to Fremantle by the US submarine *Cavalla,* was so severely damaged that it had to be scrapped.[19]

After the Japanese surrender, most of the submarines still on patrol came back to Fremantle, but it was not long before the Allied navies began to leave for home or other stations. The Americans had already begun to wind up their operations at Fremantle after the departure of Fife and his headquarters staff in March and, at the end of August, nine US submarines took their final departure from Fremantle. Now the shore facilities reverted to Australian civilian control, and much of the equipment, which had been supplied by the United States under the Lend-Lease scheme, was scrapped and dumped at sea.

HMS *Thorough* was the last British submarine to return to Fremantle at the end of the war, and it joined several others on a goodwill visit to Bunbury, Busselton and Albany before returning to Fremantle. The other British submarines began to leave Fremantle during September. HMS *Adamant* left in September, redeployed to Sydney before sailing to Hong Kong. HMS *Maidstone* returned briefly to Fremantle carrying 450 former prisoners of war from Macassar, in the Dutch Celebes (now Indonesian Sulawesi). The British government would demobilise its servicemen anywhere in the British Commonwealth, so some British servicemen did not return to Britain. RN submariner Gerry Goldman was the first

British ex-serviceman to be demobbed in Western Australia.[20]

The US submarine tender Clytie leaving Fremantle in September 1945. (West Australian Newspapers – War 921.)

The US Navy submarine tender Anthedon sailed from Fremantle on 2 October 1945. (West Australian Newspapers–War 917.)

The Dutch submarines were to be involved in Holland's attempt to re-establish colonial control in Indonesia, so Dutch submarines remained at Fremantle for some time. In December 1945, a representative of the Royal Netherlands Navy approached the manager of the Fremantle Harbour Trust to arrange to reserve a berth at North Wharf for about three months to accommodate its submarines. Berthage was made available at No.2 North Wharf from 6 December 1945, and *O 24, O 23, K XIV, K XV* and *Tigjerhaai* (a former British T-class submarine) were based there. The leasing agreement with the harbour trust eventually terminated in April 1947.[21]The Dutch navy had another former British T-class submarine, *Dolfjin,* stationed at Fremantle after the war.

After 1949 a British flotilla of three submarines was based in Sydney to provide anti-submarine training for the Australian Navy. The submarines involved were *Anchorite, Andrew, Aurochs, Tabard, Taciturn, Tactician, Tapir, Telemachus, Thorough* and *Trump.*

American submariners' memorial at the Fremantle War Memorial, Monument Hill, Fremantle. (Western Australian Museum, courtsey Michael Gregg – MHD 375/001.)

CHAPTER FIFTEEN

Remembering the Submarine Base

In the years after World War II, as the port of Fremantle resumed its peacetime role, the physical evidence of the submarine base soon disappeared. What had happened there between 1942 and 1945 had not involved many of Australia's servicemen or members of the general public, so, as people worked to establish new lives in a peacetime world, the memory blurred and faded.

The port was very busy during the 1950s. A large number of ships arrived bringing migrants from Britain and war-torn Europe. Included among them were some of the Allied submariners who had married local girls and decided to settle here. By the mid-fifties the port was experiencing something of a boom, handling over 150,000 passengers each year. In 1962 the Fremantle Passenger Terminal was built to cope with the numbers, but with the advent of cheaper air travel over the next decade, passenger numbers declined and the port began a long and slow decline.

Once again, Fremantle became a bit of a backwater, and memories of its wartime importance faded. People who had been involved, or were interested in the port's history, kept the memory alive, however, and in the 1960s and 1970s there were signs that the submarines had not been forgotten. In 1967 the City of Fremantle joined with the United States Submariners Association to commemorate the sacrifices of those American submariners who were lost while on patrol out of Fremantle, and a monument incorporating a Mark XV torpedo was placed on Fremantle's Monument Hill near the main war memorial. Five years later, in 1972, it was joined by a memorial to the British submariners, which features a Royal Navy submarine periscope. Albany's annual memorial service for US submariners was first held in 1976, and it was about this time that David Creed's *Operations of the*

Fremantle Submarine Base 1942-1945, was published by the Naval Historical Society of Australia.[1]

By that time the general public had become more aware of Western Australia's maritime history in general. The discovery, in the 1960s, of early Dutch shipwrecks off the west coast was of great importance. For many Western Australians, this was the first time they heard that Captain Cook was not the first European to discover Australia. In 1963, when the *Vergulde Draeck* was found by a group of adventurous skindivers, the site contained many valuable items and was under threat from treasure hunters. Suddenly the state government was confronted by the urgent need to do something about preserving the site. In November 1964, an amendment to the Museum Act vested all historic shipwrecks in the Western Australian Museum board[2], and in mid-1969 a Maritime Archaeology Department was set up to handle the increasing responsibility. In late 1971 the museum appointed its first qualified maritime archaeologist, and shipwreck material first went on display in the old asylum building in Fremantle, which had been the American navy's receiving barracks during the war. Shortly afterwards, the shipwreck material found a permanent home in the historic commissariat building on the corner of Cliff Street and Marine Parade.

The establishment of the Western Australian Maritime Museum in Fremantle was timely, with the state preparing to celebrate, in 1979, the 150th anniversary of European settlement. Across the state, plans were being made for commemorative events, encouraging interest in local history. Fremantle, as the Swan River Colony's first landing place, was of particular interest, and most of its history was maritime history.

As part of the establishment of the museum's new department, a maritime archaeology advisory committee had been set up. It was this group that first raised the idea, in 1988, that the museum should obtain one of the Royal Australian Navy's Oberon-class submarines when they were decommissioned, and put it on display to commemorate Fremantle's World War

II submarine heritage. The museum's adoption of this plan in 1990 helped raise awareness of this important part of Western Australia's history.

The Commonwealth government had not decided, at this time, what it was going to do with the navy's old submarines, so although the initial request was sent to the minister for defence in 1990 it was expected that it would be at least five to ten years before a submarine could be ready for display. The serious planning began in 1991, when Maritime Museum curator Sally May set out a strategy for the project. A project team was formed and cooperative links were established with American, British, Dutch and Australian submarine veterans' groups. As part of the ambitious plan, a history of the submarine base was to be published and a major international convention held, all within the following four years.[3]

Sally May, however, was fully employed managing the growing historic boats collection, with little time left to work on the submarine project. Public interest in yachting and boats in general had been boosted when the America's Cup defence was held at Fremantle in the summer of 1986-87, and this brought more donations of historic watercraft and maritime artefacts than the Maritime Archaeology Department could manage efficiently. Then, in the early 1990s the museum underwent a number of structural changes, with one important result for the history of submarines in Western Australia: Sally May became head of a new two-person Maritime History Department, with myself as her assistant.[4]

The new department inherited two important responsibilities: to forward the plan to obtain a submarine, and to work for the return of the America's Cup yacht *Australia II* to Fremantle. We also formally took over responsibility for the large, deteriorating historic boats collection, and the other maritime history collections that were either in inadequate storage or displayed in B-Shed, one of the old wharf buildings on Victoria Quay. Despite its nautical atmosphere, the building was environmentally disastrous as a museum, being open to dust, sea air and vermin.

In April 1993, with a great deal of support from the submarine veteran groups, other museum staff and the Australian Submarine Corporation, the new Maritime History Department put on a very successful display that told the story of Fremantle's vital role as a strategic submarine base during World War II.

This was just the beginning of the campaign that led to HMAS *Ovens* going on display at Fremantle. A great deal of lobbying was required to achieve this aim, as other states were also interested in getting a submarine. To justify Western Australia's claim, the secret of Fremantle's submarine history had to be brought to the public's attention. As part of this process, I was asked to research and write a history of the World War II submarine base at Fremantle, and this project became *Fremantle's Secret Fleets,* the first edition of this book.

Some research had already been done and a list of some fifty submarines had been collated from various sources, some hearsay, some incorrect. As I delved into the subject, however, I found that many more submarines had been based here and I was able to piece together bits of information from different sources to tell the story of the submarine base. Of particular value was the information supplied by the World War II submarine veterans who had made Western Australia their home. Sadly, most have since joined their comrades on that last, long patrol.

In March 1995, fifty years after the submarine command left Fremantle for Subic Bay, an International Submarine Convention was held at the Western Australian Maritime Museum at Fremantle, now the Shipwreck Galleries.[5] It was coordinated by the Maritime History Department, and greatly assisted by the support group, Friends of the Submarine Museum, and other museum staff and volunteers. Among those attending were 160 World War II veteran submariners, many from overseas.

The Australian Submarine Service was represented by Captain Denis Mole, while the present-day British and Dutch submarine services were represented by Rear Admiral R.C. Lane-Nott, Flag Officer, Submarines, RN; and Captain J.M. van der Ham, Commanding Officer, Submarine Service, RNLN. Rear Admiral Lloyd R. (Joe) Vasey (USN Ret.) represented the USN Submarine Service. A World War II veteran, he arrived at Fremantle in *Gunnel* in April 1944, and later that year became executive officer on *Angler*.

Two other veterans who attended also went on to reach senior positions in the Allied navies: Rear Admiral Corwin Mendenhall, author of *Submarine Diary*, was torpedo-gunnery officer in USS *Sculpin*, one of the first US submarines to reach Fremantle on 3 March 1942; the RN's Admiral Sir Gordon Tait served as first lieutenant on HMS *Tudor*, which was based in Fremantle during the last year of the war, and went on to become Second Sea Lord.

Over five days, submarine veterans of the United States, British and Dutch navies told of their wartime experiences, many reminiscing fondly about their time in Fremantle and Western

Australia. American Andre Bruinhout remembered dancing at the Embassy Ballroom, eating hamburgers at Bernie's Hamburger Bar, and the smooth rides in Perth's trolley buses. Dutch veteran Jan van Hattem, who served in the Fremantle-based submarine *Zwaardvisch* between September 1944 and April 1945, recalled parties, nightclubs and dancing at the Pagoda Ballroom in South Perth.

Guests also heard from Australian RNVR veteran Max Shean, DSO, whose book *Corvette and Submarine* tells of his experiences in the British X-Craft during the war. Speakers from the younger generation of RAN submarine veterans included retired submarine commander Peter Horobin, and Michael White, author of *Australian Submarines: A History*.[6]

There were number of social events, including a tour to World War II venues that held fond memories for the veterans, and a visit to HMAS Stirling, where the old submariners were able to see modern submarine training facilities. There was a cocktail party hosted by the British Consul, and guests enjoyed a twilight dinner on the wharf at Victoria Quay to the strains of wartime melodies played by the RAN band. During the convention, *Fremantle's Secret Fleets* was launched.

Shortly after the International Submarine Convention, all the effort was rewarded when the Minister for Finance, Kim Beazley, announced that HMAS *Ovens* was to be gifted to the Western Australian Maritime Museum.[7] The submarine was decommissioned on 1 December 1995, but was retained by the RAN for training purposes.[8]

Eleven months after paying off from training duties at the end of 1997, *Ovens* was moved from the submarine base at HMAS Stirling to Victoria Quay, where the batteries were removed before it was formally handed over to the Western Australian Museum in December 1998. A great deal of work was necessary to get the submarine ready for display, and it was slipped on the historic Fremantle slipway for conservation work in February the following year. On 18 December 1999, Western Australia's minister for the arts, Peter Foss, opened the Western

Ausralian Maritime Museum's Oberon-class submarine, HMAS *Ovens*, to the public for the first time.[9]

Meanwhile, the years of lobbying for *Australia II* had also borne fruit, and the Western Australian Government promised that a state-of-the-art maritime museum would be built to house it. The new maritime museum became a reality in 2001, a very busy year for museum staff. Though I had retired by then, I was involved in setting up the Naval Defence Gallery, which displays artefacts and models illustrating the whole of Australia's naval history, since the days when isolated settlements relied on the Royal Navy ships for protection and communication with their homeland. Here is the story of the first HMAS *Sydney* (I), the ship that sank the German cruiser *Emden* in World War I; and of its famous successor, HMAS *Sydney* (II), tragically sunk in 1941, its resting place now finally located. Here, also, one can learn the tragic and heroic stories of the Z-Force commandos, the exploits of the Royal Navy's X-Craft, and of course, well represented submarine history.[10]

The landmark Western Australian Maritime Museum building was opened on 1 December 2001.[11] It stands at the entrance to Fremantle harbour, right next to the World War II slipway where HMAS *Ovens* is permanently displayed.

The submarine, 89.91 metres long with a beam of 8.07 metres, is very popular with visitors. Knowledgeable volunteer guides, many ex-submariners themselves, show visitors what life was like on a submarine. Most people will have difficulty imagining how seven officers and 56 ratings survived long patrols in the cramped quarters,[12] but HMAS *Ovens* is more comfortably fitted out than some of the submarines that set out on patrol from Fremantle during the years of World War II.

'Australia's submarine AE2, Gallipoli 1915'—AE2 plaque erected accompanying the Submariners' Memorial next to HMAS Ovens on the historic WWII submarine slipway at the Western Australian Maritime Museum, Victoria Quay. (Western Australian Museum, courtesy Michael Gregg – MHD 375/025).

HMAS Ovens under way. (Western Australian Museum, courtesy the Royal Australian Navy–MHS 0216/29.)

CHAPTER SIXTEEN

Submarines Return to Western Australia

Australia had no submarines of its own during World War II, except for the former Dutch submarine *K IX,* which was used by the RAN for antisubmarine training. By the end of the war, however, navies the world over had accepted that submarines were an integral part of a modern fleet, so the Australian Government felt it needed a navy that included a submarine element as part of its post-war defence policy.

The world was a different place after 1945 than it had been before the war. The old colonial system was falling apart as former colonies struggled to gain independence. The Japanese conquest and occupation of South-East Asia and the islands to the north of Australia had broken the colonial ties with European powers. The peoples of these countries, having been left to endure conquest with no protection from their colonial masters, were not prepared to just hand back control. All over the world, former colonies were seeking independence, and there was much support in Australia and other Western countries for their aspirations.

Of special interest to Australia was what would be the outcome in the former Dutch East Indies. There was considerable ambivalence in public opinion. At first the Australian Government allowed the Dutch to use Australian bases, including Fremantle, for their reconquest attempts, but this was not universally supported. Many felt that the Indonesians had a right to run their own country, but there was concern that an aggressive, and possibly communist, regime could come to power there and threaten Australia. In the end the Dutch had to accept that they could not turn back the clock, and Indonesia gained its independence in 1949.

Although the USSR had been an ally during the war, Marxist/Leninist ideologues talked of world communism. Consequently the consolidation of Soviet power across Eastern Europe, together with the establishment of a communist government in China, was viewed with apprehension by Western countries, especially the United States of America. After 1949, when the Soviet Union matched the US in developing nuclear weapons, relations between east and west deteriorated into a kind of armed truce, known as the Cold War.

Despite the fact that the Allied submarines based in Australia had been very effective in helping to defeat the Japanese navy during World War II, Australia's navy heads remained blind to the full potential of an RAN submarine fleet. The only use they seemed to see for submarines was for training the crews of other types of vessels to fight against enemy submarines.

At first the British Royal Navy provided Australia with a submarine defence and anti-submarine training capability. Some British submarines stayed on for a time after the end of the war and, from 1949, under a cost-sharing agreement with the British government, the Royal Navy's 4th Submarine Flotilla was based in Sydney[1] This arrangement provided

Australia with a tactical presence and the opportunity to train Australian submariners. By 1950, six RN submarines were based at Sydney, and over the following nineteen years exchanges of officers and crew between the two navies led to greatly improved training.

It was not until the late 1950s, mainly at the instigation of then minister for defence John Gorton, that the subject of the navy acquiring a submarine fleet again came up for discussion, with the navy chiefs of staff accepting the idea in principle in 1959.[2] They still failed to see the full potential of submarines in warfare, or their future role in reconnaissance and surveillance.

Even in 1959, Gorton's successor was hesitant about the idea of Australia having its own submarine force,[3] but the Royal Navy submarines were leaving in 1969 so the Australian Government needed to take action to fill the gap. In 1963 four of the new British Oberon-class submarines were ordered, and the following year RAN submariners began serving in the RN Oberons to give them the necessary experience to operate the new boats. The first of Australia's new submarines, HMAS *Oxley* (2) arrived in Australia in 1967, the same year that the new land submarine base, HMAS Platypus, was commissioned at Neutral Bay, New South Wales. During the next two years, *Otway* (2) and *Ovens* arrived, so by the time the RN finally went home Australia had the nucleus of its submarine fleet. The fourth submarine, HMAS *Onslow,* arrived in 1970.[4]

The Oberons could operate in remote areas without having to return to their base, so it is almost certain that they were involved in deterrence and surveillance operations during the Cold War, including top-secret Cold War spying missions on Russia and China between 1978 and 1992, according to a media report. One mission was believed to have taken a submarine to the waters off Libya. The report suggests only certain members of the submarine's complement would have been aware of the purpose of the mission.[5]

By the 1980s a more independent defence policy, concentrating on the primary defence of Australia itself, had begun to take shape. A Defence White Paper of 1987 put forward a 'two-ocean navy policy', which included the basing of submarines in Western Australia, at HMAS Stirling, the new land naval base in Cockburn Sound, which had been commissioned in 1978.[6]

By this time the final two Oberon-class submarines, *Orion* and *Otama,* had arrived, completing the First Australian Submarine Squadron. The submarines' equipment had been upgraded to include long-range sonar, which required a redesigned bow dome to house it. Integrated data-processing and fire-control systems, and attack sonar systems were also installed. After 1984, the submarines were fitted with an underwater-launched version of the Harpoon anti-ship missile and MK 48 torpedoes.

The Oberon submarines were in service for over thirty years and served Australia well, but by the late 1970s it was obvious that they were becoming obsolete. Refits were becoming more difficult and costly, sometimes involving the replacement of corroded sections of the pressure hull.[7]Finding a replacement for them soon became a priority.

In 1983, seven European submarine companies were invited to submit proposals for the design and production of a new submarine class for the Australian navy. The requirements for the selected design showed a new awareness, as a result of experience with Oberons, of the unique role submarines could play in defending Australia. In wartime they must be capable of taking the war to the enemy, as the Allied submarines had done during World War II, and in peacetime to act as a deterrent, while gathering information about the possibly aggressive actions of other nations. It was recognised, probably for the first time, that the simple fact of the submarines' presence could act as a deterrent in peacetime and tie up enemy resources in wartime.

RAN Oberon class submarine HMAS Ovens alongside Victoria Quay, 25 August 1995, before being decommissioned at Garden Island. (Western Australian Museum, courtesy Patrick Baker–HB OVN/07.)

It was planned that at least some of the new vessels would be built or assembled in Australia. Several states hoped to attract this prestigious contract and, in 1985, the Western Australian Government began lobbying for the submarines to be assembled in Cockburn Sound. Hopes were raised in February 1986 when a local company won the $11m contract to build the navy's submarine escape training facility at HMAS Stirling. The facility meant that submariners no longer had to go to Britain for this important training.[8]

Western Australia missed out on the big contract, however. In 1987, it was announced that the newly designed Kockums Type 471 submarine, based on the Royal Swedish Navy's Vastergotland class, had been chosen, and that they were to be built in South Australia by the Australian Submarine Corporation. The submarines were to be fitted with sophisticated electronic and computerised equipment, and six were to be ordered for delivery between 1995 and 1999.[9] The choices provoked considerable controversy. Accusations were made that the selection of design and construction location were affected by bias, and there was criticism of the decision to build them in Australia, and of the choice of a new design rather than a class that was already in use. This did prove to be a problem, with the first submarine, HMAS *Collins,* effectively being a prototype and a trial run for the whole project.

There was some justification for choosing to produce a new design, however. The RAN's earlier submarine classes had all been built for operations in European waters, but these new Collins-class submarines were designed to cope with long distances and the specific climatic conditions they were likely to encounter in Australia's strategic region. It was planned that they would be quieter than the Oberons, able to travel faster and for longer periods underwater, capable of diving to greater depths, and more easily manouevred. They were intended to be capable of patrols of 70 days, over a range of 9,000 nautical miles in order to cover the vast expanse of ocean surrounding Australia.

The first of the new submarines, HMAS *Collins,* was launched in 1993, but it was not commissioned until 1996, as a whole raft of minor problems needed to be corrected. Problems with the combat system, diesel engines and noise, continued to plague the project. The five other submarines were completed by 2001, only two years later than originally planned. *Farncomb* and *Waller* were launched in 1998, *Dechaineux* in 1999, *Sheehan* in 2000 and *Rankin* in 2001. The submarines, all named after RAN personnel who served with distinction during the world wars, were to be based in Western Australia at HMAS Stirling.

An important aspect of the saga of the Collins class was the effect of the accelerated technological advances that have revolutionised not only defence but all aspects of Western culture and industry during the last twenty years. Everyone in the developed world has some experience of the rapid changes, and early obsolescence of computer and digital technology. So it is easy to imagine how such problems impinge on the use of highly sophisticated weapons and other systems such as those incorporated in submarines. When the project began in the late 1980s, for instance, computer memory was miniscule by today's standards and the compact personal computer we take for granted did not exist.

The computerised Combat System, in particular, was a victim of changes in computer technology and was eventually scrapped and replaced, in 2000, by an American system. There is some suggestion that political pressure led to the choice of this system over another possible choice, but, as the rate of change in computer technology shows no sign of slowing down, perhaps it may be the best long-term option, given the length and strength of Australia's alliance with the US.[10]

Meanwhile, the RAN continues to struggle to train enough submariners to operate the submarines, while the politicisation of the issue, plus a negative press that emphasises the faults, has given rise to a public perception that they have been a costly failure.

Nevertheless, Navy sources suggest that the Collins class is generally seen to have been a success.

> The Collins has been described as 'probably Australia's most important strategic asset for the decades starting 2000' with the 'potential to be an extremely potent

strategic and tactical defence asset'.[11]

It is expected that the Collins-class submarines will remain in service until the 2020s. This would be an active life similar to that of the Oberons. Planning for a replacement class began in 2007, and in 2009 the Australian Government issued a Defence White Paper that included long-term plans for a fleet of twelve submarines. Development would involve a number of overseas companies, but it was intended that they would, once again, be assembled in South Australia. The White Paper emphasised that it was necessary to begin the 'complex task of capability definition, design and construction' now, given the technical challenges involved. These submarines will have greater range, longer endurance than the Collins class and be equipped with highly sophisticated capabilities.[12]

The Submariners' Memorial at the Western Australian Maritime Museum, Victoria Quay, comprises the submarine HMAS Ovens, the historic WWII submarine slipway, the 'in memoriam' plaque and the four flagpoles to fly the Australian, American, British and Dutch flags. (Western Australian Museum, courtesy Michael Gregg – MHD 375/026.)

CONCLUSION

This book, as it was originally conceived, was really a local history intended to fill a gap in Western Australians' knowledge of their own story, to show that there had been a substantial submarine base at Fremantle during World War II, and that Fremantle was an appropriate resting place for one of the Australian Navy's obsolescent Oberon-class submarines. My starting point was a list of about fifty submarines provided by oral history and hearsay evidence, but research soon showed that was less than one-third of the total number operating from Fremantle during the war and that, rather than just a footnote to history, Fremantle had been a strategically important base.

The results were published in 1995 as *Fremantle's Secret Fleets,* and surprisingly, and mainly thanks to the internet, the book has become known beyond Western Australia. I still am amazed to find it listed in bibliographies, while a television adaptation, *Secret*

Fleets,[1] was produced in 1995. The book has even inspired a song: Bernard Carney's 'Barbed Wire Round the Harbour'.[2]

It is no longer necessary to prove Fremantle was an important Allied submarine base, but what happened here during those years is an important part of Australia's history and should not be forgotten. Some readers have asked why Fremantle was an appropriate site for a major base, and I have tried to show more clearly why it was a suitable choice. Without the safe havens provided by the harbours of Fremantle and Albany, it would have been impossible for the submarine fleet to continue playing its vital role among the islands directly to the north of Western Australia.

The secrecy surrounding the operation of the Fremantle submarine base not only allowed its existence to be largely forgotten after 1945; it continues to hinder research into the subject. Even the Fremantle harbour authorities' records of arrivals and departures failed to capture all the comings and goings of Allied submarines during the war years, and some submarines only appear in local records because they spent time on the port's slipway undergoing maintenance or repairs.

When I began researching the subject in the early 1990s the internet had only just emerged from the realms of science fiction. Historical research usually meant poring over old and often illegible documents in archives. Most of Western Australia's wartime documents had ended up in Canberra or Melbourne, while the Allied navies' records were kept in their homelands. For a thorough examination of the relevant documents, therefore, a researcher would need to spend quite some time interstate or overseas, and I had neither the time nor the resources to do that. Fortunately, copies of some important documents were loaned by veteran submariners and other researchers, allowing me to complete the original edition of this book in time for it to be launched on 20 March 1995, fifty years after the transferral of the USN flag from Fremantle to Subic Bay.

That is only fifteen short years ago, but the rapid development of computer technology and the internet has largely revolutionised how historians go about their work. At the National Archives of Australia website one can search for relevant records and read a digital copy of one of the most important sources. *The Dictionary of American Naval Fighting Ships,* which recounts the activities of all US submarines, has been digitised and is easily accessible. Where this record disagreed with other sources, I have been able to go to another site to find the original USN War Patrol Reports and read the daily journal entries recorded by the skippers. There is a useful site listing Dutch submarines and some of their wartime exploits, but they were heavily involved in secret missions so some of the details are obscure. Unfortunately, internet records of the British submarines' wartime activities are sparse and sometimes misleading, so the most reliable source remains the British Admiralty publication that I used previously.

Most of the submarines that were stationed at Fremantle belonged to the

United States Navy, and between 1942 and 1945 they conducted a total of 278 patrols. Several Dutch submarines also arrived in 1942, and these served with the Americans during the early years. In 1944, when they could be spared from the other theatres of war, British submarines of the Royal Navy, and more belonging to the Royal Netherlands Navy, joined the Fremantle fleet. These submarines were responsible for 63 patrols out of Fremantle between September 1944 and July 1945.

Because the history of the submarine base is part of the broader history of Australia's role in the international conflict, it can only be understood in relation to the military, social and economic history of the war. It has been important, therefore, to provide some background information, both local and worldwide, to place the story in context.

Contrary to what many Australians believe, during the first year after they entered the war the Japanese were quite capable of launching destructive attacks on Australia's coastal towns. During February and early March 1942, enemy submarines were active in Australian waters and spy planes even made surveillance flights over our major cities. With enemy submarines patrolling off the Western Australian coast, Fremantle was very vulnerable, even after the arrival of the USN Asiatic Fleet submarines in March. When they stayed, the port was identified as an important international base, making it a strategic target that had to be adequately defended.

The war brought radical changes to Fremantle. The port was closed, and barbed wire and sentries appeared at various strategic points. In the weeks after the fall of Singapore, the harbour was crowded with merchant and naval vessels seeking refuge from the war zone, transforming it, almost overnight, from a relatively quiet place to a hive of activity. Then the battered submarines arrived and their support vessels immediately began repair and maintenance work, while shore-based support facilities were being established. There was also an enormous mobilisation of civilian forces to supply food and other necessities for the base, and the services of local firms and government agencies were used. Furthermore, both commercially and informally, the people of Western Australia fed and entertained Allied servicemen on leave.

When the American submarines left shortly after the end of hostilities, however, the base infrastructure was quickly dismantled and there is little trace of it on North Wharf today. The Dutch submarines stayed for some time, as the Netherlands still hoped to regain its possessions in the East Indies. The old colonial days were drawing to a close, however, and the Dutch were finally forced to accept the reality of an independent Indonesia. After the British submarines left Western Australia, some were stationed in Sydney for several years.

For the local population in general, the submarine base had been a valuable source of employment during the war, but it seems to have provided no lasting economic stimulus. Most of the new buildings at North Wharf were removed within a few years, while the wharf sheds reverted to their former use.

The history of Australia's home front role in World War II was largely ignored after the war and, sadly, many Australians have little knowledge of this crucial period in the lives of their parents and grandparents. The relationship with the US, in particular, is often misunderstood, and younger people, unaware of the facts, have found it hard to understand why many of the older generation felt so grateful to the Americans.

In the post-war decades, Australia maintained close ties with the United States. American music, films and television shows dominated the lives of the young and, as time went by, some people were disturbed that the old homegrown culture seemed to be slipping away. Politically, also, there was disenchantment with American Cold War diplomacy and the tendency for Australian leaders to follow the US lead too slavishly. It is difficult now to see that, in 1942, the move towards a closer alliance with America was actually an act of independence, as previously Australia's foreign policy had been tied to that of Britain.

As with all the countries involved in the war, Australian industry responded to the challenge of producing the necessities of war at a pace sadly unknown in peacetime. Australians produced aircraft, ships, munitions and other war goods in large quantities, and constructed the roads, ports, airfields and barracks needed to support the Allied victory. The presence of the American forces, and the new products and ideas they brought, played an important part in this industrial development. America had a very efficient war industry and, unlike the European countries, its industrial cities were not under attack. Rapid technological advances were made and Australia was introduced to many innovations.

British submarines arriving alongside depot ship HMS Adamant in Fremantle Harbour 16 August 1945. (Western Australian Museum – MHP 0147/27.)

The Australia of 1942 was not, however, a backward, parochial and unimaginative society whose inefficient economy was somehow saved by the injection of American 'know-how', although, of course, Australia's economy was 'backward' when compared to the United States. The US was settled by Europeans in the early 1600s, independent twelve years before the First Fleet arrived at Sydney, and already highly industrialised before Australia became a nation in 1901.

An overwhelming amount of American equipment entered the country during the war, and the evidence of American industrial superiority seems to have inhibited the diversification of Australian manufacturing after 1945. Where, before the war, there had been a move to develop some level of economic self-sufficiency, in the post-war period many questioned the practicality of trying to develop competitive secondary industries.3 Western Australia continued to rely on primary products, with increasing emphasis on its vast mineral resources, and some of the secondary industries that had supported the war effort in this state began to decline.

Everyday life in Australia was never going to be the same as it was in the 1930s, of course, but people longed for the stability of family life and servicemen returning to civilian life needed jobs, so many women went back to the traditional female roles of stay-at-home wives and mothers as reunited couples initiated the post war 'baby boom'. The post-war decades also brought an influx of migrants to Australia's shores, bringing subtle changes to the national culture. British and Dutch submariners swelled the ranks of migrants arriving from Britain and Europe after the war, and a number of Americans who had married local women also returned to live here. The personal recollections of these people help to fill out the bare statistical bones of the submarine base story, giving us some insight into the lives of the men who braved the ocean depths to help defend Australia.

The US Navy lost a total of 3,637 submariners during the war, and 570 of them died in the eight submarines that were lost while on patrol from Fremantle.4 Others were lost in individual tragedies, or when their submarines had moved on from Fremantle and were operating from other bases. We should never forget them.

In the decades after 1945, though most Australians seemed unaware that there had been a major Allied submarine base at Fremantle, the memory was kept alive by a few people who were determined that that part of our history should not be completely forgotten. HMAS *Ovens,* on the historic slipway at the entrance to Fremantle harbour next to the Western Australian Maritime Museum, is an ongoing reminder that submarines played a part in Fremantle's history, while Cockburn Sound, where the Z-Force commandos once trained with their miniature submarines, is now home to Australia's own submarines.

APPENDIX

Submarines at Fremantle, March 1942 – August 1945[1]

The following information is as correct as possible given available sources, some of which disagree on details. For information on the American submarines, I have relied on *The Dictionary of American Naval Fighting Ships* where the information agrees with other sources. Where there was disagreement, I have gone to the contemporary Submarine War Patrol Reports now published on the internet. Some disagreement between American and local sources about precise dates may reflect the date difference caused by the international dateline. The British submarines (and the Dutch vessels that served with them) appear to be adequately covered by the Naval Staff History series of books if they made official war patrols from Fremantle, but there is some doubt about the movements of British vessels that came to Fremantle late in July and August 1945. Records for Dutch submarines are sometimes unclear. Some that appear to have been officially based at Fremantle were engaged in special missions from Darwin.

American Submarines

Alternative ID	Name	Class	Commissioned	Arrival at Fremantle	Final Departure
SS-240	Angler	Gato	1/10/43	9/4/44	4/12/44
SS-309	Aspro	Balao	31/7/43	16/6/44	10/9/44
SS-316	Barbel	Balao	3/4/44	7/12/44	5/1/45
SS-317	Barbero	Balao	29/4/44	4/10/44	Jan 45
SS-241	Bashaw	Gato	25/10/43	31/12/44	26/1/45
SS-310	Batfish	Balao	21/8/43	12/9/44	8/10/44
SS-318	Baya	Balao	20/5/44	22/10/44	20/6/45
SS-319	Becuna	Balao	29/5/44	10/44	21/6/45
SS-320	Bergall	Balao	12/6/44	8/11/44	19/1/45
SS-321	Besugo	Balao	19/6/44	4/12/44	29/8/45
SS-286	Billfish	Balao	20/4/43	10/10/43	18/4/44
SS-322	Blackfin	Balao	4/7/44	4/12/44	7/7/45
SS-324	Blenny	Balao	27/7/44	13/1/45	5/7/45
SS-325	Blower	Balao	10/8/44	19/3/45	29/8/45
SS-326	Blueback	Balao	28/8/44	17/4/45	12/5/45

SS-222	Bluefish	Gato	24/5/43	4/10/43	31/8/45
SS-242	Bluegill	Gato	11/11/43	24/8/44	12/3/45
SS-327	Boarfish	Balao	23/9/44	15/2/45	5/7/45
SS-223	Bonefish	Gato	31/5/43	21/10/43	5/9/44
SS-287	Bowfin	Balao	1/5/43	10/10/43	28/2/44
SS-243	Bream	Gato	24/1/44	22/11/44	20/4/45
SS-330	Brill	Balao	26/10/44	30/3/45	31/8/45
SS-331	Bugara	Balao	15/11/44	17/8/45	31/8/45
SS-332	Bullhead	Balao	4/12/44	2/7/45	31/7/45
SS-333	Bumper	Balao	9/12/44	15/8/45	31/8/45
SS-288	Cabrilla	Gato	24/5/43	6/11/43	31/8/45
SS-323	Caiman	Gato	26/1/45	22/1/45	22/7/45

Other Information

Four patrols from Fremantle departing 3/5/44 (ongoing problem with contaminated water supply), 21/6/44 (damaged at Exmouth returned to Fremantle for repairs & departed again 29/6/44), 18/9/44, 4/12/44.

Two patrols from Fremantle departing 9/7/44, 10/9/44.

One patrol from Fremantle departing 5/1/45. Lost during that patrol in Feb 45.

One patrol from Fremantle departing 26/10/44. Returned damaged 2/1/45, and was sent to the US.

One patrol from Fremantle departing 26/1/45.

One patrol from Fremantle departing 8/10/44. Damaged and returned to Darwin for repairs. Departed there 17/10/44.

Three patrols from Fremantle departing 19/11/44, 19/2/45, 20/6/45 (to Subic Bay).

Three patrols from Fremantle departing 16/11/44, Feb 45, 21/6/45 (to Subic Bay).

One patrol from Fremantle departing 2/12/44 (Damaged 15/12/44, transferred 55 crew to Angler and returned to Fremantle for repairs with a skeleton crew), 19/1/45 for Subic Bay.

Four patrols from Fremantle departing 24/12/44, 24/3/45, 16/4/45. Returned to Fremantle after June patrol from Subic Bay.

Three patrols from Fremantle departing 1/11/43, 19/1/44, 18/4/44.

Two patrols from Fremantle departing 2/1/45, 7/5/45.

Two patrols from Fremantle departing 5/2/45, 5/7/45.

One patrol from Fremantle departing 14/4/45.

One patrol from Fremantle departing 12/5/45.

Five patrols from Fremantle departing 26/10/43, 20/12/43, 13/2/44, 7/5/44, 22/7/44. Returned 29/7/45 and was at Fremantle at time of ceasefire.

Three patrols from Fremantle departing 18/9/44, 19/12/44, 12/3/45.

Two patrols from Fremantle departing 11/3/45, 5/7/45.

Five patrols from Fremantle departing 22/11/43, 12/1/44, 13/4/44, 25/6/44, 5/9/44.

Three patrols from Fremantle departing 1/11/43, 8/1/44, 28/2/44.

Three patrols from Fremantle departing 19/12/44, 7/3/44, 20/4/44.

One patrol from Fremantle departing 27/4/45. Back at Fremantle at time of ceasefire.

No patrols from Fremantle. Arrived 17/8/45 after patrol from Subic Bay.

One patrol from Fremantle departing 31/7/45. Lost with all hands during that patrol.

No patrols from Fremantle. Arrived day of ceasefire.

Five patrols from Fremantle departing 1/12/43, 6/3/44, 6/5/44, 3/7/44, 13/9/44 (to Pearl Harbor). Returned 3/8/45.

Two patrols from Fremantle departing 18/2/45, 22/7/45.

Alternative ID	Name	Class	Commissioned	Arrival at Fremantle	Final Departure
SS-336	Capitaine	Gato	26/1/45	13/7/45	22/7/45
SS-244	Cavalla	Gato	29/2/44	21/10/44	24/6/45
SS-328	Charr	Balao	23/9/44	3/3/45	29/8/45
SS-329	Chub	Gato	21/10/44	18/4/45	31/8/45
SS-245	Cobia	Gato	29/3/44	5/11/44	18/7/45
SS-224	Cod	Gato	21/6/43	16/12/43	31/8/45
SS-291	Crevalle	Gato	24/6/43	7/12/43	22/10/44
SS-246	Croaker	Gato	21/4/44	12/2/45	1/7/45
SS-247	Dace	Gato	23/7/43	6/11/44	2/12/44
SS-230	Finback	Gato	31/1/42	26/6/43	18/7/43
SS-249	Flasher	Gato	25/9/43	29/2/44	29/1/45
SS-250	Flier	Gato	18/10/43	5/7/44	2/8/44
SS-251	Flounder	Gato	29/11/43	13/12/44	14/1/45
SS-252	Gabilan	Gato	28/12/43	15/2/45	20/3/45
SS-206	Gar	Tambor	14/4/41	8/6/42	8/8/43

SS-207	Grampus	Tambor	23/5/41	17/6/42	30/8/42
SS-209	Grayling	Tambor	1/3/41	13/12/42	30/7/43
SS-208	Grayback	Tambor	30/6/41	22/6/42	3/9/42
SS-210	Grenadier	Tambor	1/5/41	18/9/42	20/3/43
SS-215	Growler	Gato	20/3/42	26/9/44	20/10/44
SS-362	Guavina	Balao	23/12/43	27/12/44	23/1/45
SS-211	Gudgeon	Tambor	21/4/41	2/9/42	15/4/43
SS-363	Guitarro	Balao	26/1/44	27/6/44	9/4/45
SS-253	Gunnel	Gato	20/8/42	6/4/44	21/10/44

Other Information

One patrol from Fremantle departing 22/7/45.

Three patrols from Fremantle departing 14/11/44, 8/2/45 (to Subic Bay). Returned to Fremantle (escorting HMS Terrapin) 27/5/45), departed on patrol 24/6/45.

Escorted RNN submarine Zwaardvisch to Fremantle, arriving 3/3/45. One patrol from Fremantle 27/3/45. Arrived Fremantle 26/7/45 after June patrol from Subic Bay. At Fremantle at time of ceasefire.

One patrol from Fremantle departing, 14/5/45. Arrived back at Fremantle 17/8/45 after July patrol from Subic Bay.

Three patrols from Fremantle departing 30/11/44, 18/2/45 (returned for repairs 4/3 to 8/3/45), 18/7/45.

Four patrols from Fremantle departing 11/1/44, 6/4/44, 3/7/44, 18/9/44. Brought crew of O 19 to Fremantle 13/8/45, and was there at time of ceasefire.

Four patrols from Fremantle departing 30/12/43, 4/4/44, 21/6/44, 1/9/44.

Two patrols from Fremantle departing 12/3/45, 1/7/45. Returned to Subic Bay after ceasefire. Brought crew of Darter to Fremantle.

One patrol from Fremantle departing 2/12/44.

One patrol from Fremantle departing 18/7/43.

Five patrols from Fremantle departing 4/4/44, 19/6/44, 30/8/44, 15/11/44, 29/1/45.

One patrol from Fremantle departing 2/8/44. Lost in Balabac Strait. Eight men rescued by Redfin.

One patrol from Fremantle departing 14/1/45 (departed 7/1/45, but returned for repairs).

One patrol from Fremantle departing 20/3/45.

Seven patrols from Fremantle departing 3/7/42, 17/9/42, 28/11/42, 9/2/43, 23/4/43, 18/6/43, 8/8/43.

One patrol from Fremantle departing 8/7/42. Departed 30/8/42 to Albany for refit, departing there for Brisbane 25/9/42. Subsequently lost while operating out of Brisbane.

Four patrols from Fremantle departing 7/1/43, 18/3/43, 18/5/43, 30/7/43. Lost on that patrol with all hands.

One patrol from Fremantle departing 15/7/42. Subsequently lost while operating from Pearl Harbor.

Three patrols from Fremantle departing 13/10/42, 1/1/43, 20/3/43. Lost during that patrol. Scuttled by crew, who became POWs.

One patrol from Fremantle departing 20/10/44. Lost with all hands during that patrol.

One patrol from Fremantle departing 23/1/45.

Went to Albany 4/9/42 to 25/9/42, then to Brisbane. Returned 18/2/43. Two patrols from Fremantle departing 13/3/43, 15/4/43.

Four patrols from Fremantle departing 21/7/44, 8/10/44, 11/12/44, 9/4/45.

Three patrols from Fremantle departing 3/5/44, 29/7/44, 21/10/44.

Alternative ID	Name	Class	Commissioned	Arrival at Fremantle	Final Departure
SS-254	Gurnard	Gato	18/9/42	11/6/44	10/3/45
SS-255	Haddo	Gato	9/10/42	4/2/44	20/10/44
SS-256	Hake	Gato	30/10/42	21/2/44	12/1/45
SS-364	Hammerhead	Gato	1/3/44	17/8/44	21/6/45
SS-257	Harder	Gato	2/12/42	3/5/44	5/8/44
SS-365	Hardhead	Balao	18/4/44	26/9/44	18/6/45
SS-366	Hawkbill	Balao	17/5/44	18/10/44	5/5/45
SS-258	Hoe	Gato	16/12/42	5/3/44	8/2/45
SS-367	Icefish	Perch	10/6/44	4/7/45	29/7/45
SS-259	Jack	Gato	6/1/43	13/3/44	27/10/44
SS-234	Kingfish	Gato	20/5/42	3/9/43	16/12/43
SS-370	Kraken	Balao	8/9/44	14/2/45	29/7/45
SS-372	Lamprey	Balao	14/1/44	22/4/45	21/5/44
SS-260	Lapon	Gato	23/1/43	1/4/44	23/11/44

SS-373	Lizard-fish	Balao	30/12/44	2/6/45	28/6/45
SS-374	Loggerhead	Balao	9/2/45	19/7/45	13/8/45
SS-261	Mingo	Gato	12/2/43	30/7/44	19/2/45
SS-262	Muskalunge	Gato	15/3/43	5/7/44	19/10/44
SS-167	Narwhal	Narwhal	15/5/30	18/12/43	12/8/44
SS-168	Nautilus	Narwhal	1/7/30	27/7/44	27/8/44
SS-263	Paddle	Gato	29/3/43	12/5/44	25/11/44
SS-383	Pampanito	Balao	6/11/43	30/12/44	23/1/45
SS-264	Pargo	Gato	26/4/43	24/5/44	15/1/45
SS-313	Perch II	Balao	7/1/44	15/2/45	15/4/45
SS-178	Permit	Plunger	17/3/37	7/4/42	12/7/42
SS-177	Pickerel	Porpoise	26/1/37	19/3/42	10/7/42
SS-173	Pike	Porpoise	2/12/35	28/3/42	19/4/42
SS-387	Pintado	Balao	1/1/44	20/3/45	15/4/45
SS-267	Pompon	Gato	17/3/43	5/11/43	29/11/43

Other Information

Four patrols from Fremantle departing 8/7/44, 9/10/44, 11/12/44, 10/3/45.

Four patrols from Fremantle departing 29/2/44, 18/5/44, 8/8/44, 20/10/44.

Five patrols from Fremantle departing 18/3/44, 23/5/44, 5/8/44, 20/10/44, 12/1/45.

Four patrols from Fremantle departing 9/9/44, 25/11/44, 19/2/45, 21/6/45 (to Pearl Harbor).

Two patrols from Fremantle departing 26/5/44, 5/8/44. Lost during that patrol.

Four patrols from Fremantle departing 24/10/44, 24/12/44, 20/3/45, 18/6/45. Returned to Onslow due to illness. Left on sixth and last patrol from there. Went to Subic Bay.

Three patrols from Fremantle departing 15/11/44, 5/2/45, 5/5/45.

Five patrols from Fremantle departing 4/4/44, 29/6/44, 15/9/44, 23/11/44, 8/2/45.

One patrol from Fremantle departing 29/7/45 to Saipan.

Four patrols from Fremantle departing 6/4/44, 4/6/44, 6/8/44, 27/10/44.

Two patrols from Fremantle departing 24/9/43, 16/12/43.

Two patrols from Fremantle departing 15/3/45, 29/7/45. On patrol at ceasefire.

One patrol from Fremantle departing 21/5/45 to Subic Bay.

Four patrols from Fremantle departing 25/4/44, 29/6/44, 4/9/44, 23/11/44.

One patrol from Fremantle departing 28/6/45. Went to Subic Bay.

One patrol from Fremantle departing 13/8/45.

Three patrols from Fremantle departing 27/8/44, 6/11/44, 6/2/45. Returned briefly and departed again on 19/2/45.

Two patrols from Fremantle departing 1/8/44, 19/10/44.

Three patrols from Fremantle departing 18/1/44, 7/5/44, 12/8/44.

One patrol from Fremantle departing 27/8/44.

Three patrols from Fremantle departing 5/6/44, 22/8/44, 25/11/44.

One patrol from Fremantle departing 23/1/45.

Four patrols from Fremantle departing 13/6/44, 3/9/44, 28/10/44, 15/1/45.

Two patrols from Fremantle departing 12/3/45, 15/4/45.

Two patrols from Fremantle departing 5/5/42, 12/7/42.

Two patrols from Fremantle departing 15/4/42, 10/7/42.[2]

One patrol from Fremantle departing 19/4/42.

No patrols from Fremantle. Returned to Pearl Harbor. Left there on patrol 1/6/45.

One patrol from Fremantle departing 29/11/43 went to Darwin. Next patrol 22/2/44 possibly from there.

Alternative ID	Name	Class	Commissioned	Arrival at Fremantle	Final Departure
SS-172	Porpoise	Porpoise	15/8/35	30/3/42	26/4/42
SS-268	Puffer	Gato	27/4/43	24/10/43	7/8/45
SS-269	Rasher	Gato	8/6/43	24/11/43	22/7/44
SS-270	Raton	Gato	13/7/43	25/1/44	6/10/44
SS-271	Ray	Gato	27/7/43	12/1/44	23/9/44
SS-272	Redfin	Gato	31/8/43	17/2/44	26/10/44
SS-273	Robalo	Gato	28/9/43	6/3/44	22/6/44
SS-274	Rock	Angler	26/10/43	8/11/44	7/3/45
SS-142	S-37	S-1	16/6/23	19/3/42	Apr 42
SS-143	S-38	S-1	11/5/23	13/3/42	16/3/42
SS-144	S-39	S-1	14/9/23	18/3/42	20/4/42

SS-145	S-40	S-1	20/11/23	9/3/1942	28/3/42
SS-146	S-41	S-1	15/1/24	10/3/1942	25/3/42
SS-192	Sailfish	Sargo	1/3/39	19/3/42	28/8/42
SS-182	Salmon	Salmon	15/3/38	23/3/42	10/10/42
SS-381	Sand Lance	Balao	9/10/43	5/6/44	10/9/44
SS-188	Sargo	Sargo	7/2/39	5/3/42	29/10/42
SS-189	Saury	Sargo	3/4/39	17/3/42	18/10/42
SS-191	Sculpin	Sargo	16/1/39	3/3/42	8/9/42
SS-315	Sealion II	Balao	8/3/44	24/1/45	19/2/45
SS-407	Sea Robin	Balao	7/8/44	29/1/45	24/2/45
SS-194	Seadragon	Sargo	23/10/39	4/3/42	23/10/42
SS-183	Seal	Salmon	30/4/37	9/4/42	24/10/42
SS-196	Searaven	Sargo	2/10/39	12/3/42	18/12/42
SS-197	Seawolf	Sargo	1/12/39	7/4/42	7/10/42
SS-184	Skipjack	Gato	30/6/38	10/3/42	27/9/42
SS-185	Snapper	Salmon	15/12/37	3/3/42	4/10/42

Other Information

One patrol from Fremantle departing 26/4/42.

Five patrols from Fremantle departing 24/11/43, 4/2/44, 30/4/44,

14/7/44. Then, after absence due to overhaul and patrols from other stations, 7/8/45.

Four patrols from Fremantle departing 19/12/43, 19/2/44, 30/4/44, 22/7/44 (to Pearl Harbor and US).

Four patrols from Fremantle departing 18/2/44, 10/5/44, 18/7/44, 6/10/44 (to Pearl Harbor).

Four patrols from Fremantle departing 6/2/44, 23/4/44, 9/7/44, 23/9/44.

Four patrols from Fremantle departing 19/3/44, 26/5/44, 6/8/44, 26/10/44.

Two patrols from Fremantle departing 10/4/44, 22/6/44. Lost east of Borneo. Four survived but died as POWs.

Two patrols from Fremantle departing 14/12/44, 7/3/45 (special mission).

No patrols from Fremantle. Departed for Brisbane Apr 42.

No patrols from Fremantle. Departed for Brisbane 16/3/42.

No patrols from Fremantle. Departed for Brisbane Apr 42.

No patrols from Fremantle. Departed for Brisbane 28/3/42.

No patrols from Fremantle. Departed for Brisbane 25/3/42.

Three patrols from Fremantle departing 22/3/42, 13/6/42, 28/8/42 to Brisbane.[3]

Three patrols from Fremantle departing 3/5/42, 21/7/42, 10/10/42.

One patrol from Fremantle. Departed 3/7/44 (but returned for repairs). Departed 10/9/44 (to Pearl Harbor).

Three patrols from Fremantle departing 8/6/42, 27/8/42, 29/10/42 (to Brisbane).

Two patrols from Fremantle departing 7/5/42 (earlier departure but returned damaged), 31/7/42. Refitted at Albany in July. Departed 18/10/42 for Brisbane.

Three patrol from Fremantle departing 13/3/42, 29/5/42, 8/9/42. Subsequently lost 19/11/43 while on patrol from Pearl Harbor.

One patrol from Fremantle departing 19/2/45.

One patrol from Fremantle departing 24/2/45.

Three patrols from Fremantle departing 18/3/42, 11/6/42, 26/8/42. Left for Brisbane 23/10/42.

Three patrols from Fremantle departing 12/5/42, 10/8/42, 24/10/42. Damaged on patrol, went to Pearl Harbor for temporary repairs, then to US.

Four patrols from Fremantle departing 2/4/42, 28/6/42, 27/9/42, 18/12/42.

Three patrols from Fremantle departing: 12/5/42, 25/7/42, 7/10/42.

Three patrol from Fremantle departing 14/4/42, 18/7/42, 27/9/42.

Three patrols from Fremantle departing 6/3/42 (towed disabled Searaven to Fremantle on return), 28/5/42, 8/8/42. Returned 3/10/42, went to Albany for refit, then to Brisbane.

Alternative ID	Name	Class	Commissioned	Arrival at Fremantle	Final Departure
SS-190	Spearfish	Sargo	17/7/39	7/3/42	8/9/42
SS-186	Stingray	Salmon	15/3/38	3/3/42	After 23/2/45
SS-187	Sturgeon	Salmon	25/6/38	3/3/42	4/9/42

SS-193	Swordfish	Sargo	22/7/39	9/3/42	18/10/42
SS-198	Tambor	Tambor	3/6/40	19/9/42	20/7/43
SS-175	Tarpon	Porpoise	12/3/36	5/3/42	28/3/42
SS-199	Tautog	Tambor	3/7/40	11/6/42	11/5/43
SS-200	Thresher	Tambor	21/8/40	15/8/42	Jun (?) 43
SS-283	Tinosa	Gato	15/1/43	16/12/43	10/1/44
SS-202	Trout	Tambor	15/11/40	8/12/42	12/8/43
SS-203	Tuna	Tambor	2/1/41	14/10/43	13/4/45

British Submarines

Alternative ID	Name	Class	Built	Arrival at Fremantle	Final Departure
12F	Clyde	River	15/3/34	29/7/44	Sep 44 (?)
N 14	Porpoise	Porpoise	30/8/32	10/8/44	After 11/10/44
N 74	Rorqual		21/7/36	Apr 45 (?)	After 20/5/45
P 218	Sea Rover	S3	1/2/43	5/9/44	Jan 45
P 253	Sea Scout	S3	1/3/44	4/5/45	May/Jun 45

P 254	Selene	S3	24/4/44	May 45	May 45
P 259	Sidon	S3	4/9/44	16/6/45	7/7/45
P 226	Sirdar	S3	26/3/43	18/9/44	Apr 45, with escort to Ceylon
P 261	Sleuth	S3	1/7/44	Mar 45	14/4/45
P 262	Solent	S3	8/6/44	Mar 45	14/4/45

Other Information

Three patrols from Fremantle departing 29/3/42 (left Albany 27/3/42), 26/6/42, 8/9/42 (to Brisbane).

Two patrols from Fremantle departing 16/3/42, 27/5/42. Operated elsewhere and returned 23/2/45.

Three patrols from Fremantle departing 15/3/42, 5/6/42. Departed 26/7/42 to Albany for refit then went to Brisbane.

Four patrols from Fremantle departing 1/4/42, 15/5/42, 27/7/42, 18/10/42 (to Brisbane).

Five patrols from Fremantle departing 14/10/42, 18/12/42 (had departed 15 Dec, but returned damaged), 18/2/43, 7/5/43, 20/7/43.

One patrol from Fremantle departing 28/3/42.

Five patrols from Fremantle departing 17/7/42, 8/10/42, 15/12/42, 24/2/43, 11/5/43.

Five patrols from Fremantle departing 15/9/42, 16/12/42, 25/1/43, 4/4/43, Jun(?) 43.

One patrol from Fremantle departing 10/1/44.

Three patrols from Fremantle departing 29/12/42, 22/3/43, 27/5/43, 12/8/43. Subsequently lost on patrol from Pearl Harbor.

One patrol from Fremantle departing 7/11/43. Special mission from Darwin 16/1/45. Returned to Fremantle 13/3/45 for training duty.

Other Information

Was on Fremantle slipway in Aug and Sep 44. No patrols recorded from Fremantle.4

One patrol from Fremantle departing 11/9/44 (Operation Rimau). Returned to Fremantle 11/10/44.

Minelaying submarine. One patrol from Fremantle departing 30/4/45. Returned 20/5/45.

Two patrols from Fremantle departing 23/9/44, 11/11/44. Damaged in collision with HMAS Bunbury. Returned to UK.

One patrol from Fremantle departing between 4/5/45 and 16/6/45 when it left on patrol from Subic Bay.

Appears to have made no patrols from Fremantle. At Subic Bay by 7/6/45.

One patrol from Fremantle departing 7/7/45 (to join 8th Flotilla at Subic Bay).

Three patrols from Fremantle departing 7/10/44, 25/11/44, 8/2/45 (returned damaged).

One patrol from Fremantle departing 14/4/45.

One patrol from Fremantle departing 14/4/45.

Alternative ID	Name	Class	Built	Arrival at Fremantle	Final Departure
P 236	Spark	S3	28/12/43	Dec 44	May 45
P 245	Spirit	S3	20/7/43	9/12/44	May 45
P 227	Spiteful	S3	6/10/43	30/8/44	Mar 45

P 231	Stoic	S3	9/4/43	Sep 44	2/12/44
P 233	Storm	S3	1/5/43	Sep 44	31/1/45
P 238	Stubborn	S3	20/2/43	14/6/45	3/10/45
P 248	Sturdy	S3	30/9/43	6/9/44	19/4/45
P 249	Stygian	S3	30/11/43	Feb 45	10/5/45
P 252	Supreme	S3	23/2/44	4/4/45	21/4/45
P 334	Taciturn	T3	7/6/44	Apr 45	After end of war
P 318	Tantalus	T3	1/2/43	26/9/44	25/3/45
P 319	Tantivy	T3	6/4/43	13/9/44	14/1/45
P 335	Tapir	T3	1/8/44	Jul/Aug 45	After end of war
P 339	Taurus	T3	1/6/42	Jul 45	
P 321	Telemachus	T3	1/6/43	6/9/44	24/2/45
P 323	Terrapin	T3	22/11/44	Late Mar 45	Aug 45
P 324	Thorough	T3	30/10/43	24/4/45	3/10/45
P 325	Thule	T3	22/10/42	May 45	14/10/45
P 332	Tiptoe	T3	25/2/44	Apr 45	6/10/45
P 352	Totem	T3	28/9/43	Before 1/8/45	14/10/45
P 329	Tradewind	T3	11/12/42	Dec 44	After 23/5/45
P 331	Trenchant	T3	24/3/43	Apr 45	After end of war

P 333	Trump	T3	25/3/44	13/4/45	14/10/45
P 326	Tudor	T3	23/9/42	13/2/45	After end of war
P 354, S 54	Turpin	T2	5/8/44	Before 5/8/45	6/10/45
P 75	Virtue	V	29/11/43	5/3/45	Mar (?) 45
P 78	Voracious	V	1/11/43	Feb 45	Mar (?) 45
P 73	Vox II	V	23/1/43	Feb 45	Mar (?) 45

Other Information

Two patrols from Fremantle departing 16/1/45, 14/3/45. Returned 14/4 and departed for Subic Bay.

Two patrols from Fremantle departing 31/12/44, 23/2/45.

Three patrols from Fremantle departing 22/9/44, 16/11/44, 12/1/45.

Two patrols from Fremantle departing 3/10/44, 2/12/44 (to Sri Lanka and UK).

Three patrols from Fremantle departing 10/10/44, 4/12/44, 31/1/45 (to Sri Lanka and UK). One patrol from

Fremantle departing 13/7/45. Returned 9/8/45.

Five patrols from Fremantle departing 24/9/44, 12/11/44, 3/1/45, 23/2/45, 19/4/45 (to Sri Lanka and UK).

One patrol from Fremantle departing 15/3/45. Returned 19/4/45 and transferred to Subic Bay.

One patrol from Fremantle departing 21/4/45 to join 8th Flotilla at Subic Bay.

Two patrols from Fremantle departing 13/5/45, 25/7/45. Returned 21/8/45.

Three patrols from Fremantle departing 16/10/44, 3/1/45, 25/3/45.

Three patrols from Fremantle departing 9/10/44, 24/11/44, 14/1/44 (to Sri Lanka and Britain).

No recorded patrols. Was still off Norway 12/4/45. Loaned to RNN 1948 and renamed Zeehond.

No patrols from Fremantle. On Fremantle slipway Jul 45. Loaned to RNN 1948 and renamed Dolfijn.

Three patrols from Fremantle departing 14/9/44, 4/12/44, 24/2/45 (to Trincomalee via Darwin).

One patrol from Fremantle departing 3/5/45 (damaged 19/5/45). Returned to Fremantle 27/5/45.

Two patrols from Fremantle departing 13/5/45, 25/7/45. Returned 21/8/45.

One patrol from Fremantle departing 5/7/45. Returned 31/7/45.

Two patrols from Fremantle departing 6/5/45, 16/7/45.

Returned 21/8/45. On slipway at Fremantle 1/8/45 to 3/8/45. Does not appear to have made any patrols from Fremantle.

Two patrols from Fremantle departing 12/1/45, 22/3/45.

One patrol from Fremantle departing 13/5/45. Returned 23/7/45.

Two patrols from Fremantle departing 4/5/45, 16/7/45. Returned 21/8/45.

Three patrols from Fremantle departing 7/3/45, 7/5/45, 9/7/45. Returned 11/8/45.

On slipway at Fremantle 5/8/45 to 8/8/45. Apparently made no patrols from Fremantle during WWII.

No patrols from Fremantle. On slipway Mar 45. Probably en route to Subic Bay.

Left Malta 21/11/44 for Fremantle. No patrols from Fremantle.5

No patrols from Fremantle. On slipway Feb 45. Probably en route to Subic Bay.

Dutch Submarines

Alternative ID	Name	Class	Commissioned	Arrival at Fremantle	Final Departure
	K VIII	K VIII	15/9/22	17/3/42	Scrapped at Fremantle
N 39	K IX	K VIII	21/6/23	13/3/42	20/4/42
N 53	K XI	K XI	24/3/25	22/3/45	
N 61	K XII	K XI	19/5/25	20/3/42	2/5/44
N 22	K XIV	K XIV	6/7/33	13/4/44	29/9/45
	K XV	K XIV	30/12/33	28/2/44	29/9/45
P 19, N 54	O 19	O 19	3/7/39	18/9/44	25/6/45
S 801, P 21	O 21	O 19	10/5/40	24/8/43	3/10/45
P 23, K XXIII	O 23	O 19	13/5/40	Aug 45	Departed after war

| S 804, P 24, | O 24 | O 19 | 13/5/40 | Mar/Apr 45 | Departed after war |
| p332, O 29, O3, S 814 | Zwaard-visch | Zwaard-vis, British T-class | 23/11/43 | 7/9/44 | 9/4/45 |

Other Information

No patrols from Fremantle. Decommissioned and sold as scrap Aug 1943.

No patrols from Fremantle. Went to RAN, and was commissioned 22/6/42 as K9. Returned to RNN 1944. Beached 1945.

No patrols from Fremantle. Decommissioned Apr 45.

Three patrols from Fremantle departing 17/11/42, 21/1/43, 10/3/44. Other activities obscure, submarine involved in special missions.

Refit Dec 42 to May 43. Based Fremantle Apr 44 to Aug 45, but no recorded patrols. Several patrols and special missions from Darwin during this time. Returned Aug 44 and Feb 45 for repairs.

Refit Nov 1942 to May 1943. Based at Fremantle Feb 44 to Sep 45, but conducted ten secret NEFIS missions from Darwin and Exmouth during that time. Also at Fremantle in 1946.

Four patrols from Fremantle departing 23/10/44, 19/12/44, 1/4/45 (returned damaged), 25/6/45 (for Subic Bay). Ran aground en route and was scuttled, crew rescued by USS Cod.

Based at Fremantle 25/8/43 to 28/11/43, but no patrols recorded. Returned in May 45 and made one patrol from Fremantle departing 7/7/45. Returned 8/8/45. In harbour at Ceasefire.

No patrols from Fremantle during World War II. Arrived after ceasefire.

Two patrols from Fremantle departing 7/4/45, 29/5/45. Returned 20/6/45. On slipway at ceasefire.

Four patrols from Fremantle departing 26/9/44, 28/11/44, 30/1/45, 9/4/45.

1 These submarine movements have been compiled from various sources, including, 'Submarine War Patrol Reports', Historic Naval Ships Association; Dictionary of American

Naval Fighting Ships; 'Arrivals and Departures at the Port of Fremantle, February 1939-March 1942'; Harbour and Light Department Records; 'Submarine operations ex Australian bases. USN, RN & RAN—World War 2'; Naval Staff History, Second World War Vol.III: Submarines, Operations in Far Eastern Waters; D. Creed, Operations of the Fremantle Submarine Base 1942-1945; 'The submarines of the Royal Netherlands Navy 1906-2005'

2 Correct according to Pickerel's War Patrol Reports. Dictionary of American Naval Fighting Ships suggests the July patrol departed Brisbane

3 Sailfish was the former Squalus, which sank during a trial dive in 1939 It was repaired and recommissioned

4 One internet source (http://home.co geco.ca/~gchalcraft) suggests Clyde made six or even seven patrols from Fremantle 18/6/44, 18/11/44, then Jan, Feb and Mar 45. There are no records of these patrols elsewhere.

They may have been special missions out of Darwin or Exmouth.
5 On slipway Feb 45. Probably en route to Subic Bay. Struck submerged wreck off Sydney on 13/4/45.

ENDNOTES

Introduction

[1] W.J. Holmes, *Double-Edged Secrets: U.S. Naval Intelligence Operations in the Pacific During World War II,* Naval Institute Press, Annapolis, 1979, p.80.

[2] *Daily News,* 11 December 1942, p.4.

[3] For details of individual USN submarines' activities as used throughout, see: *The Dictionary of American Naval Fighting Ships,* Department of the Navy, Naval Historical Centre, Washington DC. http://www.history.navy.mil/danfs/index.html (28 June 2010); 'Submarine War Patrol Reports', Historic Naval Ships Association. http://hnsa.org/doc/subreports.htm? (28 June 2010); 'Arrivals and Departures at the Port of Fremantle, February 1939–March 1942', Harbour and Light Department Records, Western Australian Archives, Accession

number 1076; 'Submarine operations ex Australian bases. USN, RN & RAN—World War 2', Department of Defence, Navy Office. NAA: B6121, 173F. (digital copy online @ http://www.naa.gov.au (20 June 2010); and C. Blair junior, *Silent Victory*, Bantam, New York, 1976.

[4] For details of individual RN submarines' activities as used throughout, see: *Naval Staff History, Second World War Vol.III: Submarines, Operations in Far Eastern Waters,* Historical Section Admiralty; D. Creed, *Operations of the Fremantle Submarine Base 1942–1945,* Naval Historical Society of Australia, Garden Island, NSW, c.1979; and 'Arrivals and Departures at the port of Fremantle, February 1939–March 1942'.

[5] For details of individual RNN submarines' activities as used throughout, see: *Naval Staff History, Second World War Vol.III: Submarines, Operations in Far Eastern Waters;* D. Creed,

Operations of the Fremantle Submarine Base 1942–1945; 'Arrivals and Departures at the port of Fremantle, February 1939–March 1942'; and 'The submarines of the Royal Netherlands Navy 1906–2005', http://www.dutchsubmarines.com (28 June 2010).

[6] D. Jones and P. Nunan, *U.S. Subs Down Under: Brisbane, 1942–1945.* Naval institute Press, Annapolis, MD, 2005.

1. The Development of the Submarine

[1] This account of the early evolution of submarines was compiled from various sources including: A. Preston, *Submarines: The History and evolution of Underwater Fighting Vessels,* Octopus Books, London, 1975; B. Harris, 'World Submarine History Timeline', www.submarine-history.com/NOVAone.htm (29June 2010); and 'History of Submarines', Wikipedia, http://

en.wikipedia.org (Search by topic) (30 March 2011).
[2] Blair., *Silent Victory,* pp.25, 26.
[3] 'Submarines 1900-1914', About Facts Net, http://aboutfacts.net/Weapons20.htm (28 June 2010).
[4] Blair, *Silent Victory,* p.32: See also 'British Submarines 1900 to 1918', http://www.historylearningsite.co.uk/british_submarines_1900_to_1918.htm (28 June 2010)., and 'History of Submarines' http://en.wikipedia.org/wiki/History_of_submarines (28 June 2010).
[5] 'The submarines of the Royal Netherlands Navy 1906-2005'.
[6] 'Submarines during World War I', Wikipedia, http://en.wikipedia.org/wiki/History_of_submarines (28 June 2010).

2. Australia's Submarines in WWII

[1] M.W.D. White, *Australian Submarines: A History,* AGPS Press, Canberra, 1992, pp.14, 15.
[2] R. Gillett, *Australian & New Zealand Warships 1914-1945,*

Golden Press, Drummoyne, NSW, p.47.
[3] ibid. pp.29–37.
[4] J.N. Green, *The Search for the AE2: Magnetometer and Side Scan Sonar Survey Duke of York Islands, East New Britain, 22–28 November 2003*, WA Maritime Museum, Fremantle, 2001.
[5] 'HMAS *AE.2*', Royal Australian Navy', http://www.navy.gov.au/HMAS_AE2 (29 June 2010).
[6] V. Basarin, *Beneath the Dardanelles*, Allen & Unwin, Crows Nest, NSW, 2008, pp.22–24, 34–41.
[7] A.E. Knaggs, 'The Diary of Able Seaman 7893 Albert Edward Knaggs R.A.N.', http://homepage.ntlworld.com/jeffery.knaggs/diary.html (28 June 2010).
[8] Basarin, *Beneath the Dardanelles*, pp.48, 49.
[9] A. Moorehead, *Gallipoli*, Cornstalk, Pymble, NSW, 1992, p.126.
[10] White, *Australian Submarines*, pp.46–75.

[11] F. and E. Brenchley, *Stoker's Submarine,* HarperCollins, Sydney, 2001, pp.168–187.

[12] 'Treaty relating to the Use of Submarines and Noxious Gases in Warfare, Washington, 6 February 1922' International Humanitarian Law—Treaties & Documents, International Red Cross, http://www.icrc.org/ihl.nsf/FULL/270?OpenDocument (29 June 2010).

[13] I. Cowman, '"The Vision Splendid": Australian Maritime Strategy 1911–23', in D, Stevens (editor), *In Search of a Maritime Strategy,* ANU, Canberra, 1997, pp.46–52.

[14] White, *Australian Submarines,* pp.82–92; 115–120, 128–164.

3. World War II Begins

[1] F. Alexander, *Australia Since Federation,* Nelson, Melbourne, 1980, p.132.

[2] Gillett, *Australian & New Zealand Warships 1914–1945,* pp.91–236.

[3] Rhodesia became Zimbabwe after gaining independence.
[4] 'Crete, ΚρhthΣ, Kreta: The Battles of May 1941' Australian War Memorial, http://www.awm.gov.au/atwar/crete.asp (29 June 2010).
[5] Blair, *Silent Victory,* pp.46-76.

4. Japan Enters the War

[1] F.K. Crowley, *Modern Australia in Documents: 1939-1970,* Wren, Melbourne, 1973, pp.46-47 (quotation from *Sydney Morning Herald,* 9 December 1941).
[2] *The War in Pictures: Third Year,* Odhams Press, London, Undated (1940s), pp.73-91.
[3] Tatsuwaka Shibuya (compiler), *Japanese Monograph No.102: Submarine Operations December 1941-April 1942,* US Military History Section, Headquarters, Army Forces Far East, 1952, p.21.
[4] Creed, *Operations of the Fremantle Submarine Base 1942-1945,* pp.1-2, 47-48.
[5] Crowley, *Modern Australia in Documents,* pp.49-52, (quoted

from *Herald*, Melbourne, 27 December 1941).
[6] P. Adam-Smith, *Australian Women at War,* Nelson, Melbourne, 1984, pp.140–142.
[7] Creed, *Operations of the Fremantle Submarine Base 1942–1945,* p.3.
[8] B. and F. Pitt, *The Month-by-Month Atlas of World War II,* Summit, New York, 1989, pp.64–65.
[9] M. McCarthy, 'The Flamingo Bay Voyage', Report, Department of Maritime Archaeology, Western Australian Maritime Museum: No.45, 1991, pp.10–52.

5. Australia Prepares for an Invasion

[1] P. Firkins, *Of Nautilus and Eagles: History of the Royal Australian Navy,* Hutchinson, Richmond, 1975, p.6.
[2] G. McKenzie-Smith, *Defending Fremantle Albany and Bunbury 1939–1945,* Grimwade

Publications, Mt Pleasant, WA, 2009, p.1.

[3] 'Press reports of bombing of Darwin. Advisory War Council Agendum No.2/1942'. NAA: A5954, 327/12. Digital copy online @: http://recordsearch.naa.gov.au/scripts/imagine.asp?B=646070&I=1&SE=1 (29 June 2010).

[4] NAA: Fact Sheet 195: 'The Bombing of Darwin', http://www.naa.gov.au/about-us/publications/fact-sheets/fs195.aspx (29 June 2010).

[5] Darwin Raids—Casualty Lists and Enquiries' pp.17, 26., NAA: Series Number F1, Control Symbol 1942/364. Digital copy online @: http://recordsearch.naa.gov.au/scripts/ItemDetail.asp?M=0&B=334209 (29 June 2010).

[6] Tatsuwaka Shibuya, *Japanese Monograph No.102.*

[7] *West Australian,* 24 February 1942, p.5.

[8] ibid., 23 February 1942, p.5.

[9] ibid., 24 February 1942, p.7.

[10] ibid., 7 March 1942, p.4.

[11] ibid.

[12] ibid., 26 February 1942, p.7; 27 February 1942, p.7.
[13] ibid., 23 February 1942, p.5.
[14] Creed, *Operations of the Fremantle Submarine Base 1942–1945,* p.6.
[15] S. Alomes, *A Nation at Last? The Changing Character of Australian Nationalism 1880–1988,* Angus & Robertson, North Ryde, NSW, 1988, p.117.
[16] Holmes, *Double-edged Secrets,* p.80.
[17] D. Jenkins, *Battle Surface! Japan's Submarine War Against Australia 1942–44,* Random House, Sydney, 1992, pp.161–255.
[18] Pitt, *The Month-by Month Atlas of World War II,* pp.73–75.
[19] Holmes, *Double-edged Secrets,* p.80.
[20] R. and H. Walker, *Curtin's Cowboys: Australia's Secret Bush Commandos,* Allen & Unwin, Sydney, 1986, pp.59–70.
[21] The *West Australian,* 1 January 1943, p.3.

THE PORT OF FREMANTLE

[1] 'Fremantle Harbour Trust Annual Report: Year Ending 30 June 1945', Fremantle Harbour Trust, 1945, p.10.

[2] 'USN Base Facilities Report Southwest Pacific Area, 15 September 1944', (compiled by Commander Seventh Fleet). State Library Service of Western Australia (Battye Library), PR 6185, pp.9–10.

[3] Fremantle Harbour Trust Annual Report: Year Ending 30 June 1945, p.11.

[4] D. Connell, *The War at Home,* pp.96–100.

[5] Fremantle Harbour Trust Annual Report: Year Ending 30 June 1945, p.11.

[6] 'USN Base Facilities Report; Southwest Pacific Area', 15 September 1944, pp.9–11.

[7] ibid., 15 September 1944, p.35.

[8] P. Kemp (editor), *The Oxford Companion to Ships and the Sea,* Oxford University Press, London, 1976, p.238.

[9] J.S.H. Le Page, *Building a State: The Story of the Public Works Department of Western Australia 1829–1985,* Water Authority of Western Australia, Perth, 1986, p.416.

6. The US Submarines come to Fremantle

[1] *Dictionary of American Naval Fighting Ships.*
[2] 'History of U.S. Naval Operations from Western Australian bases'. pp.3–4., in: 'Submarine operations ex Australian bases. USN, RN & RAN—World War 2' (pp.22–23 of online digital copy).
[3] Rear Admiral C. Mendenhall, 'International Submarine Convention Oral History Tape no.4, Side A'. Western Australian Maritime Museum Records.
[4] *'Arrivals and Departures at the Port of Fremantle'.*
[5] *Dictionary of American Naval Fighting Ships.*
[6] 'History of U.S. Naval Operations from Western Australian bases'

pp.4–5. (pp.23–24 of 'Submarine operations ex Australian bases'—online digital copy). See also: *'Arrivals and Departures at the Port of Fremantle'.*

[7] Information from Mr S. Jones, 4 January 1988, Fremantle Library Local History Collection File 940.53.

[8] Theodore Roscoe., *United States Submarine Operations in World War II,* US Naval Institute, Annapolis, 1949, p.96.

[9] *Fremantle Port Authority, Annual Report for Year Ending 30 June 1945,* p.10.

[10] LePage, *Building a State,* p.416.

[11] 'History of U.S. Naval Operations from Western Australian bases', p.6 (p.25 of 'Submarine operations ex Australian bases'—online digital copy).

[12] 'Albany Harbour-master's Logbook', Harbour and Light Dept Records, Western Australian Archives, Accession number 726).

[13] Creed, *Operations of the Fremantle Submarine Base 1942–1945,* p.7. Also:

Information from USN veteran, Homer White.
[14] *The War in Pictures: Third Year,* pp.146–168.
[15] 'History of U.S. Naval Operations from Western Australian bases', p.5. (p.24 of 'Submarine operations ex Australian bases'—online digital copy).
[16] Creed, *Operations of the Fremantle Submarine Base 1942–1945,* pp.47–51.
[17] 'USN Base Facilities Report; Southwest Pacific Area, 15 September 1944'. See also: Dept of Interior Records.
[18] Department of the Interior Files (Requisition files). NAA: K1141, USN1943/44/1—USN1943/44/91.
[19] M. McCarthy, *Jervoise Bay Shipwrecks,* Report, Department of Maritime Archaeology, Western Australian Maritime Museum, No.15, 1979), pp.5–7.
[20] Creed, *Operations of the Fremantle Submarine Base 1942–1945,* pp.48–49. Also: Information from RNN submarine veteran, Pieter Andriessen.

7. 1942: Submarines on the Offensive

[1] Blair, *Silent Victory,* pp.17, 18.
[2] Roscoe, United States Submarine Operations in World War II, p.145.
[3] Blair, *Silent Victory,* p.910.
[4] ibid., pp.273–281, 435–439.
[5] Information from USN submarine veteran, Andy Andersen.
[6] 'Albany Harbour-master's Logbook', Harbour and Lights Dept Records.
[7] Information from USN submarine veteran, William Pouleris.
[8] 'History of U.S. Naval Operations from Western Australian bases', p.7 (p.26 of 'Submarine operations ex Australian bases'—online digital copy).
[9] Fremantle Harbour Trust Records.
[10] *The War in Pictures: Third Year,* pp.353. See also: Pitt, *The Month-by-month Atlas of World War II,* p.79–93.
[11] 'History of U.S. Naval Operations from Western Australian bases', pp.7–10 (pp.26–29 of 'Submarine

operations ex Australian bases'—online digital copy).

8. 1943: The Fremantle Submarines at War

[1] 'History of U.S. Naval Operations from Western Australian bases', p.12 (p.31 of 'Submarine operations ex Australian bases'—online digital copy).
[2] *The Dictionary of American Naval Fighting Ships.*
[3] Blair, *Silent Victory,* pp.365–368. See also; Creed. *Operations of the Fremantle Submarine Base 1942–1945,* pp.15–16.
[4] ibid., p.396.
[5] Fremantle Slipway records.
[6] *West Australian,* 23 April 1943, p.5.
[7] Blair, *Silent Victory,* pp.389–390.
[8] 'History of U.S. Naval Operations from Western Australian bases', p.14 (p.33 of 'Submarine operations ex Australian bases'—online digital copy).
[9] ibid.

[10] *Dictionary of American Naval Fighting Ships.*

[11] Edward C. Whitman, *Rising to Victory: The Pacific Submarine Strategy in World War II,* http://www.navy.mil/navydata/cno/n87/usw/issue_11/rising_victory.html (28 June 2010).

[12] 'History of U.S. Naval Operations from Western Australian bases' p.14 (p.33 of 'Submarine operations ex Australian bases'—online digital copy).

[13] Fremantle Slipway records.

[14] Information from RNN veteran, Pieter Andriessen.

[15] Blair, *Silent Victory,* pp.487–490.

[16] Creed, *Operations of the Fremantle Submarine Base 1942–1945,* pp.16–17.

[17] Whitman, *Rising to Victory: The Pacific Submarine Strategy in World War II,*

[18] Blair, *Silent Victory,* pp.925–947; see Also: 'Submarine operations ex Australian bases'.

THE SUBMARINE REPAIR UNIT AT NORTH WHARF

[1] *Fremantle Harbour Trust Annual Report: Year Ending 30 June 1945,* p.10
[2] Base Facilities Report; 'USN Southwest Pacific Area, 15 September 1944'. pp.26-28.

9. Meanwhile, on the Home Front

[1] Alomes, *A Nation at Last,* p.119.
[2] Gillett, *Australian & New Zealand Warships 1914-1945,* pp.150-270.
[3] A Gunzberg, *WAGR Locomotives 1940-1968,* (Australian Railway Historical Society, Perth, 1968).
[4] 'Government Aircraft Factories', <http://en.wikipedia.org/wiki/Government_Aircraft_Factories>
[5] M. McKernan, *All In: Australia during the Second World War.* Nelson, Melbourne, 1983, p.204
[6] ibid., p.147.
[7] ibid., p.187.

[8] *West Australian,* 26 March 1943, p.6.
[9] Alomes, *A Nation at Last,* p.119.
[10] Connell, *The War at Home,* pp.89–91.
[11] L. Peet, 'The Men who stayed behind', in J. Gregory (editor), *On The Home Front: Western Australia and World War II,* pp.48–9.
[12] Adam-Smith, *Australian Women at War,* p.328.
[13] *Instructions for American Servicemen in Australia 1942,* (Reproduced from the original prepared by Special Services Division, Services of Supply, United States army and issued by War and Navy Departments Washington, D.C.), Penguin, Camberwell, 2007, p.4.
[14] L. Jackson, 'The Moment When Image and Reality Met: The social impact of the American servicemen based in Perth during the Second World War', unpublished Honours dissertation, 1991, p.38.

[15] M. Critch (compiler), *Our Kind of War: The History of the VAD/AAMWS,* Artlook, Perth, 1981, p.131.

[16] Pitt, *The Month-by-month Atlas of World War II,* pp.92–95.

[17] *West Australian,* 24 March 1943, p.2.

[18] Fr Eugene Perez, *The Kalumburu War Diary,* Artlook, Perth, 1981, pp.123–137.

[19] Jenkins, *Battle Surface!* p.266. Also G. Kennedy McDonald, 'The Little Boat Harbour: History of Port Gregory', Unpublished Report, Western Australian Maritime Museum Records, File MA 117/80.

[20] Interview with former AWAS Searchlight Unit member, Rosemary Shepherd, *Fremantle Gazette,* 5 October 1993, p.36.

[21] Information from author's parents, R. and G. Wheeler (deceased).

[22] Information from Kevin Carter.

10. A Submariner's Life

[1]   C. Mendenhall, *Submarine Diary,* Algonquin Books, Chapel Hill, NC, 1991, p.8.
[2]   ibid., p.8.
3   Information from various RN veterans.
[4]   Wikipedia, http://en.wikipedia.org/wiki/Gato_class_submarine (29 June 2010).
[5]   Information from Franz Dohmen.
[6]   Edwin Young (RN), personal diary, Courtesy Mrs S. Davey.
[7]   Information from RNN veteran, Pieter Andriessen.
[8]   Information from Selby Longmire (Reminiscences of Mrs Rita Collins).
[9]   Information from USN veteran, William Pouleris.
[10]   Information from RN veteran, Alf Jobson.
[11]   Edwin Young, personal diary.
[12]   S. Graham-Taylor, 'The War for Health', in J. Gregory (ed.), *On the Homefront: Western Australia and World War II,* p.221.

[13] 'Minutes of Conference on Venereal Disease', Dept. of Defence Correspondence File. NAA: MP742/1, 211/6/619.
[14] W.J. Ruhe, *War in the Boats: My WWII Submarine Battles,* Brassey's Inc, New York, 1994, pp.268–298.
[15] Information from Sylvia Dohmen.

11. Early 1944: The Allies Fight Back

[1] Pitt, *The Month-by-month Atlas of World War II,* pp.116–122.
[2] *The Dictionary of American Naval Fighting Ships.*
[3] Creed, *Operations of the Fremantle Submarine Base 1942–1945,* p.24.
[4] 'History of U.S. Naval Operations from Western Australian bases', p.18 (p.38 of 'Submarine operations ex Australian bases'—online digital copy).
[5] Fremantle Slipway records.
[6] Information from RNN veterans, P. Andriessen and F. Dohmen.

[7] 'Fremantle Harbour-master to Manager, Fremantle Harbour Trust, 13 March 1944', Fremantle Harbour Trust Records. See also: 'Arrivals and Departures at Port of Fremantle'.
[8] Information from Bill Archibald.
[9] Fremantle Slipway records.
[10] McKenzie-Smith, *Defending Fremantle Albany and Bunbury 1939 to 1945*, WA, 2009, p.28.
[11] Blair, Silent Victory, p.616–618. Also information from Pieter Andriessen.
[12] Fremantle Slipway records.
[13] Creed, *Operations of the Fremantle Submarine Base 1942–1945*, p.27.
[14] Blair, *Silent Victory*, pp.622–624. See also: *The Dictionary of American Naval Fighting Ships.*
[15] 'History of U.S. Naval Operations from Western Australian bases', p.18. (p.38 of 'Submarine operations ex Australian bases'—online digital copy).
[16] Pitt, *The Month-by-month Atlas of World War II,* p.125.
[17] Blair, *Silent Victory,* pp.627–637.

[18] Pitt, *The Month-by-month Atlas of World War II,* p.130–131.
[19] Creed, *Operations of the Fremantle Submarine Base 1942–1945,* p.28.
[20] 'History of U.S. Naval Operations from Western Australian bases', p.17. (p.37 of 'Submarine operations ex Australian bases'—online digital copy).
[21] Blair, *Silent Victory,* p.687.
[22] ibid., p.688.

UNITED STATES NAVY ACCOMODATION

[1] Base Facilities Report; 'USN Southwest Pacific Area, 15 September 1944'.

12. Late 1944: British Submarines Arrive

[1] Fremantle Slipway records.
[2] Pitt, *The Month by-month Atlas of World War II,* pp.130–137.
[3] Creed, *Operations of the Fremantle Submarine Base 1942–1945,* p.42.

[4] ibid., p.24. Also: Information from RN submarine veteran, Herbert Gardner.

[5] *Naval Staff History, Second World War: Submarines, Vol.III,* pp.69–72.

[6] Arrivals and Departures at the Port of Fremantle.

[7] *Naval Staff History, Second World War: Submarines, Vol.III,* p.76. See also: Fremantle Slipway records.

[8] Information from RN submarine veteran, Arnold Hole.

[9] *The Dictionary of American Naval Fighting Ships.* See Also, M. Sturma, *The U.S.S. Flier: Death and Survival on a World War II Submarine,* University Press of Kentucky, Lexington, 2008.

[10] 'U.S.S. *Flier* (SS–250), Press Release of Confirmed Discovery', Commander Submarine Force, U.S. Pacific Fleet, Public Affairs Office, Pearl Harbor, 1/2/2010, www.ussflier.com/release.htm (29 June 2010).

[11] *The Dictionary of American Naval Fighting Ships.* See Also, M.

Sturma, *Death at a Distance: The Loss of the Legendary USS Harder,* Naval Institute Press, Annapolis, 2006.
[12] *Naval Staff History, Second World War Vol.III,* pp.69–70.
[13] Information from RN submarine veteran, Eric Theedom.
[14] Arrivals and Departures at the Port of Fremantle.
[15] Ruhe, *War in the Boats: My WWII Submarine Battles,* p.268–298.
[16] Blair, *Silent Victory,* pp.743. See also 'The Submarines of the Royal Netherlands Navy 1906—2005'.
[17] Pitt, *The Month-by-Month Atlas of World War II,* pp.136–139.
[18] Creed, *Operations of the Fremantle Submarine Base 1942–1945,* p.35.
[19] Edward C. Whitman, *Rising to Victory: The Pacific Submarine Strategy in World War II,* http://www.navy.mil/navydata.
[20] Blair, *Silent Victory,* p.783. See also *Dictionary of American Naval Fighting Ships.*

[21] Fremantle Slipway Records.
[22] *Arrivals and Departures at the Port of Fremantle.*
[23] *Naval Staff History, Second World War: Submarines, Vol.III,* p.83. Also: information from RN submarine veteran John Meek.
[24] 'History of U.S. Naval Operations from Western Australian bases', pp.25–32 (pp.45–52 of 'Submarine operations ex Australian bases'—online digital copy).

13. Clandestine Operations

[1] *Dictionary of American Naval Fighting Ships.*
[2] Information from RNN veteran, Pieter Andriessen (personal experience and material from P. Jalhay, *Nederlandse Onderzeedienst 75jaar: de Boer Maritiem,* Unieboek bv., Bussum, 1982; and *Comité voor de viering van dit Jubileum, Veertig Jaren Onderzeedienst 1906–1946* (Schelters & Gillray, Amsterdam, 1947).

[3] Michael Jeffery (Major General), in foreword to Sue, Jack Wong. *Blood on Borneo,* WA Skindivers Publication, Perth, c.2001, p.v.

[4] Gladys Whyte (sister of Jack Sue), in Sue, *Blood on Borneo,* p.353.

[5] A.B. Feuer, *Australian Commandos: Their Secret War Against the Japanese in WWII.* Stackpole Books, Mechanicsburg, PA, 1996, pp.1–9.

[6] R. Horton, *Ring of Fire: Australian Guerilla Operations Against the Japanese in World War II,* Macmillan, Melbourne, 1983, pp.9–15.

[7] ibid., pp.9–15. See also: 'Operation Jaywick', Wikipedia, http://en.wikipedia.org/wiki/Operation_Jaywick.

[8] 'Double Tenth Incident', Wikipedia, http://en.wikipedia.org/wiki/Double_Tenth_Incident (28 June 2010).

[9] Feuer, *Australian Commandos,* p.25. 'Welman submarine'. See also: Wikipedia, http://en.wikipedia.org/wiki/Welman (28 June 2010).

[10] Gillett, *Australian & New Zealand Warships 1914–1945*, pp.188–190.

[11] Feuer, *Australian Commandos,* pp.27–43.

[12] Blair, *Silent Victory,* pp.192–197, 497, 581, 906–975.

[13] Information from RNN veteran, Pieter Andriessen.

[14] Ruhe. *War in the Boats: My WWII Submarine Battles,* pp.215–234.

[15] L. Ramsay Silver, *The Heroes of Rimau,* Sally Milner Publishing, Birchgrove NSW, 1990. See also:'1941–1950 (World War II)'. See also: http://www.mindef.gov.sg/imindef/about_us/history/world_war2.html (29 June 2010).

[16] *Naval Staff History, Second World War: Submarines, Vol.III,* pp.76–77. Also information from RN veteran Arnold Hole.

[17] Feuer, *Australian Commandos,* pp.45–84.

[18] Sue, *Blood on Borneo.* Also personal information from Z-Force veteran, Jack (Wong) Sue.

[19] Feuer, *Australian Commandos*, pp.51–55, 95–116.
[20] 'Special Missions Performed by Submarines Operating from Fremantle', pp.1–7 (pp.11-17 of 'Submarine operations ex Australian bases'—online digital copy).

THE BRITISH MINIATURE SUBMARINES

[1] M. Shean, Corvette and Submarine, The author, Claremont, WA, 1992. See also: 'Welman submarine', Wikipedia, http://en.wikipedia.org/wiki/Welman (28 June 2010).

14. The War Comes to an End

[1] *The War in Pictures: Sixth Year*, pp.94–150. See also Pitt, *The Month-by-Month Atlas of World War II*, pp.144–147.
[2] Blair, *Silent Victory*, p.819. See also: Creed, *Operations of the*

Fremantle Submarine Base 1942–1945, pp.39–40.

[3] 'History of U.S. Naval Operations from Western Australian bases', p.33 (p.53 of 'Submarine operations ex Australian bases'—online digital copy).

[4] Creed, *Operations of the Fremantle Submarine Base 1942–1945,* p.39.

[5] *Naval Staff History, Second World War: Submarines, Vol.III,* p.73, 90–97. See also: Blair, *Silent Victory,* pp.845–851, 947–948; and Vic Jeffery, 'Crisis in the Port of Fremantle', in *Port of Fremantle,* Winter 1983.

[6] *Naval Staff History, Second World War: Submarines, Vol.III,* p.91.

[7] McCarthy, *Jervoise Bay Shipwrecks,* pp.53–59.

[8] 'History of U.S. Naval Operations from Western Australian bases', p.33 (p.53 of 'Submarine operations ex Australian bases'—online digital copy).

[9] *Naval Staff History, Second World War: Submarines, Vol.III,* p.73.

[10] Information from RN submarine veteran, Alf Jobson.
[11] Edwin Young (RN), personal diary.
[12] *Naval Staff History, Second World War: Submarines, Vol.III,* pp.73, 94–95.
[13] ibid. pp.100–105.
[14] Pitt, *The Month-by-month Atlas of World War II,* pp.148–161.
[15] Blair, *Silent Victory,* p.856.
[16] ibid., p.856. See also: www.history.navy.mil/danfs/b10. Also information from William Pouleris.
[17] Creed, *Operations of the Fremantle Submarine Base 1942–1945,* p.53.
[18] *Naval Staff History, Second World War: Submarines, Vol.III,* pp.94–111.
[19] G. Cudden, 'HMS Terrapin's Final War Patrol', http://www.bbc.co.uk/ww2peopleswar/stories/77/a2207477.shtml (29 June 2010).
[20] Information from RN veteran, Gerry Goldman.
[21] Fremantle Harbour Trust Records.

15. Remembering the Submarine Base

[1] Creed, *Operations of the Fremantle Submarine Base 1942–1945.*
[2] *Western Australian Museum: Annual Report 1963–1964* (Perth, 1964), p.11.
[3] 'Australian Submarine Heritage HMAS Ovens: Department of Maritime History's Oberon Submarine Project—1991–1995', http://www.museum.wa.gov.au/collections/maritime/submarine/whyovens.asp (29 June 2010).
[4] Western Australian Museum: Annual Report 1993–1994, Perth, 1994, pp.10,13, 80
[5] 'Australian Submarine Heritage HMAS Ovens: Department of Maritime History's Oberon Submarine Project, 1991–1995'.
[6] WA Maritime Museum Records, Maritime History files ISC Oral history tapes.
[7] 'Australian Submarine Heritage HMAS *Ovens:* Department of

Maritime History's Oberon Submarine Project, 1991–1995'.
[8] *HMAS Ovens 15 April 1919–1 December 1995,* Decommissioning Ceremony program, 1995.
[9] 'Australian Submarine Heritage', HMAS *Ovens* Events, http://www.museum.wa.gov.au/collections/maritime/submarine/HMASovensevents.asp (29 June 2010).
[10] ibid.
[11] 'Welcome to the Maritime Museum', http://www.museum.wa.gov.au/oursites/maritime/maritime.asp (29 June 2010).
[12] 'Australian Submarine Heritage: HMAS Ovens' http://www.museum.wa.gov.au/collections/maritime/submarine (29 June 2010).

16. Submarines Return to Western Australia

[1] White, *Australian Submarines: A History,* AGPS Press, Canberra, 1992, p.189.
[2] Yule and Woolner, *The Collins Class Submarine Story: Steel, Spies and Spin,* Cambridge

University Press, Pt Melbourne, 2008, p.11.
[3] ibid., p.12.
[4] White, *Australian Submarines: A History,* pp.193–200.
[5] Brendan Nicholson, 'Secret spy missions forced to the surface', *Age,* 08/09/2006, http://www.theage.com.au/news/national/secret-spy-missions-forced-to-the-surface/2006/09/07/1157222265317.html (29 June 2010).
[6] S. Woodman, 'Defending the Moat; Maritime Strategy and Self Reliance', in D. Stevens (editor), *In Search of a Maritime Strategy,* ANU, Canberra, 1997, pp.117–132
[7] Yule and Woolner, *The Collins Class Submarine Story: Steel, Spies and Spin,* p.18–25.
[8] *West Australian,* 18 Feb.1986, p.32.
[9] White, *Australian Submarines: A History,* pp.206–7.
[10] Yule and Woolner, *The Collins Class Submarine Story: Steel, Spies and Spin,* pp.244–253.
[11] Lee Willett, 'Tomahawk for Collins?' in Official Journal Of

Navy League Of Australia, http://navyleag.customer.netspace.net.au/fc_07th.htm (29 June 2010).

[12] *Defence White Paper 2009,* Department of Defence, Australian Government, Canberra, 2009. http://www.defence.gov.au/whitepaper/(29 June 2010).

Conclusion

[1] G. Colgan and M. Kelley, *Secret Fleets,* Mask Productions, 1995.
[2] B. Carney© 'Barbed Wire Round the Harbour'. 'West' Album, Bernard Carney, 2004.
[3] N.G. Butlin, A. Barnard and J.J. Pincus, *Government and Capitalism: Public and Private Choice in Twentieth Century Australia,* George Allen & Unwin, Sydney, 1982, pp.111–113. See also: E.A. Boehm, *Twentieth Century Economic Development in Australia* (third edition), Longman Cheshire, Melbourne, 1993, p.188.
[4] 'On Eternal Patrol: Submarines that Sustained Losses in World War II', http://www.oneternalpatr

ol.com/submarine-losses.htm (28 June 2010).

SOURCES AND SUGGESTED READING

Publications

Adam-Smith, P. *Australian Women at War.* Nelson, Melbourne, 1984.

Alexander, F. *Australia Since Federation: A Narrative and Critical Analysis.* Nelson, Melbourne, 1980.

Alomes, S. *A Nation at Last? The Changing Character of Australian Nationalism 1880–1988.* Angus &Robertson, North Ryde, NSW, 1988.

Basarin, V. *Beneath the Dardanelles: The Australian Submarine at Gallipoli.* Allen & Unwin, Crows Nest, NSW, 2008.

Battle, L. *War Brides.* W.H. Allen, London, 1982.

Blair, C. Jnr. *Silent Victory: The US submarine war against Japan.* Bantam, New York, 1975.

Boehm, E.A. *Twentieth Century Economic Development in Australia* (third edition). Longman Cheshire, Melbourne, 1993.

Brenchley, F. and E. *Stoker's Submarine.* HarperCollins, Sydney, 2001.

Brenkley, D. *World War II Geraldton 1941–45: Early Surveillance of Air, Land and Sea and Secret Operations: Historical Record of 47 RDF (RADAR).* The author, Sorrento, WA, Undated.

Butlin, N.G., Barnard, A., and Pincus, J.J. *Government and Capitalism: Public and Private Choice in Twentieth Century Australia.* George Allen & Unwin, Sydney, 1982.

Butlin, S.J. and Schedvin, C.B. *War Economy 1942–1945.* Canberra War Memorial, Canberra, 1977.

Butlin, S.J. *War Economy 1939–1942.* Canberra War Memorial, Canberra, 1955.

Compton-Hall, R. *Sub Vs Sub: The Tactics and Technology of Underwater Warfare.* Orion, New York, 1988.

Connell, D. *The War at Home, Australia 1939–1949.* ABC, Crows Nest NSW, 1988.

Courtney, G.B. *Silent Feet: The History of 'Z' Special Operations 1942–1945.* R.J. & S.P. Austin, Melbourne, 1993.

Creed, D. *Operations of the Fremantle Submarine Base 1942–1945.* Naval Historical Society of Australia, Garden Island NSW, Undated (possibly 1976).

Critch, M. (compiler). *Our Kind of War: The History of the VAD/AAMWS.* Artlook, Perth, 1981.

Crowley F. (editor). *A New History of Australia.* William Heinemann, Melbourne, 1974.

Crowley, K.F. *Modern Australia in Documents: 1939–1970.* Wren, Melbourne, 1973. *Daily News,* Perth, 1941–1946.

Davies, J. *The Lady was Not a Spy.* The author, Sorrento, WA, 1992. (World War II security issues in Western Australia.)

Ewer, P. *Wounded Eagle: The Bombing of Darwin and Australia's Air Defence Scandal.* New Holland Publishers (Australia), Sydney, 2009.

Feuer, A.B. *Australian Commandos: Their Secret War Against the Japanese in WWII.* Stackpole Books, Mechanicsburg, PA, US, 1996.

Firkins, P. *Of Nautilus and Eagles: History of the Royal Australian Navy.* Hutchinson, Richmond, 1875.

Frances, R. *Women at Work in Australia from the Gold Rushes to World War II.* Cambridge University Press, Cambridge, 1993.

Fremantle Gazette, 5 October 1993, Fremantle.

Gillett, R. *Australian & New Zealand Warships 1914–1945.* Golden Press,

Drummoyne, NSW. (Includes information on auxiliary and requisitioned craft.)

Green, J.N. *The Search for the AE2: Magnetometer and Side Scan Sonar Survey: Duke of York Islands, East New Britain, 22–28 November 2003,* WA Maritime Museum, Fremantle, 2001.

Gregory, J. (editor). *On the Homefront: Western Australia and World War II.* University of Western Australia Press, Nedlands, 1996.

Gunzberg, A. *WAGR Locomotives 1940–1968.* Australian Railway Historical Society, Perth, 1968. Hammond Moore, J. *Over-sexed, Over-paid and Over Here: Americans in Australia, 1941–1945.* University of Queensland Press, St Lucia, 1981.

Holmes, W.J. *Double-edged Secrets: US Naval Intelligence Operations in the Pacific during World War II.* US Naval Institute Press, Annapolis, 1979.

Hopkins, W.B. *The Pacific War: The Strategy, Politics, and Players that Won the War.* Zenith, Minneapolis, c.2008.

Horton, D. *Ring of Fire: Australian Guerilla Operations Against the Japanese in World War II.* Macmillan, Melbourne, 1983.

Instructions for American Servicemen in Australia 1942 (reproduced from the original prepared by Special Services Division, Services of Supply, United States Army and issued by War and Navy Departments Washington, DC). Penguin, Camberwell, 2007.

Jeffery, V. 'Crisis in the Port of Fremantle', in *Port of Fremantle,* Winter 1983. (About the fire on board the Panamanian.)

Jenkins, D. *Battle Surface! Japan's Submarine War against Australia 1942–44.* Random House, Sydney 1992.

Jones, D. and Nunan, P. *U.S. Subs Down Under: Brisbane, 1942–1945.*

Naval Institute Press, Annapolis, MD, 2005.

Kemp, P. (editor). *The Oxford Companion to Ships and the Sea.* Oxford University Press, London, 1976.

Le Page, J. *Building a State: The Story of the Public Works Department of Western Australia 1829– 1985.* Water Authority of Western Australia, Perth, 1986.

Lind, L. *Toku-Tai: Japanese Operations in Australian Waters.* Kangaroo Press, Melbourne, 1992.

Longstaff, R. *Submarine Command: A Pictorial History.* Robert Hale, London, 1984. (RN submarines.)

McKenzie-Smith, G. *Defending Fremantle, Albany and Bunbury, 1939 to 1945.* Grimwade Publications, Mt Pleasant, 2009.

McKernan, M. *All In: Australia during the Second World War.* Nelson, Melbourne, 1983.

McKernan, M. *All In: Fighting the War at Home.* Allen & Unwin, St Leonards, NSW, 1995.

McKernan, M. *The Strength of a Nation: Six Years of Australians Fighting for the Nation and Defending the Home Front in WWII.* Allen & Unwin, Crows Nest, NSW, 2008.

McKie, R. *The Heroes: Daring Raiders of the Pacific War.* Eden, North Ryde, 1989.

Mendenhall, C. *Submarine Diary.* Algonquin Books, Chapel Hill, NC, 1991.

Moorehead, A. *Gallipoli.* Cornstalk, Pymble, NSW, 1992.

Neumann, K. *In the Interest of National Security: Civilian Internment in Australia During World War II.* National Archives of Australia, Canberra, c.2006.

Naval Staff History: Second World War: Submarines, Vol.III: Operations in Far

Eastern Waters. History Section, Admiralty.

Odgers, G. *The Royal Australian Navy: An Illustrated History.* Child & Henry, Hornsby NSW, 1982.

Parker, J. *The World Encyclopedia of Submarines.* Anness Publishing (Lorenz Books), London, 2007.

Perez, E. *The Kalumburu War Diary.* Artlook, Perth, 1981.

Pfennigworth, I. *The Royal Australian Navy and MacArthur.* Rosenberg, NSW, 2009.

Pitt, B., and F. *The Month-by-Month Atlas of World War II.* Summit, New York, 1989.

Preston, A. *Submarines.* Bison, Greenwich, 1982.

Roscoe, T. *United States Submarine Operations in World War II.* United States Naval Institute, Annapolis, 1949.

Ruhe, W.J. *War in the Boats: My WWII Submarine Battles.* Brassey's Inc., New York, 1994.

Sarantakes, N.E. *Allies Against the Rising Sun: The United States, the British Nations, and the Defeat of Imperial Japan.* University Press of Kansas, Lawrence, KS, US, c.2009.

Shean, M. *Corvette and Submarine.* The author, Claremont, WA, 1992. (The British X-Craft.)

Sheiner, R. *Smile, the War is Over: A Novel.* Macmillan, South Melbourne, 1983. (Novel based on experiences of Western Australian women who married US servicemen.)

Silver, L. Ramsay. *The Heroes of Rimau: Unravelling the Mystery of One of World War II's Most Daring Raids.* Sally Milner Publishing, Birchgrove NSW, 1990.

Stanley, P. *Invading Australia: Japan and the Battle for Australia, 1942.* Penguin, Camberwell, 2008.

Stevens, D, (editor). *In Search of a Maritime Strategy.* ANU, Canberra, 1997

Sue, J.W. *Blood on Borneo.* WA Skindivers Publication, Perth, c.2001.

Tatsuwaka Shibuya, (compiler). *Japanese Monograph No.102: Submarine Operations December 1941–April 1942.* Military History Section, Headquarters, Army Forces Far East, 1952. (Excerpt in Paine, T. (compiler): *'HIJMS I–124, HMAS Sydney and Related Naval History'.* Wreck Inspection files, Maritime Archaeology Records, Western Australian Maritime Museum.)

The War in Pictures: Sixth Year. Odhams Press, London, Undated (1940s).

The War in Pictures: Third Year. Odhams Press, London, Undated (1940s).

Walker, R. and H. *Curtin's Cowboys: Australia's Secret Bush Commandos.* Allen & Unwin, Sydney, 1986.

West Australian, 1941–1946, Perth.

White, M.W.D. *Australian Submarines: A History.* AGPS Press, Canberra, 1992.

Yule, P. and Woolner, D. *The Collins Class Submarine Story: Steel, Spies and Spin.* Cambridge University Press, Pt Melbourne, 2008.

Web Sites

'1941 to 1950 (World War II)', Mindef, Singapore government, http://www.mindef.gov.sg/imindef/about_us/history/world_war2.html (29 June 2010).

'Australian Submarine Heritage', Western Australian Maritime Museum, http://www.museum.wa.gov.au/collections/maritime/submarine/links.asp (28 June 2010).

Australian War Memorial, http://www.awm.gov.au/atwar/ww2.asp (29 June 2010).

'British Submarines 1900–1918', http://www.historylearningsite.co.uk/british_s

ubmarines_1900_to_1918.htm (28 June 2010).

'Crete: The Battles of May 1941', Australian War Memorial, http://www.awm.gov.au/atwar/crete.asp (29 June 2010).

'Double Tenth Incident', Wikipedia, http://en.wikipedia.org/wiki/Double_Tenth_Incident (28 June 2010).

'Government Aircraft Factories', Wikipedia, http://en.wikipedia.org/wiki/Government_Aircraft_Factories (28 June2010).

'HMAS *AE.2'*, Royal Australian Navy, http://www.navy.gov.au/HMAS_AE2 (29 June 2010).

'Submarine operations ex Australian bases. USN, RN & RAN—World War 2', Department of Defence, Navy Office. National Archives of Australia: B6121, 173F, http://www.naa.gov.au/collection/recordsearch/index.aspx (22 July 2010). (Digital copy online).

'Submarine War Patrol Reports', Historic Naval Ships Association, http://hnsa.org/doc/subreports.htm? (28 June 2010).

'Submarine', Wikipedia, http://en.wikipedia.org/wiki/Submarines (28 June 2010) (for historical and other information).

'Submarines 1900–1914', About Facts Net, http://aboutfacts.net/Weapons20.htm (28 June 2010).

'Submarines during World War I', Wikipedia, http://en.wikipedia.org (search by topic) (30 March 2011).

'The Submarines of the Royal Netherlands Navy 1906–2005', http://www.dutchsubmarines.com (28 June 2010).

'Treaty for the Limitation and Reduction of Naval Armaments, (Part IV, Art 22, relating to submarine warfare). 'London, 22 April 1930', http://www.icrc.org/ihl.nsf/WebART/310-440001?OpenDocument (29 June 2010).

'Treaty relating to the Use of Submarines and Noxious Gases in Warfare, Washington, 6 February 1922', International Humanitarian Law, Treaties & Documents, International Red Cross, http://www.icrc.org/ihl.nsf/FULL/270?OpenDocument (29 June 2010).

'WA Shipping Arrivals and Departures' database, Western Australian Museum website at http://www.museum.wa.gov.au

'Welman submarine', Wikipedia, http://en.wikipedia.org/wiki/Welman (28 June 2010).

'World War II U.S. Submarine List', FleetSubmarine.com, http://www.fleetsubmarine.com/sublist.html (28 June 2010).

Harris, B. 'World Submarine History Timeline Part 4: 1941–2000', http://www.submarine-history.com/NOVAfour.htm (29 June 2010).

Knaggs, A.E. 'The Diary of Able Seaman 7893 Albert Edward Knaggs R.A.N.' *(AE11* crewman), http://homepage.ntlworld.com/jeffery.knaggs/diary.html (28 June 2010).

National Archives of Australia, http://www.naa.gov.au/collection/recordsearch/index.aspx (28 June 2010).

Dictionary of American Naval Fighting Ships, Department of the Navy, Naval Historical Centre, Washington DC. http://www.history.navy.mil/danfs/index.html (28 June 2010)

Official Journal of Navy League Of Australia, Navy League of Australia, http://www.navyleague.org.au/ (31 July 2010).

Western Australian Maritime Museum, (Maritime History topics), http://www.museum.wa.gov.au/maritime/(28 June 2010).

Whitman, E.C. *Rising to Victory: The Pacific Submarine Strategy in World War II,* http://www.navy.mil/navydata/c

no/n87/usw/issue_11/rising_victory.html (28 June 2010).

'On Eternal Patrol: Submarines that Sustained Losses in World War II', http://www.oneternalpatrol.com/submarine-losses.htm (28 June 2010).

Unpublished Sources

Base Facilities Report; USN Southwest Pacific Area, compiled by Commander Seventh Fleet, 15 September 1944. State Library Service of Western Australia (Battye Library), PR 6185.

Bruce, W. Oral History Transcript, 28 August 1987, Maritime History Records, Western Australian Maritime Museum.

'Conference on Venereal Disease Held in the Conference Room Hyde Park Gate' (Dept of Army File). NAA: MP742/1, 211/6/619

Edwin Young's *Trenchant* diary (courtesy Mrs S.G. Davey). Copy of excerpt in

Maritime History Records, Western Australian Maritime Museum.

Farrington, B & Gregg, M, 'Lots of ups and downs: the operations of the Government Slipways at Fremantle 1899-1999' (proposed title). Manuscript in preparation, Western Australian Museum

Fremantle Harbour Trust Records. Western Australian State Records Office, WAA–71, WAS 91.

Fremantle Library Local History Collection File 940.53.

Fremantle Slipway Records. Maritime History Records, Western Australian Maritime Museum.

Gregg, M, 'Secret sailings—operations of the WWII Allied Submarine Base at Fremantle' (proposed title). Manuscript in preparation, Western Australian Museum.

Harbour and Light Department Records. Western Australian State Records Office,

WAS–4044 (formerly Accession numbers 726, 1076).

International Submarine Convention Oral History Tapes. Western Australian Maritime Museum Records.

Jackson, L. 'The Moment When Image and Reality Met: The Social Impact of the American Servicemen Based in Perth during the Second World War'. Honours dissertation, University of Western Australia, 1991.

Kennedy McDonald, G. 'The little boat harbour: History of Port Gregory.' Unpublished report, Western Australian Maritime Museum Records, File MA 117/80.

Longmore Papers, State Library of WA Heritage Collection, Accession No.1298A, File 42.

McCarthy, M. 'Jervoise Bay shipwrecks.' Report, Department of Maritime Archaeology, Western Australian Maritime Museum, No 15, 1978.

McCarthy, M. 'The Flamingo Bay Voyage', including reports on *I 124*, the *Ann Millicent*, and a wreck believed to be the *Koombanah*. Report, Department of Maritime Archaeology, Western Australian Maritime Museum, No.45, 1991.

Reekie, G. 'Women's paid work during World War II in Western Australia: Government direction and women's response 1942–1947.' Honours dissertation, Murdoch University, 1982.

'Requisition files, financial annual single number series with alphabetical prefix' (Allied Works Council files). NAA: K1141, USN1943/4/1–USN1943/4/91.

Rourke papers, Maritime History Records, Western Australian Maritime Museum.

Oral and Written Information

Obtained from:

Andy Andersen, USN (Rtd)

Pieter Andriessen, RNN (Rtd)

Bill Archibald

Kevin Carter

Franz and Sylvia Dohmen, RNN (Rtd)

Merle Drayson (RN war bride)

Herbert Gardner, RN (Rtd)

Isaac Goldman, RN (Rtd)

Alf Jobson, RN (Rtd)

Selby Longmire (reminiscence from Mrs Rita Collins)

John Meek, RN (Rtd)

Elaine Porter (RN war bride)

William and Kathleen Pouleris, USN (Rtd)

Eric Theedom, RN (Rtd)

Jack Sue, AIF (Rtd) (Z-Force)

Homer White, USN (Rtd)

Lynne Cairns worked as a graphic artist before studying history during the 1980s. Between 1990 and 1995 she worked at the Western Australian Maritime Museum, where she co-wrote *Unfinished Voyages: Western Australian shipwrecks 1881– 1900,* with Graeme Henderson, before producing a history of the World War II submarine base at Fremantle, published in 1995 as *Fremantle's Secret Fleets: Allied submarines based in Western Australia during World War II.* After retiring from the Museum, she researched the role of women in the settlement of Western Australia for her MA thesis.

In 1942 Australia's northern ports were repeatedly bombed, spy planes made surveillance flights over our major cities and Japanese submarines were patrolling off the Western Australian coast. With the arrival of the US submarines in March, Fremantle was set to become an important international base.

Index

A

accommodation, of US personnel, *231*
AIF (Australian Imperial Force), *39, 43, 73, 126, 129, 178, 307*
aircraft production, *38, 165*
Albany, *106, 115, 117, 124, 126, 194, 209, 221, 313, 321*
America's Cup, *323*
Anderson, Andy, *124*
Andriessen, Pieter, *150, 193, 219, 224*
Archibald, Bill, *158, 163*
Army, Australian, see AIF,
atomic bomb, *309*
attacks on Australian territory, *46, 68, 74, 77, 81, 84, 87, 89, 109, 178, 182, 219, 221, 224*
Australia as Allied base, *81, 84, 98, 219*
Australian Submarine Corp, *323, 343*
Australian Submarines: A History (M. White), *330*
American,
Alden, *70*
Angler, *217, 219, 227, 268, 327*
Anthedon, *249, 292, 299, 315*
ARD, *158, 163, 219, 221, 249*
Aspro, *236*
Balao, *187*
Barbel, *247, 294*
Bashaw, *294*
Baya, *297, 304, 307*
Becuna, *297, 307*
Bergall, *294*
Besugo, *247, 294, 301, 311*
Billfish, *150, 154*

Black Hawk, *98*
Blackfin, *292, 294, 299, 301, 304*
Blenny, *297, 309*
Blower, *301, 309, 311*
Blueback, *299, 301, 304, 307*
Bluefish, *150, 219, 227, 236*
Bluegill, *278, 299*
Boarfish, *281, 299, 309*
Bonefish, *150, 153, 224, 236*
Bowfin, *150, 153, 154, 155, 217*
Bream, *274, 276, 278, 301*
Brill, *311*
Bugara, *309, 311*
Bullhead, *307, 309*
Bumper, *311*
Cabrilla, *124, 227, 236, 311*
Caiman, *297, 307, 309*
Canopus, *65*
Capelin, *150, 153*
Capitaine, *309*
Cavalla, *304, 309, 313*
Chanticleer, *148, 219, 221, 249*
Charr, *297, 301, 311*
Childs, *106, 126, 148*
Chub, *301, 304, 307, 309*
Cisco, *150*
Clytie, *209, 299, 315*
Cobia, *294, 297, 307, 309*
Cod, *150, 153, 217, 236, 309, 311*
Corpus Christi, *236, 249, 292*
Coucal, *249*
Crevalle, *150, 153, 201, 224, 236, 242, 268, 270*
Croaker, *297, 309*
Dace, *245*
Darter, *245*
David (Confederate 1863), *5*
Edsall, *70*
Euryale, *242, 249, 292, 299*
Finback, *148*
Flasher, *217, 219, 224, 227, 294, 311*
Flier, *236, 239, 249, 270*
Flounder, *276, 294*

Fred C Ainsworth, *203, 209*
Fulton, *299*
Gabilan, *294, 301*
Gar, *124, 129, 141, 142, 144, 148, 150, 187*
Gato, *187*
Goldstar, *112*
Grampus, *124, 129*
Grayback, *124, 129*
Grayling, *129, 141, 142, 144, 148, 150*
Grenadier, *126, 129, 141, 142, 148*
Griffin, *148, 227, 236, 249*
Growler, *245, 249*
Guavina, *294*
Gudgeon, *126, 129, 142, 144, 148*
Guitarro, *236, 268*
Gunnel, *224, 227, 236, 327*
Gurnard, *227, 236*
H.L. Hunley (Confederate 1863), *3, 5*
Haddo, *217, 219, 221, 224, 236, 239, 268*
Hake, *217, 219, 224, 236, 239, 245, 294*
Hammerhead, *297, 307*
Harder, *227, 236, 239, 242, 249, 268*
Hardhead, *245, 299*
Hawkbill, *247, 297, 301, 304*
Heron, *126, 148*
Hoe, *217, 224, 236*
Holland (1897), *8, 10*
Holland, *65, 98, 103, 106, 126, 129, 209*
Housatonic (1864), *5*
Hutchinson, *292*
Icefish, *309*
Isabel, *126, 148, 249*
Jack, *219, 224, 236*
Kingfish, *150, 155, 209, 266*
Kraken, *307, 309*
Lamprey, *301, 304*
Lanakai, *126*
Lapon, *224, 227, 236*
Lark, *126, 148*
Lizardfish, *307*

Loggerhead, *309*
Meigs, *74*
Memphis (1864), *5*
Mingo, *236*
Missouri, *311*
Muskalunge, *236*
Narwhal, *150, 153, 187, 236, 266, 268*
Nautilus, *221, 236, 268*
New Ironsides (1863), *5*
Number, *249*
Ondina, *144*
Orion, *219, 236*
Otus, *65, 98, 100, 126, 144, 148*
Paddle, *227, 236*
Pampanito, *294*
Pargo, *227, 236, 276, 294*
Peary, *77*
Pelias, *65, 126, 129, 144, 148, 227*
Perch, *106, 278, 281, 294*
Permit, *121, 126*
Peter Silvester, *278*
Phoenix, *126*
Pickerel, *106, 126*
Pigeon, *65*
Pike, *106, 112*
Pompon, *150, 153, 219*
Pope, *106*
Porpoise, *106, 112, 187, 258*
Protector (1901), *10*
Puffer, *150, 219, 227, 236*
Rasher, *150, 153, 227, 236*
Raton, *227, 236*
Ray, *219, 236*
Redfin, *224, 227, 236, 239, 270*
Robalo, *229, 239, 249*
Rock, *278*
S-36 to S-39, *106*
S-40, *100, 106*
S-41, *106*
Sailfish, *106, 129*
Salmon, *106, 121, 129, 187*
Sand Lance, *236*
Saratoga, *227*
Sargo, *100, 106, 129, 187*
Saury, *106, 121, 124, 129*

SC-739, *148*
Sculpin, *98, 106, 108, 121, 129, 186, 327*
Sea Robin, *297*
Seadragon, *100, 106, 108, 129, 258*
Seal, *121, 129*
Sealion, *297*
Searaven, *109, 129, 131, 258*
Seawolf, *121, 129*
Shark, *106*
Skipjack, *106, 124, 129*
Snapper, *98, 106, 108, 109, 121, 129, 258*
Spearfish, *106, 109, 129, 258*
Stingray, *98, 100, 106, 108, 121*
Sturgeon, *100, 106, 108, 129*
Swordfish, *106, 121, 129, 258*
Tambor, *126, 129, 131, 141, 142, 144, 148, 187, 264*
Tarpon, *100, 106, 109, 112*
Tautog, *112, 124, 129, 131, 141, 144, 148*
Thresher, *126, 129, 131, 141, 144, 148, 150*
Tinosa, *155, 266*
Trout, *129, 142, 148, 150*
Tuna, *276*
Turtle (1776), *1, 3*
Wabash (1864), *5*
Whippoorwill, *126, 148*
William B Preston, *126, 148*
Yuma, *219*
YP 286, *148*
YP 288, *148*
Australian,
  Adelaide, *38, 39, 247*
  AE1, *18, 19, 28*
  AE2, *18, 19, 23, 25, 28*
  Australia (HMAS), *38, 39*
  Australia II (yacht), *323, 330*
  Bunbury, *247, 249*
  Canberra, *38, 39, 129*
  Centaur, *182*
  Collins, *345*
  Dechaineux, *345*
  Deloraine, *68, 70*
  Farncomb, *345*

Grass Snake, *264*
Hobart, *38, 43*
J1 to J7, *28*
Katoomba, *70*
Kookaburra, *38*
Krait, *262, 264*
Lithgow, *70*
Mother Snake, *264*
Onslow, *340*
Orion, *340*
Otama, *340*
Otway (1), *32*
Otway (2), *340*
Ovens, *323, 327, 330, 334, 340*
Oxley (1), *32*
Oxley (2), *338*
Perth, *38, 73*
Platypus, *28*
Rankin, *345*
River Snake, *264*
Sheehan, *345*
Stuart, *38*
Swan, *38*
Sydney (I), *334*
Sydney (II), *38, 39, 43, 46, 334*
Uco, *219*
Vampire, *38*
Vendetta, *38*
Voyager, *38*
Waller, *345*
Waterhen, *38*
Wyola, *219*
Yarra, *38, 73*

B

Balabac Strait, *229, 239, 294*
Beazley, Kim, *330*
Bertrand, Commander John, *153*
Besant, Commander T.F., *18*
Biak Island, *236*
Bismarck Archipelago, *18, 236*
Bismarck Sea, Battle of, *177*
Blind, Lieutenant Howard, *242*
Blind, Mary, *201, 242*
Blood on Borneo (J. Sue), *276*
Borneo, *68, 87, 120, 121, 142, 155, 227, 245, 260, 266, 268, 276, 289, 294, 301, 307*

brawls, between Australian and US servicemen, *177*
Brisbane, submarine base at, *112, 124, 129, 141, 148, 150, 155, 217, 236, 247*
Britain, Battle of, *41*
British Empire, *60, 163, 236*
British Sailors' Society, *197*
Broome, *77, 84*
Bruinhout, Andre, *330*
buildings in Fremantle, *100, 109, 132, 231, 323*
British,
    Adamant, *236, 301, 315*
    Anchorite, *315*
    Andrew, *315*
    Athenia, *35*
    Aurochs, *315*
    Bonaventure, *289*
    Clyde, *236, 239, 242*
    Eagle (1776), *1*
    Holland, *209*
    Illustrious, *227*
    London, *227*
    Lusitania, *25*
    Maidstone, *209, 211, 236, 242, 292, 294, 297, 301, 315*
    Nigeria, *242*
    Porpoise, *211, 239, 270, 272, 274*
    Prince of Wales, *62*
    Queen Elizabeth, *227*
    Renown, *227*
    Repulse, *60, 62*
    Resurgam (1879), *8*
    Sea Rover, *242, 247*
    Selene, *304*
    Sidon, *309*
    Sirdar, *187, 242, 297*
    Sleuth, *301*
    Solent, *301*
    Spark, *247, 289*
    Spearhead, *289*
    Spirit, *247, 297*
    Spiteful, *242*
    Storm, *297*
    Stubborn, *311*
    Sturdy, *301*

Stygian, *252, 289, 307*
Suffolk, *227*
Supreme, *301*
Tabard, *315*
Taciturn, *301, 309, 315*
Tactician, *315*
Talent, *245*
Tantalus, *187, 274*
Tapir, *315*
Taurus, *309*
Telemachus, *187, 239, 242, 274, 276, 297, 315*
Terrapin, *313*
Thorough, *194, 214, 301, 309, 311, 315*
Tiptoe, *309, 311*
Totem, *309*
Trenchant, *252, 255, 284, 301, 304, 307, 311, 313*
Trump, *214, 309, 315*
Tudor, *299, 309, 327*
Turpin, *309*
Valiant, *227*
Victorious, *203, 211*
Virtue, *299*
Vox, *299*
Voracious, *299*
XE 1, *289*
XE 3 toXE-5, *289*

C
Cairns, Lynne, *323, 327, 334*
Campbell, Sergeant Lloyd, *281*
Careening Bay, *182, 264*
Carpenter, Operation, *239, 274*
Celebes Island, *121, 131, 153, 315*
Celebes Sea, *108, 121, 144, 227*
Ceylon,
   see Sri Lanka,
Chaffey, Lieutenant William, *281*
Changi Gaol, *264*
Christie, Rear Admiral Ralph, *142, 153, 155, 217, 221, 227, 242, 292*
Christmas Island, *141, 268*
Civil Alien Auxiliary Corps, *171*
Civil Construction Corps, *171*

civilian life, impact of war on, *43, 68, 89, 117, 163, 167, 197, 199, 201, 203*

clandestine operations, *141, 144, 148, 150, 153, 155, 219, 227, 236, 239, 258, 260, 262, 264, 266, 268, 270, 272, 274, 276, 278, 281, 313*

Cockburn Sound, *182, 221, 264, 343*

code-breaking, *46, 221, 224, 245*

Cold War, the, *338, 340*

commandos, *141, 165, 219, 258, 260, 268*

   see also Z-Force,

computerised systems, *345, 346*

conditions, of submariners, *184, 186, 187, 192, 193, 194, 197*

Coral Sea, Battle of the, *87, 120, 124, 126*

Corregidor, *65, 108, 120, 258*

Corvette and Submarine (M. Shean), *289, 330*

Creed, David, *311, 321*

Curtin, John, *62, 68, 178*

D

Darwin, *65, 68, 74, 77, 81, 84, 98, 108, 144, 150, 178, 217, 247, 276, 297*

Davao, *121, 217*

Dealey, Commander Sam, *239*

Dohmen, Franz, *211, 219*

Dohmen, Sylvia, *203, 211*

Dooland, Sergeant Bruce, *281*

Drayson, Derek, *209*

Drayson, Merle, *209*

Dutch East Indies, *41, 65, 68, 81, 84, 87, 98, 106, 112, 121, 148, 155, 236, 258, 336*

   see also Indonesia,

Dutch (Netherlands),

Dolfjin, *315*
K1 (pre-1914), *14*
K VII, *106*
K VIII, *106, 109*
K IX, *106, 109, 336*
K X, *106*
K XI, *106, 297, 299*
K XII, *65, 106, 109, 150, 219, 236, 258*
K XIII, *106*
K XIV, *106, 219, 268, 315*
K XV, *106, 193, 211, 219, 268, 315*
K XVI, *65*
K XVII, *65*
K XVIII, *106*
O 1 (Luctor et Emergo 1906, *12, 14*
O 2 and O 3 (pre-1914), *14*
O 16, *65*
O 19, *106, 242, 304, 309*
O 20, *65*
O 21, *150, 155, 192, 260, 304, 309, 311*
O 23, *260, 315*
O 24, *211, 260, 304, 315*
Tigjerhaai, *315*
Zwaardvisch, *242, 245, 297, 304, 330*

E

El Alamein, Battle of, *178*
Elder, Claudie, *203, 209*
Elder, Teresa, *203, 209*
engines, internal combustion, *5, 8, 10*
English, Rear Admiral Robert, *141*
ethics of submarine warfare, *12, 25*
Exmouth Gulf, *98, 100, 144, 178, 221, 236, 262, 278*

F

Fife, Rear Admiral James, *124, 292, 299, 307, 313*
Fisher, Andrew, *35*
Fitzgerald, Lt Commander John, *142*
floating dock (ARD 10), *158, 163, 219, 221, 249*
Flores Sea, *121, 141, 144, 153, 217, 299, 301*

Folbots (folding boats or folboats), *258, 262, 264, 272, 274, 276, 278, 281*
food supplies, *167, 168*
Foss, Peter, *330*
Fraser, Lieutenant I.E., *289*
Fremantle Harbour Trust, *91, 92, 96, 126, 315*
Fremantle's Secret Fleets (L. Cairns), *327, 330*
Friends of the Submarine Museum, *327*
Fulton, Robert, *3*

G

Gallipoli, *19, 23, 25*
Garrett, George, *8*
Geraldton, *182, 224*
Goldman, Isaac (Gerry), *211, 315*
Goldman, Miriam, *211*
Gorton, John, *338*
Great Depression, *32, 163*

Griffith, Commander Walter, *154, 155*
Guadalcanal, *129, 178*
German,
  Emden, *334*
  Kormoran, *46*
  Tirpitz, *286*
  U-1 (1906), *14*
  U-30, *35*
  U-168, *245*
  U-183, *301*
  U-862, *278*
  Aden Maru, *227*

H

Halmahera, *217*
Helbert, Commander, *242*
Hole, Arnold, *274*
Holland, John P, *8, 14*
Hong Kong, *62, 236, 289, 309, 315*
Horobin, Peter, *330*
Horrocks, Sergeant W., *281*
Hunley, H.L., *5*

I

Indochina, *108, 120, 121, 142, 144, 227, 239, 276, 281, 289, 294, 297, 299*

Indonesia, *227, 315, 336*
  see also Dutch East Indies,
industrial development, *163*
infrastructure, *168, 171*
invasion, threat of, *60, 68, 73, 74, 77, 79, 81, 84, 87, 89, 103, 178, 224*

Iwo Jima, *304*

J

Java, *65, 68, 77, 79, 100, 120, 148, 217, 258, 260, 309, 313*

Java Sea, *108, 131, 217, 245, 276, 297, 299, 301, 307, 309*

Jaywick, Operation, *262, 264, 270*

Jervoise Bay, *109*

Jobson, Alf, *194, 214, 301*

Jobson, Audrey, *214*

Jongejan, Ary, *211*

Jongejan, Joy, *211*

Japanese,

Amato Maru, *297*

Araosan Maru, *299*

Asahi, *121*

Ashigara, *252, 255, 304, 307*

Banshu Maru No.2, *131*

Daizen Maru, *297, 301*

Eifuku Maru, *294*

Eiski Maru, *144*

Engen Maru, *294*

Fulton (1903), *14*

Ganges Maru, *121*

Haguro, *304*

Haichan Maru, *131*

Hasshu Maru, *131*

Honan Maru, *278, 299*

I-2, *77, 100*

I-3, *77, 100*

I-25, *77*

I-121, *68*

I-122, *68*

I-123, *68*

I-124, *68, 70*

I-165, *182*

I-182, *150*

Indus Maru, *144*

Isuzu, *301, 304*
Isuzu Maru, *148*
Kamakura Maru, *144*
Meigen Maru, *142*
Meikai Maru, *144*
Meiten Maru, *144*
Meizan Maru, *150*
Nampo Maru, *121*
Nichiryo Maru, *153*
Nichiryu Maru, *297*
Protector (1903), *14*
Ryotoku Maru, *150*
Sanraku Maru, *148*
Shinei Maru, *144*
Shoyu Maru, *217*
Suez Maru, *153*
Taijima Maru, *227*
Tenshinzan Maru, *227*
Toen Maru, *141*
Toko Maru, *142*
Yamashiro Maru, *150*
Yoneyama Maru, *150*
Yoshida Maru I, *224*

K
Kalumburu Mission, *178*
Katanning, *194*
Keith, Commander, *126*
Koga, Admiral Mineichi, *217*
Kokoda Track, *126, 178*
Kolay, Selçuk, *25*

L
Lae, *68, 178*
Lake, Simon, *10, 14*
Lane-Nott, Rear Admiral R.C., *327*
Lend-Lease, *163, 313*
Leyte Gulf, Battle of, *245*
Lockwood, Vice Admiral Charles, *120, 121, 124, 141, 142, 299*
Lombok Strait, *221, 227, 242, 262, 276, 278, 294, 297, 301, 304, 307, 309*
losses of submarines, *106, 142, 150, 153, 229, 239, 242, 245, 247, 249, 294, 307, 309, 311*

Lyon, Lt Colonel Ivan, *270, 274*

M

MacArthur, General Douglas, *84, 245*
Mackerel, Operation, *258*
maintenance, of submarines,
  see repair facilities,
Makassar Strait, *108, 121, 141, 150, 153, 229*
Malacca Straits, *142, 236, 242*
Malay Archipelago, *106, 120*
Malaya, *39, 62, 68, 70, 73, 77, 81, 87, 236, 260*
Maritime History Dept, Western Australian Museum, *323, 327*
Maritime Museum, Western Australian, *25, 321, 323, 327, 330, 334*
marriages, wartime, *203, 206, 209, 211, 214, 319*

May, Sally, *323*
McCallum, Lt Commander James, *278*
McMillan, Captain Leslie, *281*
memorials, to submariners, *319, 321*
Mendenhall, Rear Admiral Corwin, *98, 100, 184, 186, 327*
Menzies, Sir Robert, *35*
midget submarines, *87, 109, 182, 270, 284, 286, 289*
  see also Welfreighter; Welman; SB submarines,
Midway Island, *87, 121, 124, 219*
Midway, Battle of, *87, 121, 124*
Milne Bay, Battle of, *126, 129*
minelaying, *68, 98, 142, 299*
Missions to Seamen, *197*

Mitchell, Sir James, *174*
Mole, Captain Denis, *327*
Molucca Sea, *108, 144*
Monturiol, Narcis, *5*
Monument Hill, Fremantle, *319*
munitions production, *38, 171*

N

Naval Historical Society of Australia, *321*
naval strategy,
   American, *60, 62, 65, 68, 84, 98*
     Australian, *338, 340, 343, 345, 346*
Navy, *229*
  see Submarine Repair Unit,
New Guinea, *18, 68, 77, 84, 106, 126, 148, 178, 224, 227, 236, 245, 260, 268*
Nimitz, Admiral Chester, *84*
Nordenfeldt, Thorsten, *8*
North Australia Observer Unit, *89*
North Wharf, *92, 100, 109, 126, 158, 192, 315*

O

Operation, *276*
oil supplies, Japanese, *106, 108, 120, 148, 155, 217, 229, 245, 247*
Operations of the Fremantle Submarine Base 1942–1945 (D. Creed), *321*
Other nations,
  Aigette (France 1904), *10*
  Bartolomeo Colleoni (Italy), *43*
  Gymnote (France 1888), *8*
  Ictineo II (Spain 1864), *5*
  Mustika (Malaya), *272*

Narval (France 1900), *10*
Panamanian (Panama), *294*
Peyki Sevket (Turkey), *23*
Recina (Yugoslavia), *182*
Richelieu (France), *227*

P

Palawan, *229, 294*
Pearl Harbour, *62, 65, 68, 109, 112, 121, 124, 126, 129, 131, 144, 148, 155, 219, 224, 227, 247, 258, 299*
Philippine Sea, Battle of the, *227, 229*
Philippines, *62, 65, 108, 109, 121, 141, 144, 148, 150, 153, 155, 236, 239, 245, 247, 258, 264, 268, 292, 299, 304*
Phyllis Dean Hostel, *197, 199, 214*
Platypus, HMAS, *340*
Platypus, Operation, *278, 281*
Politician, Operation, *270, 276*
Port Gregory, *182*
Port Hedland, *84*
Porter, Alan, *214*
Porter, Elaine, *214*
Potshot, see Exmouth Gulf,
Pouleris, Kath, *206*
Pouleris, William, *126, 206, 307*
Prawn, Operation, *268*
Purnell, Rear Admiral William, *98*
Python I, Operation, *266*
Python II, Operation, *266, 268*

R

RAAF, *74, 100, 109, 221, 258, 297, 307*
Rabaul, *68, 73, 262*
repair facilities, Fremantle, *103, 109, 112, 126, 129, 142, 158, 163, 313*
see also slipway,

Rimau, Operation, *211, 239, 264, 270, 272, 274*
Ruhe, Captain William, *242*
Russell, Ben, *194*
Russell, Scott, *194*

S

Saipan, *126, 309*
Sargent, Arthur, *194*
SB submarines, *264, 270, 272, 284*
security issues, *112*
Services Reconnaissance Department, *260*
Shean, Lt Commander Max, *284, 286, 289, 330*
shipbuilding, *163, 165*
Shipwreck Museum, *327*
Siam, Gulf of, *121, 299, 301, 304*
Singapore, *38, 39, 60, 68, 70, 73, 77, 81, 217, 236, 262, 264, 270*
sinkings by Fremantle submarines, statistics of, *131, 155, 229, 247, 311, 313*
slipway, Fremantle Harbour, *96, 103, 121, 129, 132, 142, 219, 224, 236, 239, 247, 297, 299, 330, 334*
see also repair facilities,
Smart, Lieutenant J.E., *289*
Snake Flotilla, *264*
social attitudes, *197, 199, 201, 203*
South China Sea, *120, 121, 155, 217, 219, 229, 247, 268, 276, 292, 294, 297, 299, 301, 307, 309*
Special Operations Australia, *260*
special operations, see clandestine operations,
Sri Lanka, *84, 106, 236, 297, 301, 313*
Stalingrad, Battle of, *178*
Starfish, Operation, *278*

Stirling, HMAS, *330, 340, 343, 345*
Stoker, Lt Commander Henry, *19, 23, 25*
Stott, Major Don, *278, 281*
Subic Bay, *299, 301, 304, 307, 309, 311, 327*
submarine classes, American,
    Fleet-class, *65, 112, 126, 129, 141, 184, 236*
    S-class, *65, 112, 129, 187*
submarine classes, Australian,
    Collins, *343, 345, 346*
    Oberon, *338, 340, 346*
submarine classes, British,
    A-class, *14*
    E-class, *14*
    Holland, *14*
    J-class, *28, 32*
    O-class, *32, 38*
    Oberon, *338, 340*
    S-class, *186, 187, 236, 301*
    T-class, *186, 187, 236, 301, 315*
    X-class, *286, 330, 334*
    XE-class, *289*
submarine classes, Dutch, *187*
Submarine Convention, International, *327, 330*
Submarine Diary (C. Mendenhall), *327*
submarine fleet, Australian (post-1945), *338, 340, 343, 345, 346*
Submarine Repair Unit (Navy 137), *129, 158, 163, 192*
Submariners Association, United States, *319*
Sue, Jack Wong, *276*
Sumatra, *106, 120, 155, 236, 245, 268*
Surabaya, *65, 68, 106, 131, 227, 301, 309*
surrender, Japanese, *309, 311, 313*

T

Tait, Admiral Sir Gordon, *327*
Tawi-Tawi, *217, 227*
Theedom, Eric, *242*
Tiger 1 to 5 Operations, *260*
Timor, *77, 81, 87, 109, 121, 131, 141, 150, 258*
Timor Sea, *74*
torpedoes, development of, *5, 124, 155, 217, 229*
Townsville, *178, 262*
Truk, *217*

V

van der Ham, Captain J.M., *327*
van Hattem, Jan, *330*
Vasey, Rear Admiral Lloyd (Joe), *327*
Victoria Quay, *103, 165, 323, 330*
Voluntary Aid Detachment, *177*

W

War in the Boats (W.J. Ruhe), *242*
Welfreighter submarines, *264, 284, 286*
Welman submarines, *262, 264, 266, 284, 286*
White, Ethel, *209*
White, Homer, *117, 209*
White, Michael, *330*
Whitehead, Robert, *5*
Wilkes, Captain John, *100, 103, 120*
Will, Commander John, *121*
Wilson, Admiral Sir Arthur, *12, 14*
wolf packs, *153, 154, 229, 239, 245, 294, 307, 309*
women, Australian, and Allied servicemen, *175, 193, 197, 199, 201, 203*

wartime recruitment of, *68, 171, 174, 175*
Women's Land Army, *171*
World War I, *12, 14, 18, 19, 23, 25, 46, 60*
World War II,
  campaigns in Europe and Middle East, *39, 41, 43, 73, 178, 229, 236, 292*
  outbreak of, *32, 35, 38*
  VE Day, *304*
Wyndham, *77, 84, 89*

Y

Yamamoto, Admiral Isoroku, *177, 178*
Young, Edwin, *197, 252, 255, 301, 307*

Z

Z-Force (Z Special Unit), *165, 182, 260, 262, 264, 266, 268, 270, 272, 274, 276, 278, 281, 284, 286, 334*
  see also commandos,

www.ingramcontent.com/pod-product-compliance
Lightning Source LLC
Chambersburg PA
CBHW052136300426
15CB00011B/1403